# Human Relations:
## Principles and Practices

*FIFTH EDITION*

**Barry L. Reece**
*VIRGINIA POLYTECHNIC INSTITUTE
AND STATE UNIVERSITY*

**Rhonda Brandt**
*OZARKS TECHNICAL COMMUNITY COLLEGE*

*HOUGHTON MIFFLIN COMPANY*
*Boston      New York*

Editor-in-Chief: *George T. Hoffman*

Associate Sponsoring Editor: *Susan M. Kahn*

Associate Project Editor: *Kate Hartke*

Editorial Assistant: *May Jawdat*

Senior Production/Design Coordinator: *Jill Haber*

Senior Manufacturing Coordinator: *Jane Spelman*

Marketing Manager: *Steven Mikels*

Cover Image: © *Ron Chan*

Printed in the U.S.A.

Library of Congress Catalog Card Number: 2001133330

ISBN: 0-618-21435-6

23456789-QV-06  05  04  03  02

To Vera, Lynne, Mark, Monique, Michelle, and Colleen
*BARRY L. REECE*

To Patrick, Matthew, Manda, Arabella, and Bairon
*RHONDA BRANDT*

# BRIEF CONTENTS

# CONTENTS

*Human Relations: Principles and Practices,* fifth edition, represents a compilation of twenty-five years of research by authors Barry Reece and Rhonda Brandt. Their combined years of post-secondary teaching experience and on-site consulting with business, industry, and educational institutions provide the basis for their real-world approach to human relations skill building. With their diverse backgrounds, they work together to consistently offer their readers up-to-date information and advice in this best-selling text.

**BARRY L. REECE** is a Professor at Virginia Polytechnic Institute and State University. He received his Ed.D. from the University of Nebraska. Dr. Reece has been actively involved in teaching, research, consulting, and designing training programs throughout the past three decades. He has conducted more than 500 workshops and seminars devoted to leadership, human relations, communications, sales, customer service, and small business operations. He has received the Excellence in Teaching Award for classroom teaching at Virginia Tech and the Trainer of the Year Award presented by the Valleys of Virginia Chapter of the American Society for Training and Development. Dr. Reece has contributed to numerous journals and is author or co-author of twenty-five books. He has served as a consultant to Lowe's Companies, Inc., First Union, WLR Foods, Kinney Shoe Corporation, and numerous other profit and not-for-profit organizations.

**RHONDA BRANDT** teaches interpersonal communication at Ozarks Technical Community College in Springfield, Missouri. Prior to joining the OTC staff she served as Chair of the Administrative Support Department of Springfield College in Springfield, Missouri. Prior to joining Springfield College she served for ten years as the human relations instructor at Hawkeye Community College. She received her M.Ed. from the University of Missouri—Columbia. She has been active in the training and consulting industry for over twenty-five years, specializing in human relations, communications, and self-esteem programs for small businesses, large corporations, and educational institutions throughout the nation. She was a member of the National Council on Vocational Education's working committee for the Presidential White Paper *Building Positive Self-Esteem and a Strong Work Ethic.*

It has never been easier to make a hard case for the soft skills. A solid grounding in interpersonal skills is an essential key to career success in the age of information. Persons entering the work force today encounter a work/life landscape that is more complex than at any other time in history. The New Economy is characterized by an increasing number of mergers, acquisitions, and business closings. Downsizing continues even when the economy is strong. Employees are more likely to be judged by their ability to work effectively in teams and embrace work force diversity. Organizations are increasingly oriented toward service, and in a service economy relationships are often more important than products.

## What Makes This Book Effective

*Human Relations: Principles and Practices* has been updated to reflect these important trends and developments. It features a blend of time-proven fundamentals and new practices needed to succeed in today's information economy. As in earlier editions, the fifth edition includes a number of important components that have been praised by instructors and students.

- The **"total person" approach** to human relations has been expanded and enriched in this edition. We continue to believe that human behavior at work and in our private lives is influenced by many interdependent traits such as emotional balance, self-awareness, integrity, self-esteem, physical fitness, and healthy spirituality. This approach focuses on those human relations skills needed to be well-rounded and thoroughly prepared to handle a wide range of human relations problems and issues.

- This edition, like all previous editions, provides the reader with an overview of the **seven major themes of effective human relations:** Communication, Self-Awareness, Self-Acceptance, Motivation, Trust, Self-Disclosure, and Conflict Resolution. These broad themes serve as the foundation for contemporary human relations courses and training programs.

- **Self-development opportunities** are provided throughout the entire text. One of the few certainties in today's rapidly changing work place is the realization that we must assume greater responsibility for developing and upgrading our skills and competencies. In many cases, self-development begins with self-awareness. The text provides multiple opportunities to complete self-assessment activities and then reflect on the results. Each chapter includes thinking/learning starters, application exercises, self-assessment exercises, and a case problem. Every effort has been made to encourage self-assessment, reflection, planning, and goal setting.

**xvii**

■ A hallmark of this edition, and all previous editions, is the use of many **real-world examples** of human relations issues and practices at respected organizations. These examples build the reader's interest and promote understanding of major topics and concepts. Many of the organizations cited in the fifth edition have been recognized by the authors of *The 100 Best Companies to Work for, The 100 Best Companies for Working Mothers, The 100 Best Corporate Citizens, Hispanic* magazine's "100 Best Companies for Hispanics" and *Black Professional* magazine's "200 Great Places to Work." The fifth edition also includes many examples from successful smaller companies featured in *Inc.* and *Fast Company* magazines and from America's trading partners within the international community.

## ■ *Staying on the Cutting Edge*

The fifth edition of *Human Relations: Principles and Practices* has been updated to reflect the growing importance of the human element in our service-oriented, information-saturated, global economy. Up-to-date coverage of key topics and concepts is based on a review of over 3,000 recent articles, books, and research reports. It is a practical text that is designed for persons who wish to fine-tune interpersonal skills and develop strategies for dealing with unique people-related problems in today's work place. The most significant changes include:

■ The new edition is a more concise, **tightly focused textbook.** Information not essential to coverage of the topic or concept has been removed. The finished product is very "reader friendly" because the text is focused on important "must know" information. In most cases real-world examples are provided to enhance student interest and clarify important concepts.

■ In response to suggestions from current adopters and reviewers, and a thorough review of the current literature, **many new topics** are included in this edition. Some examples include new tools for tolerance; living life less plugged in; incivility—the ultimate career killer; coping with communication barriers created by advanced technology; casual dress guidelines revisited; and coping with people who behave badly.

■ Over 25 **Human Relations in Action boxed inserts** have been included in the text. These new inserts are a mix of "how to" tips and real-world examples that advance our understanding of human relations problems and issues. These inserts also encourage reflection and self-assessment.

■ The fifth edition provides a more **contemporary examination of diversity.** Coverage of diversity issues and developments is not limited to a single chapter. The challenge of valuing diversity, working across cultures, and learning to work effectively with persons who differ in terms of national origin, race, religion, gender, and other dimensions of diversity requires support information found in several chapters. Throughout the text a diverse selection of individuals is featured in cases, boxed inserts, photos, and examples.

■ The Internet has had a major impact on the work place. A major effort has been made to integrate **Internet related content** in appropriate chapters. For example, Chapter 2 provides suggestions on how to use e-mail effectively. A new case entitled "Cybersurveillance: Big Brother Is Watching" was developed for Chapter 2.

Every chapter includes an **Internet application exercise.** These exercises include web sites complete with reliable URLs. However, because URLs and specific web site content can change over time, these exercises are repeated on the text's web site, and will be updated as necessary.

■ The new edition includes expanded coverage of strategies that can be used to **resolve work/life tensions.** Throughout the past few years we have seen an explosion of books, articles, and reports on how to achieve work/life balance. We provide greater coverage of this important area of human relations.

■ Many of the teaching/learning aids featured throughout the text have been updated. Most of the chapter opening vignettes are new to this edition. These real-world examples introduce chapter topics and build reader interest in the material. Over half of the case problems have been replaced or rewritten. Many of these focus on an employee issue or problem within the context of a specific organization. Several of the Thinking/Learning Starters within each chapter have been rewritten or replaced, and many new Total Person Insights appear throughout the text.

## ■ *Tools that Enhance the Teaching/Learning Process*

The extensive supplements package accompanying the fifth edition of *Human Relations: Principles and Practices* includes a variety of new and traditional tools that will aid both teaching and learning.

**Student and Instructor Web Sites** The **student web site** includes a **resource center** with links of general interest to anyone studying human relations, links to the specific companies highlighted in the textbook's boxes and cases, and **ACE self-test questions** to help students prepare for exams.

The **instructor web site** includes downloadable Word files from the **Instructor's Resource Manual** so that instructors can edit the outlines and other teaching materials to suit their own course needs. The site also includes downloadable **PowerPoint slides,** which provide complete lecture outlines illustrated with figures from the text.

**Instructor's Resource Manual with Test Bank** The Instructor's Resource Manual is a complete teaching guide. The opening material provides a review of the most important **teaching and learning principles** that facilitate human relations training, a review of several **teaching methods,** and a description of suggested **term projects.**

Part I, **Chapter Teaching Resources,** provides a chapter preview, chapter purpose and perspective, a presentation outline, and suggested responses to the Thinking/Learning Starters, review questions, and case problem questions for every chapter in the text. Answers, when applicable, are also provided for the text's application exercises.

**Additional application exercises** are included. Between the material in the textbook and the Instructor's Resource Manual, the instructor can now choose from over 50 application exercises.

Part II contains the **test items** and answers. True/false, multiple-choice, completion, short answer, essay, and minicase questions are provided.

Part III includes two **instructional games** entitled "Ethical Decision Making" and "Coping with Organizational Politics." The ethics game stimulates in-depth thinking about the ethical consequences of certain decisions and actions. Politics surface in every organization and the politics game prepares the student to cope effectively with common political situations. Each game simulates a realistic business environment in which employees must make difficult decisions. Students play these games to learn without having to play for keeps. This section of the Instructor's Resource Manual includes complete instructions on how to administer these learning activities in the classroom.

Part IV provides a list of **human relations–related videos** and a corresponding list of video vendors. Instructors who wish to supplement their course with videos beyond what is provided in the video program that accompanies the text may use this list for reference.

**HM Testing** This electronic version of the printed test items allows instructors to generate and change tests easily. The program includes an online testing feature by which instructors can administer tests via their local area network or over the Web. It also has a gradebook feature that lets users set up classes, record and track grades from tests or assignments, analyze grades, and produce class and individual statistics.

**Video Program** The video package that accompanies the text includes several segments that illustrate important concepts from the text. The videos focus on topics including ethics, motivation, diversity, and organizational culture. These videos provide examples from real-world organizations and bring chapter content to life. The accompanying **Video Guide** provides a description of each video, suggested uses, and issues for discussion.

**Transparency Package** Forty color transparencies are available for use by adopters of the fifth edition of *Human Relations: Principles and Practices.* This newly expanded transparency program includes figures, graphs, and key concepts featured in the text, as well as pieces that are exclusive to the transparency program.

## ■ *The Search For Wisdom*

The search for what is true, right, or lasting has become more difficult because we live in the midst of an information explosion. The Internet is an excellent source of mass information, but it is seldom the source of wisdom. Television usually reduces complicated ideas to a sound bite. Books continue to be one of the best sources of knowledge. Many new books, and several classics, were used as references for the fifth edition of *Human Relations: Principles and Practices.* A sample of the books we used to prepare this edition follows.

*Anger, Rage, and Resentment* by Kimes Gustin
*Civility—Manners, Morals, and Etiquette of Democracy* by Stephen L. Carter
*Complete Business Etiquette Handbook* by Barbara Pachter and Majorie Brody
*Creative Visualization* by Shakti Gawain
*Data Smog—Surviving the Information Glut* by David Shenk
*Do What You Love . . . The Money Will Follow* by Marsha Sinetar
*Empires of the Mind* by Denis Waitley
*Getting to Yes* by Roger Fisher and William Ury
*How to Control Your Anxiety Before It Controls You* by Albert Ellis
*How to Win Friends and Influence People* by Dale Carnegie
*The Human Side of Enterprise* by Douglas McGregor
*I'm OK—You're OK* by Thomas Harris
*Minding the Body, Mending the Mind* by Joan Borysenko
*Multiculture Manners—New Rules of Etiquette For a Changing Society* by Norine Dresser
*1001 Ways to Reward Employees* by Bob Nelson
*The Power of 5* by Harold H. Bloomfield and Robert K. Cooper
*Psycho-Cybernetics* by Maxwell Maltz
*Re-Engineering the Corporation* by Michael Hammer and James Champy
*The Seven Habits of Highly Effective People* by Stephen Covey
*The Situational Leader* by Paul Hersey
*The Six Pillars of Self-Esteem* by Nathaniel Branden
*Spectacular Teamwork* by Robert R. Blake, Jane Srygley Mouton, and Robert L. Allen
*Stress for Success* by James Loehr
*The 10 Natural Laws of Successful Time and Life Management* by Hyrum W. Smith
*Trust & Betrayal in the Workplace* by Dennis S. Reina and Michelle L. Reina
*When Talking Makes Things Worse* by David Stiebel
*Working Relationships* by Bob Wall

*Working with Emotional Intelligence* by Daniel Goleman
*You Just Don't Understand: Women and Men in Conversation* by Deborah Tannen

## ■ Acknowledgments

Many people have made contributions to *Human Relations: Principles and Practices*. Throughout the years the text has been strengthened as a result of numerous helpful comments and recommendations. We extend special appreciation to the following reviewers and advisors who have provided valuable input for this and prior editions:

James Aldrich, *North Dakota State School of Science*
Thom Amnotte, *Eastern Maine Technical College*
Garland Ashbacker, *Kirkwood Community College*
Sue Avila, *South Hills Business School*
James Bailey, *George Washington University*
Shirley Banks, *Marshall University*
Rhonda Barry, *American Institute of Commerce*
C. Winston Borgen, *Sacramento Community College*
Jane Bowerman, *University of Oklahoma*
Charles Capps, *Sam Houston State University*
Lawrence Carter, *Jamestown Community College*
Cathy Chew, *Northampton Community College*
John P. Cicero, *Shasta College*
Anne C. Cowden, *California State University—Sacramento*
Michael Dzik, *North Dakota State School of Science*
John Elias, *Consultant*
Mike Fernsted, *Bryant & Stratton Business Institute*
Dave Fewins, *Neosho County Community College*
Dean Flowers, *Waukesha County Technical College*
Jill P. Gann, *Anne Arundel Community College*
M. Camille Garrett, *Tarrant County Junior College*
Roberta Greene, *Central Piedmont Community College*
Ralph Hadl, *Community College of Southern Nevada*
Sally Hanna-Jones, *Hocking Technical College*
Daryl Hansen, *Metropolitan Community College*
Carolyn K. Hayes, *Polk Community College*
John J. Heinsius, *Modesto Junior College*
Edward Hernandez, *CSU Stanislaus*
Stephen Hiatt, *Catawba College*
Larry Hill, *San Jacinto College—Central*
Janice Lee Holmgaard, *Patrick Henry Community College*
Bill Hurd, *Lowe's Companies, Inc.*
Dorothy Jeanis, *Fresno City College*

Marlene Katz, *Canada College*
Robert Kegel, Jr., *Cypress College*
Vance A. Kennedy, *College of Mateo*
Deborah Lineweaver, *Consultant and Trainer*
Thomas W. Lloyd, *Westmoreland County Community College*
Jerry Loomis, *Fox Valley Technical College*
Roger Lynch, *Inver Hills Community College*
Edward C. Mann, *The University of Southern Mississippi*
Karen Minchella, *Consulting Management, LLC*
Russ Moorhead, *Des Moines Area Community College*
Marilyn Mueller, *Simpson College*
Erv J. Napier, *Kent State University*
Barbara Ollhoff, *Waukesha County Technical College*
Leonard L. Palumbo, *Northern Virginia Community College*
James Patton, *Mississippi State University*
C. Richard Paulson, *Mankato State University*
Naomi W. Peralta, *The Institute of Financial Education*
William Price, *Virginia Polytechnic Institute and State University*
Shirley Pritchett, *Northeast Texas Community College*
Linda Pulliam, *Pulliam Associates, Chapel Hill, NC*
Lynne Reece, *Alternative Services*
Jack C. Reed, *University of Northern Iowa*
Robert Schaden, *Schoolcraft College*
Mary R. Shannon, *Wenatchie Valley College*
J. Douglas Shatto, *Muskingum Area Technical College*
Marilee Smith, *Kirkwood Community College*
Cindy Stewart, *Des Moines Area Community College*
Rahmat O. Tavallali, *Wooster Business College*
V. S. Thakur, *Community College of Rhode Island*
Linda Truesdale, *Midlands Technical College*
Wendy Bletz Turner, *New River Community College*
Marc Wayner, *Hocking Technical College*
Tom West, *Des Moines Area Community College*
Steven Whipple, *St. Cloud Technical College*
Burl Worley, *Allan Hancock College*

We would also like to thank Dr. Denis Waitley and Mr. Charles Haefner for helping us develop a fuller understanding of human relations; Margaret Burk of Muskingum College for her assistance in revising the test items and preparing ACE questions for the student web site; and Lynn Bradman of Metropolitan Community College for preparing the PowerPoint slides.

Over 200 business organizations, government agencies, and nonprofit institutions provided us with the real-world examples that appear throughout the text.

We are grateful to organizations that allowed us to conduct interviews, observe workplace environments, and use special photographs and materials.

The partnership with Houghton Mifflin, which has spanned two decades, has been very rewarding. Several members of the Houghton Mifflin College Division staff have made important contributions to this project. Sincere appreciation is extended to Susan Kahn who has worked conscientiously on the text from the planning stage to completion of the book. We also offer a hearty thank you to other key contributors: George Hoffman, Kate Hartke, Julia Perez, May Jawdat, and Steven Mikels.

BARRY L. REECE
RHONDA BRANDT

# Introduction to Human Relations

**CHAPTER PREVIEW**

After studying this chapter, you will be able to

- Understand how the study of human relations will help you achieve career success and increased work/life balance.

- Explain the nature, purpose, and importance of human relations in an organizational setting.

- Identify major developments in the workplace that have given new importance to human relations.

- Identify major forces influencing human behavior at work.

- Review the historical development of the human relations movement.

- Identify seven basic themes that serve as the foundation for effective human relations.

Each year *Fortune* magazine publishes a list of the 100 best companies to work for in America. Job seekers study the list carefully because these are the companies where morale is high and relationships are characterized by a high level of trust and camaraderie. In addition, these companies offer excellent benefits along with extensive training and development opportunities. The list changes each year because more companies are discovering ways to attract talented new employees and to keep current employees who have helped make the company successful. Companies, in fact, compete for a place on the list.

Employees at The Container Store were thrilled to learn that their company not only made the year 2000 list but also was ranked number one. The company was also ranked number one on the year 2001 list and number two on the year 2002 list. The Container Store is a chain of twenty retail stores that sell high-quality storage and organizational products for home or office. So what's it like to work for "number one"? The first things you notice are that employees are honestly happy and that they delight in providing outstanding service to customers. Employees also display a fierce sense of ownership in the company. The owners share everything with employees, including financial information. This emphasis on communication helps nurture intense employee loyalty. In an industry where employee turnover ranges from 80 to 130 percent, it is 15 percent at The Container Store.[1]

The Container Store's emphasis on open communication, employee loyalty, and meaningful work is not an isolated case. A growing number of U.S. organizations, from hospitals to hotels, are discovering and rediscovering the benefits of work environments that put people first.

For two consecutive years the Container Store has topped *Fortune* magazine's annual list of the "100 Best Companies to Work For." Employees are enthusiastic about their work and are quick to say, "People care about each other here." The company annually provides 185 hours of training for each employee.

## The Nature, Purpose, and Importance of Human Relations

Many of America's best-managed organizations are not simply being "nice to people"; they are genuinely helping employees come alive through their work. We have learned that the goals of worker and workplace need not be in conflict. This chapter focuses on the nature of human relations, its development, and its importance to the achievement of individual and organizational goals.

### ■ Human Relations Defined

The term **human relations** in its broadest sense covers all types of interactions among people—their conflicts, cooperative efforts, and group relationships. It is the study of *why* our beliefs, attitudes, and behaviors sometimes cause relationship problems in our personal lives and in work-related situations. The study of human relations emphasizes the analysis of human behavior, prevention strategies, and resolution of behavioral problems.

### ■ Human Relations in the Age of Information

The restructuring of America from an industrial economy to an information economy has had a profound impact on interpersonal relationships. Living in an age in which the effective exchange of information is the *foundation* of most economic transactions means making major life adjustments. The information age is dynamic, but it can also be disorienting. Many people feel a sense of frustration because they must cope with a glut of information that arrives faster than they can process it. As information becomes more accessible, we often must alter traditional patterns of work and leisure.

*Fast Company* magazine asked its superbusy readers to reflect on this question: Does the new economy leave you feeling tested, bested, toasted, and roasted? Most readers probably answered with a resounding yes! Increased reliance on information technology often comes at a price—less human contact. To thrive, indeed to just survive, we need warm-hearted contact with other people. Sources of connection away from work are also being trimmed way back. Extended families are so disconnected that contact is rare. A human-contact deficiency weakens the spirit, the mind, and the body.[2]

The authors of *The Social Life of Information* describe another price we pay for living in the age of information. A great number of people are focusing on information so intently that they miss the very things that provide valuable balance and perspective. Neglecting the cues and clues that lie outside the tight focus on information can limit our effectiveness. Think about written proposals negotiated on the Internet and signed by electronic signature. Such transactions lack the essence of a face-to-face meeting: a firm handshake and a straight look in the eye. Today's knowledge worker needs to take more account of people and a little less of information.[3]

### ■ *The Importance of Human Relations*

One of the most significant developments in the age of information has been the increased importance of interpersonal skills in almost every type of work setting. Technical ability is often not enough to achieve career success. Studies indicate that many of the people who have difficulty in obtaining or holding a job, or advancing to positions of greater responsibility, possess the needed technical competence but lack interpersonal competence.

Several important developments in the workplace have given new importance to human relations. Each of the following developments provides support for human relations in the workplace.

■ *The labor market has become a place of churning dislocation caused by the heavy volume of mergers, acquisitions, business closings, and downsizing.* Each month, over 100,000 workers lose their jobs because of layoffs. During a recession, this figure will often be much higher. Some layoffs are the result of megamergers involving large companies such as Exxon and Mobil. In some cases, global economics is a major factor. When orders from Asian airlines were canceled due to an economic downturn, Boeing Company announced plans to cut as many as 48,000 jobs.[4] Downsizing has become a common practice even when the economy is strong.

WWW.RALL.COM

Downsizing has many negative consequences. Large numbers of major U.S. companies are attempting to deal with serious problems of low morale and mistrust of management, problems caused by years of upheaval and restructuring.[5] Employees who remain after a company reduces its ranks also suffer; they often feel demoralized, overworked, and fearful that in the next round of cuts, they will be targeted.

Massive downsizing has created another phenomenon in the workplace—the large-scale use of temporary workers. Some companies that still have memories of painful layoffs are turning to temporary workers as a hedge against future layoffs. Strong demand for temps has surfaced in such diverse fields as telecommunications, banking, heavy manufacturing, and computers. Temporary work is growing in popularity among people who want more flexibility in their lifestyle. Others select this employment route because it can open the door to full-time employment.[6]

■ *Organizations are increasingly oriented toward service to clients, patients, and customers.* We live in a service economy where relationships are often more important than products. Restaurants, hospitals, banks, public utilities, colleges, airlines, and retail stores all must now gain and retain the patronage of their clients and customers. In any service-type firm, there are thousands of "moments of truth," those critical incidents in which customers come into contact with the organization and form their impressions of its quality and service.

> **We live in a service economy where relationships are often more important than products.**

In the new economy almost every source of organizational success—technology, financial structure, and competitive strategy—can be copied in an amazingly short period of time.[7] To illustrate, let's revisit The Container Store. The layout of these stores, store policies, and inventory could be duplicated by a competitor in a short period of time. However, making customers the center of the company culture takes years. Most owners and managers are reluctant to embrace the idea that people are at the heart of every form of quality improvement.

---

**TOTAL PERSON INSIGHT**

*HARRY E. CHAMBERS*

Author, *The Bad Attitude Survival Guide*

*"No matter what we do, we do it with people. People create the technology. People implement the technology. People make it all happen. People ultimately use whatever it is we create. No matter how small your organization or how technical its process, it takes people to be successful."*

---

■ *Workplace incivility is increasingly a threat to employee relationships.* A popular business magazine recently featured a cover story entitled "The Death of Civility."[8] The authors describe an epidemic of coarse and obnoxious behavior

Radius restaurant, located in Boston's Financial District, has received rave reviews from food critics. The recipe for success includes generous portions of staff training and a heaping scoop of teamwork. The staff responsible for great teamwork includes Christopher Myers (left), co-owner; Michael Schlow, co-owner and chef; and Esti Benson, general manager.

that weakens worker relationships. At a team meeting, a member's cell phone rings several times and is finally answered. As the person talks loudly on the phone, the rest of the team members wait. There's the employee who routinely brushes his teeth at the drinking fountain and the boss who takes three phone calls during an important meeting with an employee. Stephen L. Carter, author of *Civility*, believes that rudeness, insensitivity, and disrespect are the result of people believing in "me" rather than "we." He says civility is the sum of many sacrifices we are called on to make for the sake of living and working together.[9]

■ *Many companies are organizing their workers into teams in which each employee plays a part.* Organizations eager to improve quality, improve job satisfaction, increase worker participation in decision making and problem solving, and improve customer service are turning to teams. Typical of the team approach is Motorola, Inc., which now has more than 5,000 specialized "customer satisfaction" teams that work on highly specific ways of improving efficiency or providing new and innovative services.[10]

Although some organizations have successfully harnessed the power of teams, others have encountered problems. One barrier to productivity is the employee who lacks the skills needed to be a team member. In making the transition to a team environment, team members need skills in group decision making, leadership, conflict resolution, and communications.[11] In the world of e-mail, Web pages, and instant messaging it's now possible to work with team members you have never met who live in places you will never visit. New software is making it easier to work as a member of an "electronic" team.[12]

■ *Diversity has become a prominent characteristic of today's work force.* A number of trends have contributed to greater work force diversity. Throughout the past two decades, participation in the labor force by Asians, African Americans, and Hispanics has increased; labor force participation by adult women has risen to a record 60 percent—defying the widespread view that it had leveled off; the employment door for people with physical or mental impairments has opened wider; and larger numbers of young workers are working with members of the 50-plus age group. Within this heterogeneous work force we will find a multitude of values, expectations, and work habits. There is a need to develop increased tolerance for persons who differ in age, gender, race, physical traits, and sexual orientation. The major aspects of work force diversity are discussed in Chapter 7.

■ *Growing income inequality has generated a climate of resentment and distrust.* Even in the midst of one of the strongest economic booms in American history, most measures of income and wage distribution indicated that the wage gap keeps getting bigger. About 36 million people live in poverty, and 44 million do not have health insurance. The gap in pay separating chief executives from the average worker continues to widen. Scientists are finding that socioeconomic status— our relative status influenced by income, job, education, and other factors—impacts our physical and mental health. Most agree that psychological factors such as pessimism, stress, and shame are burdens of low social class.[13]

## HUMAN RELATIONS *in* ACTION

### Civility Under Siege

Rude, obnoxious behavior is not illegal, according to a recent court ruling. The U.S. Court of Appeals in Chicago upheld a lower court dismissal of a lawsuit in which a black female employee of S. C. Johnson & Company charged a male coworker with sexual and racial harassment. The man had berated her with obscenities—some with racial overtones, let a door slam in her face, and cut her off in the parking lot. The court found that the man treated all his coworkers with disrespect, and concluded that "equal opportunity harassers" are not guilty of discrimination.

It is safe to say that no line of work, organization, or industry will enjoy immunity from these developments. Today's employee must be adaptable and flexible to achieve success within a climate of change and uncertainty.

## ■ *The Challenge of Human Relations*

To develop and apply the wide range of interpersonal skills needed in today's workplace can be extremely challenging. You will be working with clients, customers, patients, and other workers who vary greatly in age, work background, communications style, values, cultural background, gender, and work ethic. Because every person you come in contact with is unique, each encounter offers a new challenge.

Human relations is further complicated by the fact that we must manage three types of relationships. The first relationship is the one with ourselves. Many people carry around a set of ideas and feelings about themselves that are quite negative and in most cases quite inaccurate. People who have negative feelings about their abilities and accomplishments, and who engage in constant self-criticism, must struggle to maintain a good relationship with themselves. The importance of high self-esteem is addressed in Chapter 3.

The second type of relationship we must learn to manage is the one-to-one relationships we face in our personal and work lives. People in the health-care field, sales, food service, and a host of other occupations face this challenge many times each day. In some cases, racial, age, or gender bias serves as a barrier to good human relations. There are numerous other people differences that become barriers to effective one-to-one relationships.

The third challenge we face is the management of relationships with members of a group. As already noted, many workers are assigned to a team on either a full-time or a part-time basis. Lack of cooperation among team members can result in quality problems or a slowdown in production.

## ■ *The Influence of the Behavioral Sciences*

The field of human relations draws on the behavioral sciences—psychology, sociology, and anthropology. Basically, these sciences focus on the *why* of human behavior. Psychology attempts to find out why *individuals* act as they do, and sociology and anthropology concentrate primarily on *group* dynamics and social interaction. Human relations differs from the behavioral sciences in one important respect. Although also interested in the why of human behavior, human relations goes further and looks at what can be done to anticipate problems, resolve them, or even prevent them from happening. In other words, this field emphasizes knowledge that can be *applied* in practical ways to problems of interpersonal relations at work or in our personal life.

## ■ *Human Relations and the "Total Person"*

The material in this book focuses on human relations as the study of *how people satisfy both personal and work-related needs*. We believe, as do most authors in the field of human relations, that such human traits as physical fitness, emotional control, self-awareness, self-esteem, and values orientation are interdependent. Although some organizations may occasionally wish they could employ only a person's physical strength or creative powers, all that can be employed is the **total**

**person.** A person's separate characteristics are part of a single system making up that whole person. Work life is not totally separate from home life, and emotional conditions are not separate from physical conditions. The quality of a person's work, for example, is often related to physical fitness or one's ability to cope with stress.

Many organizations are beginning to recognize that when the whole person is improved, significant benefits accrue to the firm. These organizations are establishing employee development programs that address the total person, not just the employee skills needed to perform the job. These programs include such topics as stress management, assertiveness training, physical fitness, balancing work and family life, and values clarification. A few examples follow:

ITEM: Employees at H. A. Montgomery—a chemical manufacturing firm in Detroit, Michigan—have the option of starting each workday with 20 minutes of Transcendental Meditation.[14]

ITEM: Liz Claiborne, Inc., holds seminars on domestic violence issues for its employees.[15]

ITEM: Texas Instruments offers seminars for dads who need help juggling work and home.[16]

ITEM: The wellness center at Tires Plus corporate headquarters offers classes on nutrition and healthy cooking, work/life balance, weight loss, and smoking cessation.[17]

Some of the results of these programs may be difficult to assess in terms of profit and loss. For example, does a person in good physical health contribute more? If an employee is under considerable stress, does this mean he or she will have more accidents on the job? Specific answers vary, but most human resource management experts agree that total person development includes physical, mental, social, emotional, and spiritual development.

---

**TOTAL PERSON INSIGHT**

*DANIEL GOLEMAN*

Author, *Working with Emotional Intelligence*

*"The rules for work are changing, and we're all being judged, whether we know it or not, by a new yardstick—not just how smart we are and what technical skills we have, which employers see as givens, but increasingly by how well we handle ourselves and one another."*

---

■ ***The Need for a Supportive Environment***

Some managers do not believe that total person development, job enrichment, motivation techniques, or career development helps increase productivity or strengthen worker commitment to the job. It is true that when such practices are tried without full commitment or without full management support, there is a good chance they will fail. Such failures often have a demoralizing effect on employees and management alike. "Human relations" may take the blame, and management will be reluctant to try other human relations methods or approaches in the future.

A basic assumption of this book is that human relations, when applied in a positive and supportive environment, can help individuals achieve greater personal satisfaction from their careers and help increase an organization's productivity and efficiency.

---

### THINKING / LEARNING STARTERS

1. How important will human relationship skills be in your future career(s)?

2. Do you believe the developments in the workplace described in this chapter will continue throughout the next decade? What new developments might surface?

---

## The Forces Influencing Behavior at Work

A major purpose of this text is to increase your knowledge of factors that influence human behavior in a variety of work settings. An understanding of human behavior at work begins with a review of the six major forces that affect every employee, regardless of the size of the organization. As Figure 1.1 indicates, these are organizational culture, supervisory-management influence, work group influence, job influence, personal characteristics of the worker, and family influence.

### ■ *Organizational Culture*

Every organization, whether a manufacturing plant, retail store, hospital, or government agency, has its own unique culture. **Organizational culture** is the collection of shared values, beliefs, rituals, stories, and myths that foster a feeling of community among organizational members.[18] The culture of an organization is, in most cases, the reflection of the deeply held values and behaviors of a small group of individuals. In a large organization, the chief executive officer (CEO) and a handful of senior executives will shape the culture. In a small company, the culture may flow from the values held by the founder.[19]

Herb Kelleher, chairman of Southwest Airlines Company, has created a culture that other airlines envy. By almost every measure of efficiency in the airline industry, Southwest is at the top of the charts. Kelleher's dedication to his employees is the major reason for this success. He has proven that a large company (nearly 30,000 employees) with a unionized work force can be a place where kindness, cooperation, and human spirit abound. By contrast, the U.S. Postal

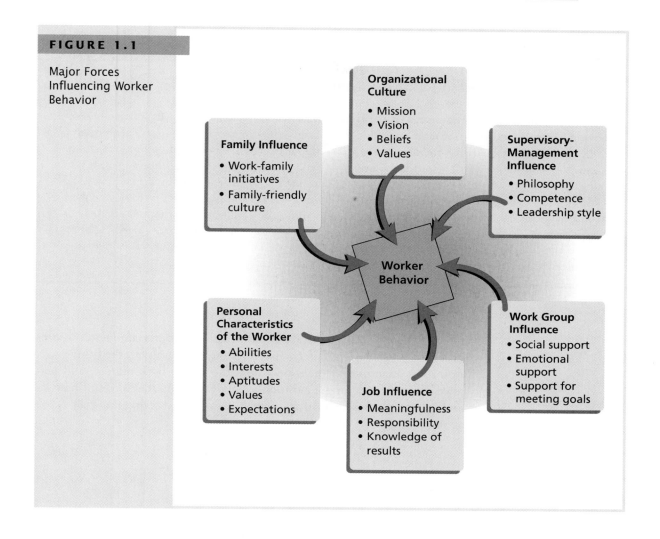

**FIGURE 1.1**

Major Forces Influencing Worker Behavior

**Organizational Culture**
- Mission
- Vision
- Beliefs
- Values

**Family Influence**
- Work-family initiatives
- Family-friendly culture

**Supervisory-Management Influence**
- Philosophy
- Competence
- Leadership style

**Worker Behavior**

**Personal Characteristics of the Worker**
- Abilities
- Interests
- Aptitudes
- Values
- Expectations

**Job Influence**
- Meaningfulness
- Responsibility
- Knowledge of results

**Work Group Influence**
- Social support
- Emotional support
- Support for meeting goals

Service's authoritarian culture has resulted in poor labor-management relations and customer service that is often mediocre.[20]

A growing number of organizations are creating vision statements that direct the energies of the company and inspire employees to achieve greater heights. Once a vision statement is created, senior management must serve as "cheerleaders" to unify employees behind the vision.

## ■ *Supervisory-Management Influence*

Supervisory-management personnel are in a key position to influence employee behavior. It is no exaggeration to say that supervisors and managers are the spokespersons for the organization. Their philosophy, competence, and leadership style establish the organization's image in the eyes of employees. Each employee develops certain perceptions about the organization's concern for his or

## HUMAN RELATIONS *in* ACTION

### Timberland Culture in the Age of Information

At a recent conference, Jeffrey Swartz, CEO of Timberland Company, described the evolution of his company. He explained that his grandfather had started the company, making boots by hand. Everything about the process was personal: "When he sold you a pair of boots and promised that the boots would last a lifetime, it wasn't a customer-service program. It was my grandfather looking you in the eye and making a personal promise that if anything went wrong, you could bring the boots back and he himself would make you another pair." Later Jeffrey Swartz's father took over Timberland and made it a national company. Today, the third-generation CEO says his challenge is to make the business personal all over again. He says, "These days, when people buy something from you, they want to know who you are, what you believe in."

Swartz also believes in giving something back to the community. Every employee gets paid for 40 hours a year of volunteer work.

her welfare. These perceptions, in turn, influence such important factors as productivity, customer relations, safety consciousness, and loyalty to the firm.

Supervisory-management personnel hold the key to both outlook and performance. They are in a unique position to unlock the internal forces of motivation and help employees channel their energies toward achieving the goals of the organization.[21]

---

**TOTAL PERSON INSIGHT**

WILLIAM RASPBERRY

Syndicated Columnist

> "Jobs do a lot more than merely provide income. They provide the opportunity to learn and enhance skills, to have some control over one's fate and, perhaps most important, to gain a sense of self-worth, a sense of carrying one's own weight."

---

### ■ *Work Group Influence*

In recent years, behavioral scientists have devoted considerable research to determining the influence of group affiliation on the individual worker. They are particularly interested in group influence within the formal structure of the organization. This research has identified three functions of group membership.[22] First, it can satisfy *social needs*. Many people find the hours spent at work enjoyable because coworkers provide needed social support. Second, the work group can provide the *emotional support* needed to deal with pressures and problems on or off the job. Finally, the group provides *assistance in solving problems and meeting goals.* A cohesive work group lends support and provides the resources we need to be productive workers.

### ■ Job Influence

Work in modern societies does more than fulfill economic needs. When we find meaning and fulfillment in our jobs, we become more complete as human beings.[23] As one organizational consultant noted, work has taken center stage in the lives of most people: "We spend most of our waking hours doing our jobs, thinking about work, and getting to and from our workplaces. When we feel good about our work, we tend to feel good about our lives. When we find our work unsatisfying and unrewarding, we don't feel good."[24] Unfortunately, many people hold jobs that do not make them feel good. Many workers perceive their jobs to be meaningless and boring because there is little variety to the work. Some workers experience frustration because they are powerless to influence their working conditions.

> **We spend most of our waking hours doing our jobs, thinking about work, and getting to and from our workplaces.**

### ■ Personal Characteristics of the Worker

Every worker brings to the job a combination of abilities, interests, aptitudes, values, and expectations. Worker behavior on the job is most frequently a reflection of how well the work environment accommodates the unique characteristics of

In our expanding service economy relationships are often more important than products. Patience and a caring attitude are two important personal characteristics needed by these two service employees.

each worker. For more than half a century, work researchers and theorists have attempted to define the ideal working conditions that would maximize worker productivity. These efforts have met with some success, but unanswered questions remain.

Identifying the ideal work environment for today's work force is difficult. A single parent may greatly value a flexible work schedule and child care. The recipient of a new business degree may seek a position with a new high-tech company, hoping to make a lot of money in a hurry. Other workers may desire more leisure time.

Coming into the workplace today is a new generation of workers with value systems and expectations about work that differ from those of the previous generation. Today's better-educated and better-informed workers value identity and achievement. They also have a heightened sense of their rights.

### ■ *Family Influence*

There is general agreement that people need to establish a balance between work life and family life. Balance implies an interconnection among many areas of work and the family.[25] We are beginning to see some work-family trends that will definitely have an impact on work in this new century.[26]

- The value workers place on time versus money will shift in favor of time. Many people feel they spend too much time at work. More employers will offer flexible work schedules and time off as an incentive.

- More employers will take steps to ease the pressure on workers who feel they need to be in two places at once. Backup child care and convenience services such as dry cleaning at the workplace will be offered by more employers.

- More young fathers will avoid jobs that require them to be emotionally and physically absent from their homes for long periods of time.

Many organizations have found that family problems are often linked to employee problems such as tardiness, absenteeism, and turnover. The discovery has led many companies to develop work-family programs and policies that help employees juggle the demands of children, spouses, and elderly parents.[27]

## The Development of the Human Relations Movement

The early attempts to improve productivity in manufacturing focused mainly on trying to improve such things as plant layout and mechanical processes. But over time, there was more interest in redefining the nature of work and perceiving workers as complex human beings. This change reflected a shift in values from a concern with *things* to a greater concern for *people*. In this section we examine a few major developments that influenced the human relations movement.

## ■ *The Impact of the Industrial Revolution*

The Industrial Revolution marked a shift from home-based, handcrafted processes to large-scale factory production. Prior to the Industrial Revolution, most work was performed by individual craftworkers or members of craft guilds. Generally, each worker saw a project through from start to finish. Skills such as tailoring, carpentry, and shoemaking took a long time to perfect and were often a source of pride to an individual or a community. Under this system, however, output was limited.

The Industrial Revolution had a profound effect on the nature of work and the role of the worker. Previously, an individual tailor could make only a few items of clothing in a week's time; factories could now make hundreds. However, the early industrial plants were not very efficient because there was very little uniformity in the way tasks were performed. It was this problem that set the stage for research by a man who changed work forever.

## ■ *Taylor's Scientific Management*

In 1874 Frederick W. Taylor obtained a job as an apprentice in a machine shop. He rose to the position of foreman, and in this role he became aware of the inefficiency and waste throughout the plant. In most cases workers were left on their own to determine how to do their jobs. Taylor began to systematically study each job and break it down into its smallest movements. He discovered ways to reduce the number of motions and get rid of time-wasting efforts. Workers willing to follow Taylor's instruction found that their productivity soared.[28]

Frederick W. Taylor started the **scientific management** movement, and his ideas continue to influence the workplace today. Critics of Taylor's approach say that the specialized tasks workers perform often require manual skills but very little or no thinking.[29] Trade unions rebelled against his principles and practices. His lack of concern for the human dimension encouraged others to search for better ways to manage workers.

---

**TOTAL PERSON INSIGHT**

JAMES BAUGHMAN

Director of Management Development, General Electric Co.

*"You can only get so much more productivity out of reorganization and automation. Where you really get productivity leaps is in the minds and hearts of people."*

---

## ■ *Mayo's Hawthorne Studies*

Elton Mayo and his colleagues accidentally discovered part of the answer to variations in worker performance while conducting research in the mid-1920s at the Hawthorne Western Electric plant, located near Chicago. Their original goal was to study the effect of illumination, ventilation, and fatigue on production workers in the plant. Their research, known as the **Hawthorne studies,** became a sweeping investigation into the role of human relations in group and individual productivity. These studies also gave rise to the profession of industrial psychology by legitimizing the human factor as an element in business operations.[30]

After three years of experimenting with lighting and other physical aspects of work, Mayo made two important discoveries. First, all the attention focused on workers who participated in the research made them feel more important. For the first time, they were getting feedback on their job performance. In addition, test conditions allowed them greater freedom from supervisory control. Under these circumstances, morale and motivation increased and productivity rose.

Second, Mayo found that the interaction of workers on the job created a network of relationships called an **informal organization.** This organization exerted considerable influence on workers' performance.

Although some observers have criticized the Hawthorne studies for flawed research methodology,[31] this research can be credited with helping change the way management viewed workers.

### ■ *From the Great Depression to the New Millennium*

During the Great Depression, interest in human relations research waned as other ways of humanizing the workplace gained momentum. During that period, unions increased their militant campaigns to organize workers and force employers to pay attention to such issues as working conditions, higher pay, shorter hours, and protection for child laborers.

After World War II and during the years of postwar economic expansion, interest in the human relations field increased. Countless papers and research studies on worker efficiency, group dynamics, organization, and motivational methods were published. Douglas McGregor, in his classic book *The Human Side of Enterprise,* argued that how well an organization performs is directly proportional to its ability to tap human potential.[32] Abraham Maslow, a noted psychologist, devised a "hierarchy of needs," stating that people satisfied their needs in a particular order.

Since the 1950s, theories and concepts regarding human behavior have focused more and more on an understanding of human interaction. Eric Berne in the 1960s revolutionized the way people think about interpersonal communication when he introduced transactional analysis, with its "Parent-Adult-Child" model. At about the same time, Carl Rogers published his work on personality development, interpersonal communication, and group dynamics. In the early 1980s, William Ouchi introduced the Theory Z style of management, which is based on the belief that worker involvement is the key to increased productivity.

There is no doubt that management consultants Tom Peters and Robert Waterman also influenced management thinking regarding the importance of people in organizations. Their best-selling book *In Search of Excellence,* published in

1982, describes eight attributes of excellence found in America's best-run companies.[33] One of these attributes, "productivity through people," emphasizes that excellent companies treat the worker as the root source of quality and productivity.

We have provided you with no more than a brief glimpse of selected developments in the human relations movement. Space does not permit a review of the hundreds of theorists and practitioners who have influenced human relations in the workplace. However, in the remaining chapters, we do introduce the views of other influential thinkers and authors.

---

### THINKING / LEARNING STARTERS

1. What do you personally find to be the basic rewards of work?

2. The book *In Search of Excellence* cites "productivity through people" as an attribute of excellent companies. Do you agree or disagree with this view?

3. What degree of worker involvement have you experienced in places where you have worked or volunteered?

---

## *Major Themes in Human Relations*

Seven broad themes emerge from the study of human relations. They are communication, self-awareness, self-acceptance, motivation, trust, self-disclosure, and conflict resolution. These themes reflect the current concern in human relations with the twin goals of (1) personal growth and development and (2) the satisfaction of organizational objectives. To some degree, these themes are interrelated (see Figure 1.2), and most are discussed in more than one chapter of this book.

### ■ *Communication*

It is not an exaggeration to describe communication as the "heart and soul" of human relations. **Communication** is the means by which we come to an understanding of ourselves and others. To grow and develop as persons, we must develop the awareness and the skills necessary to communicate effectively. John Diekman, author of *Human Connections,* says that "if we are going to do anything constructive and helping with one another, it must be through our communication."[34] Communication is the *human* connection. That is why the subject is covered in more than one section of this book. In Chapter 2 we explore the fundamentals of interpersonal communication. It is these fundamentals that provide the foundation for all efforts to improve communication. Suggestions on how to improve communication will appear in other chapters.

> **It is not an exaggeration to describe communication as the "heart and soul" of human relations.**

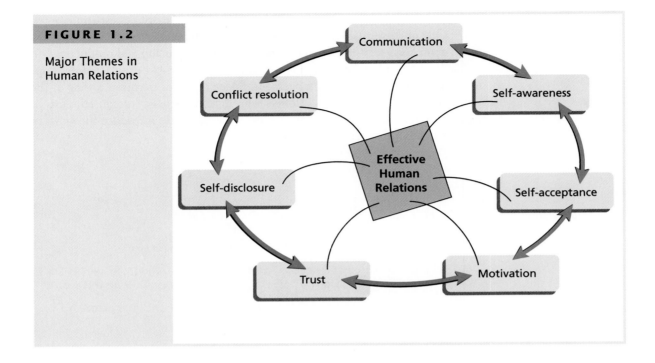

**FIGURE 1.2**

Major Themes in Human Relations

## Self-Awareness

One of the most important ways to develop improved relationships with others is to develop a better understanding of ourselves. With increased **self-awareness** comes a greater understanding of how our behavior influences others. Stephen Covey, author of *The Seven Habits of Highly Effective People,* says that self-awareness enables us to stand apart and examine the way we "see" ourselves. He states that self-awareness "affects not only our attitudes and behaviors, but also how we see other people."[35]

The importance of self-awareness is being recognized by an increasing number of authors, trainers, and educators. Daniel Goleman, author of the best-selling book *Emotional Intelligence,* has given us new insights into the importance of self-awareness. Goleman says IQ accounts for only about 20 percent of a person's success in life. The rest, he says, you can credit to "emotional intelligence." Of all the elements that make up emotional intelligence, Goleman asserts, self-awareness is the most important. He notes that a deficit in self-awareness can be damaging to one's personal relationships and career.[36]

## Self-Acceptance

The degree to which you like and accept yourself is the degree to which you can genuinely like and accept other people. **Self-acceptance** is the foundation of successful interaction with others. In a work setting, people with positive self-concepts tend to cope better with change, accept responsibility more readily, tolerate differences, and generally work well as team members. A negative self-concept, however, can create barriers to good interpersonal relations. Self-acceptance is crucial not only for building relationships with others but also for setting and achieving goals. The more you believe you can do, the more you are likely to accomplish. Chapter 3 explains why high self-esteem (complete self-acceptance) is essential for effective human relations. That chapter also helps you identify ways to achieve greater self-acceptance.

## ■ *Motivation*

Most people who engage in the study of **motivation** seek answers to two questions: "How do I motivate myself?" and "How do I motivate others?" If you are really committed to achieving peak performance, you must motivate yourself from within.[37] Inner drives for excellence can be very powerful. Chapter 4 will help you identify the priorities and values that motivate you.

## ■ *Trust*

**Trust** is the building block of all successful relationships with coworkers, customers, family members, and friends. There is compelling evidence that low levels of trust in a work force can lead to reduced productivity, stifled innovation, high stress, and slow decision-making.[38] When a lack of trust exists in an organization, a decline in the flow of information almost always results. Employees communicate less information to their supervisors, express opinions reluctantly, and avoid discussions. Cooperation, so necessary in a modern work setting, deteriorates. When a climate of trust is present, frank discussion of problems and a free exchange of ideas and information are encouraged.

## HUMAN RELATIONS *in* ACTION

### A Well-Managed Work Force Impacts the Bottom Line

Companies that do a good job of recruiting and rewarding workers, and provide them with a flexible, collegial workplace, offer a larger return to shareholders. This is the finding of research conducted by Watson Wyat Worldwide, a human resources consulting firm in Bethesda, Maryland. A well-managed workplace can increase a corporation's market value by as much as 30 percent. Personal satisfaction of the work force results in higher productivity and lower employee turnover. Low employee turnover can have a major impact on profits. The per-person cost of employee turnover often exceeds $10,000.

Is there someone who understands how

frightening a situation can be? Someone who

believes fear can be dismantled when we are

armed with confidence? Is there an insurance

company that is consistently rated superior by

independent rating services — a company with

a 146 year history of providing strength in the

face of uncertainty? Without Question.

Trust *is not being afraid even if you're vulnerable.*

*Without Question.* **The St Paul**
Property and Liability Insurance

In a two-person relationship, or a relationship with team members, trust exists when you fully believe in the integrity or character of the other person. In a work setting, trust is the cement that holds an organization together.

### ■ *Self-Disclosure*

**Self-disclosure** and trust are two halves of a whole. The more open you are with people, the more trust you build up. The more trust there is in a relationship, the safer you feel to disclose who you are. Self-disclosure is also part of good communication and helps eliminate unnecessary guessing games. Managers who let their subordinates know what is expected of them help those employees fulfill their responsibilities. Chapter 2 emphasizes the need of individuals to verbalize the thoughts and feelings they carry within them and provides many practical suggestions on how to use constructive self-disclosure.

### ■ *Conflict Resolution*

Conflict in one form or another surfaces almost daily in the lives of many workers. You may experience conflict during a commute to work when a careless driver cuts you off at a freeway exit ramp. If your job includes supervisory-management responsibilities, you will spend a great deal of time in **conflict reso-**

**lution** attempting to resolve conflicts among members of your staff. As a team member, you may assume the role of mediator when other team members clash. Resolving conflict with coworkers can require a great deal of energy. Conflict also surfaces when working parents attempt to balance the demands of both work and family. Stressful conditions at home often interfere with work performance, and on-the-job pressures create or magnify problems at home.[39]

Conflict tends to obstruct cooperative action, create suspicion and distrust, and decrease productivity. The ability to anticipate or resolve conflict can be an invaluable skill. Chapter 8 provides several valuable suggestions on how conflict can be resolved effectively.

---

### *THINKING / LEARNING STARTER*

Now that you have had an opportunity to read about the seven themes of human relations, what do you consider your strongest areas? In which areas do you feel you need improvement? Why?

---

## *Human Relations: Benefits to You*

As previously noted, the work force is currently characterized by downsizing, mergers, buyouts, and business closings. We are seeing more emphasis on quality products and quality services. In addition, diversity has become a more prominent characteristic of today's work force. These conditions will very likely continue in the new millennium. One of the best ways to cope with these changes is to develop and apply the interpersonal skills needed for success in today's working world.

A basic course in human relations cannot give you a foolproof set of techniques for solving every people-related problem that might arise. It can, however, give you a better understanding of human behavior in groups, help you become more sensitive to yourself and others, and enable you to act more wisely when problems occur. You may even be able to anticipate conflicts or prevent small problems from escalating into major ones.

Many leaders feel that courses in human relations are important because very few workers are responsible to themselves alone. These leaders point out that most jobs today are interdependent. If people in these jobs cannot work effectively as a team, the efficiency of the organization will suffer.

## *Summary*

The study of human relations helps us understand how people fulfill both personal growth needs and organizational goals in their careers. Many organizations are beginning to realize that an employee's life outside the job can have a significant impact on work performance, and some are developing training and education programs in human relations that address the total person. Increasingly, organizations are discovering that many forces influence the behavior of people at work.

Human relations is not a set of foolproof techniques for solving people-related problems. Rather, it gives people an understanding of basic behavior concepts that may enable them to make wiser choices when problems arise, to anticipate or prevent conflicts, and to keep minor problems from escalating into major ones.

The development of the human relations movement involved a redefinition of the nature of work and the gradual perception of managers and workers as complex human beings. Two landmarks in the study of motivation and worker needs are Frederick Taylor's work in scientific management and Elton Mayo's Hawthorne studies. Many industry leaders predict an increased emphasis on human relations research and application. The reasons for this trend include greater awareness that human relations problems serve as a major barrier to the efficient operation of an organization, the employment of workers who expect more from their jobs, and worker organizations and government agencies pressing for attention to employee concerns.

Seven major themes emerge from a study of human relations: communication, self-awareness, self-acceptance, motivation, trust, self-disclosure, and conflict resolution. These themes reflect the current concern in human relations with personal growth and satisfaction of organizational objectives.

## *Career Corner*

Q: The daily newspapers and television news shows are constantly reporting on mergers, business closings, and downsizing efforts. With so much uncertainty in the job market, how can I best prepare for a career?

A: You are already doing one thing that is very important—keeping an eye on labor market trends. During a period of rapid change and less job security, you must continuously study workplace trends and assess your career preparation. Louis S. Richman, in a *Fortune* magazine article entitled "How to Get Ahead in America," said, "Climbing in your career calls for being clear about your personal goals, learning how to add value, and developing skills you can take anywhere." After you clarify the type of work that would be rewarding for you, be sure you have the skills necessary to be competitive in that employment area. Keep in mind that today's employers demand more, so be prepared to add value to the company from day one. Search for your employer's toughest problems and make yourself part of the solutions.

The skills you can take anywhere are those transferable skills required by a wide range of employers. These are important because there are no jobs for life. Be prepared to work for several organizations.

## Key Terms

| | |
|---|---|
| human relations | self-awareness |
| total person | self-acceptance |
| organizational culture | motivation |
| scientific management | trust |
| Hawthorne studies | self-disclosure |
| informal organization | conflict resolution |
| communication | |

## Review Questions

1. Given the information provided in this chapter, define *human relations.*
2. List and briefly describe the major developments that have given new importance to human relations.
3. Describe the total person approach to human relations. Why is this approach becoming more popular?
4. List and describe the six major forces influencing human behavior at work.
5. In what ways can training in human relations benefit an organization?
6. How did Taylor's work help usher in the modern assembly line? What are some possible negative outcomes of the assembly-line approach?
7. Mayo's research indicated that workers could influence the rate of production in an organization. What discoveries did Mayo make that led to this conclusion?
8. Liz Claiborne provides seminars on domestic violence issues, and Tires Plus offers classes on nutrition and healthy cooking, work/life balance, weight loss, and smoking cessation. Do these programs represent a good use of company funds? Explain your answer.
9. What seven themes emerge from a study of human relations? Describe each one briefly.
10. Reread the Total Person Insight that quotes Daniel Goleman and then indicate what you feel is the meaning of this quotation.

## Application Exercises

1. Throughout this book you will be given many opportunities to engage in self-assessment activities. Self-assessment involves taking a careful look at the human relations skills you need to be well rounded and thoroughly prepared for success in your work life and fulfillment in your personal life. To assess your human relations skills, complete the self-assessment exercise at the ends of chapters 2 through 9. These assessment exercises will provide you with increased awareness of your strengths and a better understanding of those abilities you may want to improve.

2. The seven broad themes that emerge from the study of human relations were discussed in this chapter. Although these themes are interrelated, there is value in examining each one separately before reading the rest of the book. Review the description of each theme and then answer these questions:

a. When you take into consideration the human relations problems that you have observed or experienced at work, school, and home, which themes represent the most important areas of study? Explain your answer.

b. In which of these areas do you feel the greatest need for improvement? Why?

 *Internet Exercise*

Companies featured in *Fortune's* list of the 100 best companies to work for in America are characterized by openness, fairness, camaraderie among employees, job security, opportunities for advancement, and sensitivity to work/family issues. These companies are concerned about the total person, not just the skills that help the company earn a profit. Here are some of the companies that have made the "best companies" list:

| Company | Location | Type of Business |
|---|---|---|
| Southwest Airlines | Dallas, TX | Airline |
| SAS Institute | Carey, NC | Computer software |
| MBNA | Wilmington, DE | Issuer of credit cards |
| Corning | Corning, NY | Manufacturing |
| Nordstrom | Seattle, WA | Retailing |

Develop a profile of two of these companies by visiting their Web sites and reviewing the available information. Also, visit Hoover's Online, a resource that provides access to profiles of about 2,800 companies. Additional information on each of these companies may be found in *Business Week, Forbes, Working Mother,* and other business publications.

*Case Problem* *Challenges in the New Economy*

At the beginning of the new millennium, a growing number of social researchers, economists, and consultants tried to predict what the world of work would be like in the years ahead. We pay close attention to these and to even more recent forecasts because work is a central part of our identities. As one writer has noted, our working life—in a few short decades—adds up to life itself. Work can also be one of the major fulfillments in life. What will the new economy be like from a worker's viewpoint? Here are three predictions:

- *In the new economy, everyone is an entrepreneur.* This is the view expressed by Thomas Petzinger, Jr., author and former columnist for the *Wall Street Journal.* He reports on factories where shop floor employees handle customer service calls and create new ways to solve customer problems. The employees who deliver freight for Western Kansas Xpress carry business cards and search out potential customers. To become an entrepreneur in a corporate setting often means using your creativity more often, taking some risks and moving beyond your job description. The new economy will give many workers an opportunity to take more responsibility for their work.

- *The new economy features the art of the relaunch.* How often will you change jobs during your lifetime? Five times? Ten? Fifteen? The new economy offers more career options, more challenges, and more uncertainty. Chances are, you will need to relaunch your career several times. Molly Higgins held a career track job in the human resources department of a large company. When she discovered that in the entire department, there wasn't a single position she aspired to, it was time to relaunch her career. In recent years, thousands of people joined the ranks of new dot-com companies, only to lose their jobs in a matter of weeks or months. Petzinger says that changing jobs will require using your learning skills and applying the skills you have already learned.

- *In the new economy getting a job may be easier than getting a life.* We have, in recent years, seen a dramatic increase in the standard of living. The price we pay for a bigger home, a nicer automobile, or a vacation in Italy is often a more demanding work life. Some people choose to work harder in order to acquire more "things." In some cases, corporate downsizing has left fewer people to do the same amount of work. Working more hours and working harder during those hours can result in greater stress, a breakdown in family life, and a decrease in leisure time.[40]

## Questions

1. Would you feel comfortable assuming the duties of an entrepreneur within an existing company, or would you rather start your own business?
2. You are likely to relaunch yourself several times during the years ahead. Does the prospect of several relaunches seem frightening to you, or do you look forward to the challenge?
3. What steps would you take to achieve better work/life balance?

# 2 Improving Interpersonal Communications

CHAPTER PREVIEW

After studying this chapter you will be able to:

- Understand the impact advanced technology has had on today's communications.

- Differentiate impersonal from interpersonal communication.

- Understand the communication process and the filters that affect communication.

- Identify ways to improve personal communication, including developing listening skills.

- Learn how to communicate effectively through technology, including voice mail and e-mail.

When the managers at GE Capital Services were asked to define communication, they described specific, relatively infrequent things such as newsletters and meetings. GE Capital employees, however, viewed communication as an everyday electronic, verbal, and visual process that provided information needed in their jobs.[1] This particular definition gap is common. Yet both managers and employees have an accurate view of communication in an organization; they agree that multiple communication techniques are necessary in the information age.

Shari Franey, president of Performance Personnel, which has six offices in Pennsylvania, installed voice mail and e-mail to facilitate the flow of information among her employees. However, she also instituted a series of face-to-face meetings for all employees to ensure that what one employee knew, everybody else would know.[2] In Arizona, Eric Schechter, president of Great American Events, provides his employees with e-mail, Internet access, and PalmPilots, all of which enable them to share project management files and to facilitate group scheduling. He discovered, however, that many times information would be lost in an electronic folder—and the average employee wouldn't have time to search or know where to find it. So when information of a time-sensitive nature needed to be shared immediately, Schechter simply wrote a note on the whiteboard in the company conference room where employees ate lunch.[3]

In today's fast-paced communications environment, progressive organizations cannot depend on one medium to send a message. They must use a combination of face-to-face, print, and electronic methods in order to meet the needs and interests of all those involved.

## Advanced Technology's Impact on Communication

The new millennium has ushered in the age of information, led by rapid advances in technology-based communication. But technology without people won't work. **E-commerce,** the ability to instantly buy and sell products or services via the World Wide Web, has made it imperative for all of us to learn efficient and effective communication skills utilizing the latest technology advances. Yet we must not lose the human touch that keeps customers coming back. This global business boom presents individuals with the additional challenge of learning how to communicate across language and cultural barriers, often without seeing one another.

**Technology without people won't work.**

Not everyone is in the communication business, but everyone is in the business of communicating. Today many workers are consumed by over 200 messages a day through various options such as the telephone, voice mail, telephone message slips, Post-its, interoffice mail, e-mail, postal mail, overnight couriers, faxes, pagers, and personal digital appliances with wireless connections to the Internet.[4] Some of these options enhance the communication process; others can create barriers to effective communication. Often individuals must wade through useless data to

**Not everyone is in the communication business, but everyone is in the business of communicating.**

"SINCE OUR NETWORK WAS UPGRADED, WE GET 30 PERCENT MORE USELESS INFORMATION."

find the information they are seeking. Although the speed and volume of information have increased, the average person's brain cannot operate any faster. As the number of messages sent and received increases, people often find themselves distracted and unable to concentrate because of the constant interruptions and volume of information. This often leads to a breakdown in communications between individuals. The breakdown can result in human relations problems that may be hard to fix once the damage is done.

## The Communication Process

Most people take communication for granted. When they write, speak, or listen to others, they assume that the message given or received is being understood. In reality, messages are often misunderstood because they are incomplete or because different people interpret messages in different ways. The diversity of today's work force calls for a greater understanding of how to communicate effectively, through technology or face to face, with people from different cultures, countries, and lifestyles. Yet even though people and communication methods may be diverse, the basic communication process remains the same.

### ■ Impersonal Versus Interpersonal Communication

The types of communication used to exchange information can be placed on a continuum ranging from "impersonal" on one end to "interpersonal" on the other.[5] When we use such words as *transmit* or *transfer*, we are talking about a one-way information-giving process. This impersonal, one-way communication process can be used to give basic information such as company policies, instructions, or facts. Generally, organizations use memos, letters, electronic mail (e-mail), computer printouts, voice mail, manuals, and/or bulletin boards as quick, easy ways to "get the word out." The major limitation of these forms of **impersonal communication** is that people receiving the information usually have little opportunity to ask the sender to clarify vague or confusing wording. Even e-mail has its limitations because the person sending the information cannot be sure when the person receiving the information will retrieve it. If the message is retrieved hours—or even days—later, the sender may not be available to clarify any misunderstandings.

**Interpersonal communication** is the verbal exchange of thoughts or information between two or more people. Such words as *share, discuss, argue,* and *interact* refer to this form of two-way communication. Interpersonal communication can take place in meetings, over the phone, in face-to-face interviews, or even during classroom discussions between instructors and students. If interpersonal communication is to be effective, some type of **feedback,** or response, from the person receiving the information is necessary. When this verbal exchange happens, the person sending the information can determine whether or not the message has been understood in the way he or she intended. As executive assistant to the CEO of Tyco International Ltd., Mary Sullivan prefers to communicate by phone instead of e-mail. She is aware that when you talk with someone directly, you don't have to wait for a return message.[6]

The speed of conveying information has increased dramatically through the use of technology. Yet many workers say they are out of touch. A young narrator in a television commercial for Volkswagen expressed the feelings of many people:

> I've got gigabytes. I've got megabytes. I'm voice-mailed. I'm e-mailed. I surf the net. I'm on the Web. I am Cyber-Man. So how come I feel so out of touch?[7]

Technology can be invaluable when it comes to impersonal information giving, but it cannot replace the two-way, interpersonal communication process when feedback and discussion are necessary.

---

## TOTAL PERSON INSIGHT

*PAUL R. TIMM*

Educator; Author,
*The Way We Word*

"'Communication breakdown' has just about taken the place of original sin as an explanation for the ills of the world— and perhaps with good cause. As our world becomes more complex and we spend more time in organized activities, the need for interpersonal understanding has never been greater. And just as important, the cost of failure has never been higher."

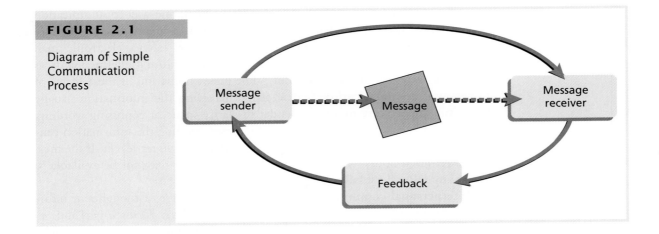

**FIGURE 2.1**

Diagram of Simple
Communication
Process

## Sender—Message—Receiver

Effective communication, in its most basic form, is composed of three elements: a sender, a receiver, and an understood message.[8] To illustrate, suppose your friend phones from your neighborhood convenience store and asks for directions to your home. You give your friend the appropriate street names, intersections, and compass directions so that he can drive to your door without getting lost. When your friend repeats his understanding of your directions, you clarify any misunderstandings, and he drives directly to your home. A simplified diagram of this communication process would look like Figure 2.1.

Now suppose you are late for an appointment, and the plumber you had requested three days ago calls you from her cellular phone and asks directions to your house. She explains that she has gotten lost in this neighborhood before,

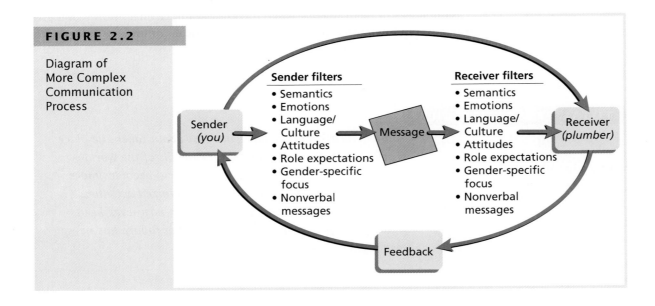

**FIGURE 2.2**

Diagram of
More Complex
Communication
Process

and it is obvious that English is her second language. The communication process becomes much more complicated, as shown in Figure 2.2. As your message travels from you to your plumber, it must pass through several "filters," each of which can alter the way your message is understood. Most communications flow through this complex process.

## Communication Filters

Messages are sent—and feedback is received—through a variety of filters that can distort the intended message. (See Figure 2.2.) When people are influenced by one or more of these filters, their perception of the message may be totally different from what the sender was attempting to communicate. Since the message received *is* the message, both sender and receiver must be keenly aware of these possible distortions so that they can intercept any miscommunication.

### ■ *Semantics*

We often assume that the words we use mean the same things to others, but this assumption can create problems. Words are not things; they are labels that stand for something. **Semantics** is the study of the relationship between a word and its meaning(s). We have agreed that particular words have associated meanings and usages. We can easily understand what words like *desk, computer,* or *envelope* mean. But more abstract terms, such as *job satisfaction, downsizing, internal customers,* or *word processing,* have less precise meanings and will be interpreted by different people in different ways. The more abstract the term, the less likely it is that people will agree on its meaning. Some professionals have been strongly criticized for using abstract words:

## HUMAN RELATIONS *in* ACTION

### Business Jargon

Communication often breaks down between individuals when they insert strange new words into their daily conversations. Although some people may be very familiar with the latest business jargon, others may not. To them, the jargon just sounds like language from another world. Being alert to the latest jargon may improve your communications skills. For example:

**Percussive maintenance:** an attempt to fix a computer or other electronic device by hitting it.

**Pink mail:** layoff notices delivered by e-mail.

**Voice-jail system:** a voice mail system that sends callers into a series of complex menus that create a vicious circle from which there appears to be no escape.

**People churner:** a boss who drives talented people away.

**Clockless worker:** committed worker who does not work strictly nine to five.

**Gender blurring:** jobs that are perceived as neither male- nor female-oriented.

**Boomerang worker:** retiree returning to work for a former employer.

ITEM: Effective 2002, all federal agencies are required to communicate in writing that is clear and easy to understand. For example, OSHA has replaced the phrase "ways of exit access" with "exit door" on all its documents.[9]

ITEM: The Securities and Exchange Commission requires that company prospectuses comply with a section of its plain-English regulations or risk delaying the stock offering.[10]

ITEM: Corporate employees often use important-sounding jargon that is almost incomprehensible. Better Communications, a firm that teaches writing skills to employers, clipped this statement from a memo circulated at a Fortune 500 company: "Added value is the keystone to exponentially accelerating profit curves."[11]

## ■ *Language and Cultural Barriers*

If you are connected to the Internet, you have automatically entered the global marketplace. English has been the dominant language throughout the free world for several decades. However, as more and more developing countries connect with the Internet, and transnational organizations (companies conducting business with more than one country) expand their global markets, multilingual transactions have become a serious communications issue. People who speak English fluently must remember to avoid slang when communicating with those whose first language is not English.

Hong Kong's chief executive Tung Chee Hwa and Mickey Mouse shake hands after making final plans to build the Walt Disney Company's new Hong Kong theme park. Through its international ventures in France and Japan, Disney officials have learned how to adapt their magic to the tastes and traditions of their multicultural park employees and guests.

Culture, which is an accumulation of values, forms of expression, beliefs, language, and the like, shapes one's interpretations of what events mean. Communication problems can be caused by conflicting cultural assumptions. For example, people living in the United States, Canada, Europe, Israel, or Australia usually prefer direct-approach communication; they tend to say more or less exactly what they mean. Their cultures value clarity, fluency, and brevity in communication. People from the Orient, the Arab world, and much of Africa prefer a more indirect style of communication and therefore value harmony, subtlety, sensitivity, and tact more than clarity. They try hard to connect with their listeners.[12]

Cultures have different customs for how fast you should talk, how much you should talk, how long you should pause between ideas, and how long you should wait after someone finishes talking before you say something.[13] Navajo people, for example, consider it impolite to begin talking immediately after another person finishes.

Today, culture is getting more attention because of globalization, rapid increases in immigrant groups, and growing support for cultural diversity by employers. As you communicate with people from other cultures, keep in mind how your words and gestures may influence how the other person is interpreting your message. At the same time, avoid making potentially incorrect judgments about others' messages if they are coming from a culture different from your own.

### Emotions

Emotions can be a powerful communication filter. Strong emotions can either prevent people from hearing what a speaker has to say or make them too susceptible to the speaker's point of view. If they become angry or allow themselves to be carried away by the speaker's eloquence, they may "think" with their emotions and make decisions or take action they regret later. They have shifted their attention from the content of the message to their feelings about it.

You may have had the experience of your spouse or parent angrily demanding to know why you forgot to run an errand. If you allow someone else's anger to trigger your own, the conversation quickly deteriorates into an argument. The real issue—what happened and what is to be done about it—is lost in the shouting match. Detaching yourself from another's feelings and responding to the content of the message is often difficult. Yet many jobs require that employees remain calm and courteous regardless of a customer's emotional state. Emotional control is discussed in Chapter 8.

### Attitudes

Attitudes can be a barrier to communication in much the same way emotions can—by altering the way people hear a message. The listener may not like the speaker's voice, accent, gestures, mannerisms, dress, or delivery. Perhaps the listener has preconceived ideas about the speaker's topic. For instance, a person who is strongly opposed to abortion will most likely find it difficult to listen with objectivity to a pro-choice speaker. Negative attitudes create resistance to the message and can lead to a breakdown in communication. Overly positive attitudes can also be a barrier to communication. Biased in favor of the message, the listener may fail to evaluate it effectively. More is said about forming attitudes in Chapter 5.

### ■ Role Expectations

Role expectations influence how people expect themselves, and others, to act on the basis of the roles they play, such as boss, customer, or subordinate. These expectations can distort communication in two ways. If people identify others too closely with their roles, they may discount what the other person has to say: "It's just the boss again, saying the same old thing." A variation of this distortion occurs when we do not allow others to change their roles and take on new ones. This often happens to employees who are promoted from within the ranks of an organization to management positions. Others may still see the new manager as a secretary instead of a supervisor, as "old Chuck" from accounting rather than as the new department head.

### ■ Gender-Specific Focus

When discussing the same topic, men and women may be on completely different wavelengths because their gender-specific focus is different. This filter makes it appear that men and women are communicating through different "genderlects," just as people from different cultures use different dialects.[14] For example, men are more likely to focus on the financial aspects of a business situation; women often focus on the feelings and relationships of the people involved. Neither view is wrong, but the resulting conversation can frustrate both parties. In her book *Genderflex: Men and Women Speaking Each Other's Language at Work*, Judith Tingley states:

> Men and women assume that the other gender is trying to accomplish the same goal as their own gender, but assume the other gender is going about it the wrong way. . . . Both men and women often become critical and angry at the other gender for not using the "correct" means to the desired end.[15]

This anger and frustration can create a major filter that interferes with effective communication between the genders.

### ■ Nonverbal Messages

When we attempt to communicate with another person, we use both verbal and nonverbal communication. **Nonverbal messages** are "messages without words" or "silent messages." These are the messages (other than spoken or written words) we communicate through facial expressions, voice tone, gestures, appearance, posture, and other nonverbal means. Research indicates that our nonverbal messages have much more impact than verbal messages. Albert Mehrabian, author of

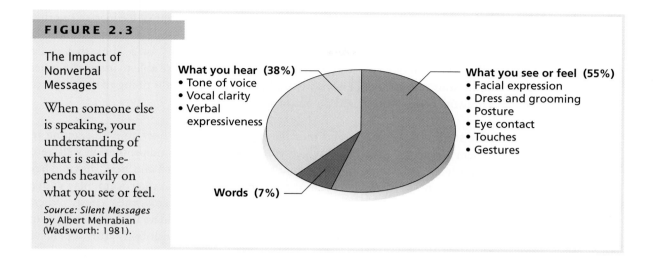

**FIGURE 2.3**

The Impact of Nonverbal Messages

When someone else is speaking, your understanding of what is said depends heavily on what you see or feel.

*Source: Silent Messages* by Albert Mehrabian (Wadsworth: 1981).

**What you hear (38%)**
- Tone of voice
- Vocal clarity
- Verbal expressiveness

**What you see or feel (55%)**
- Facial expression
- Dress and grooming
- Posture
- Eye contact
- Touches
- Gestures

**Words (7%)**

*Silent Messages,* indicates that only 7 percent of the meaning attached to our messages is conveyed through our choice of words and 55 percent is conveyed by what is seen—facial expressions, posture, eye contact, and gestures. About 38 percent of the message meaning is conveyed by what others hear—tone of voice, vocal clarity, and verbal expressiveness.[16] This chapter limits its discussion to the form of nonverbal communication commonly referred to as "body language."

Many of us could communicate more clearly, more accurately, and more credibly if we became more conscious of our body language. We can learn to strengthen our communications by making sure our words and our body language are consistent. When our verbal and nonverbal messages match, we give the impression that we can be trusted and that what we are saying reflects what we truly believe. But when our body language contradicts our words, we are often unknowingly changing the message we are sending. If a manager says to an employee, "I am very interested in your problem," but then begins to look at his watch and fidget with objects on his desk, the employee will most likely believe the nonverbal rather than the verbal message.

Individuals can improve their communications by monitoring the nonverbal messages they send through the use of eye contact, facial expressions, gestures, and personal space.

**Eye Contact**   Eyes transmit more information than any other part of the body. Because eye contact is so revealing, people generally observe some unwritten rules about looking at others. People who hold direct eye contact for only a few seconds, or avoid eye contact altogether, risk communicating indifference. However, a direct, prolonged stare between strangers is usually considered impolite, even potentially aggressive or hostile.

As a general rule, when you are communicating in a business setting, your eyes should meet the other person's about 60 to 70 percent of the time. This timing is an effective alternative to continuous eye contact.

**Facial Expressions**   If you want to identify the inner feelings of another person, watch facial expressions closely. A frown or a smile will communicate a great deal. We have all encountered a "look of surprise" or a "look that could kill." Most of our observations are very accurate. If we are able to assess the inner emotions of the other person, we can be sure that person is doing the same to us, drawing conclusions based on our facial expressions.

**Gestures**   Gestures send messages to people about how you are reacting to them and to the situation in which you find yourself. Some people will walk into a business meeting with their shoulders slumped forward and head down. They will slouch into their chair, lean their chin on the palm of their hand, play with a pencil or paperclip on the table, or clutch their arms across their chest. Others will walk into the room with chin held high and shoulders back, sit straight in their chairs and lean slightly forward, and take notes with both arms "open" to whoever is speaking during the meeting. Experts agree that during a meeting

Your nonverbal messages can enhance or weaken your credibility and effectiveness when working with others.

with others, the words you say—no matter how powerful—are often forgotten or disregarded unless your gestures command respect.[17]

**Be aware that some gestures that may be common in the American culture may have dramatically different meanings to people from outside the United States.**

Be aware that some gestures that may be common in the American culture may have dramatically different meanings to people from outside the United States. Although nodding your head up and down means "yes" in most countries, it means "no" in Greece and Bulgaria.[18] To use your fingers to call someone forward in a crowd is insulting to most Middle and Far Easterners.[19] And that common American gesture of folding your arms in front of you shows disrespect in Fiji.[20]

**Personal Space**   Research conducted by Edward Hall provides evidence that people use the space around them to define relationships. It is possible to make others uncomfortable by standing too close to, or too far away from, them. A customer may feel uncomfortable if a salesperson stands too close. A job applicant may feel uncomfortable if the interviewer maintains a distance of several feet. Hall identified four "zones" of comfortable distances that help us understand this nonverbal effect on others:[21]

1. *Intimate distance* includes touching to approximately 18 inches from another person. Most people will respond with defensiveness when strangers intrude into this territory.

2. *Personal distance* ranges from 18 inches to 4 feet. This distance is usually reserved for people we feel close to, such as spouses or close friends.

3. *Social distance* is 4 to 12 feet and is used for business meetings and impersonal social gatherings. Business can be conducted with a minimum of emotional involvement.

4. *Public distance,* which usually involves one-way communication from a speaker to an audience, is 12 to 15 feet.

It is important to keep in mind that these distances vary from one culture to another. For example, Asians are accustomed to close contact, but Americans want more space around them.

## Who Is Responsible for Effective Communication?

The sender and the receiver share *equal* responsibility for effective communication. The communication loop, as shown in Figure 2.2, is not complete if the message the receiver hears, and acts upon, differs from the one the sender intended. When the sender accepts 100 percent of the responsibility for sending a clear, concise message, the communication process begins. But the receiver must also accept 100 percent of the responsibility for receiving the message as the sender intended. Receivers must provide senders with enough feedback to ensure that an accurate message has passed through all the filters that might alter it. In other words, rather than assuming that everyone understands what you are saying, take the time to make sure everyone really hears it.

---

### THINKING / LEARNING STARTERS

1. Are you aware of the messages you send through body language? Recall your nonverbal behavior in various situations, including a difficult meeting with a supervisor or a dinner party with friends. Was your behavior consistent with your words? Explain.

2. Acute sensitivity to nonverbal messages is an important skill for people to develop. In general, do you feel that nonverbal messages are more trustworthy than verbal ones? Describe specific nonverbal messages that you have learned to trust in your friends or coworkers.

---

## How to Improve Personal Communication

Now that you understand the communication process and the various filters messages must pass through, you can begin to take the necessary steps to improve your own personal communication skills.

### ■ Send Clear Messages

Become a responsible sender by always sending clear, concise messages with as little influence from filters as possible. A general rule of thumb is to give clear instructions and ask clear questions so you won't be misunderstood. A new employee stood before the paper shredder in her new office. An administrative assistant noticed her confused look and asked if she needed some help. "Yes, thank you. How does this thing work?" "It's simple," said the assistant and took the thick report from the new employee and fed it through the shredder. "I see," she said, "but how many copies will it make?" This kind of miscommunication could easily have been avoided if both parties had followed these simple rules:

■ *Use words carefully.* As noted previously, abstract words, whether spoken or written, often become barriers to effective communication. Use words that are simple, clear, and concise. Avoid buzzwords or complex, official language. Tailoring the message to the receiver by using words the listener understands will help ensure that your message is understood.

■ *Use repetition.* When possible, use parallel channels of communication. For example, by sending an e-mail and making a phone call, you not only gain the receiver's attention through dialogue but also make sure there is a written record in case specific details need to be recalled. Many studies show that repetition, or redundancy, is an important element in ensuring communication accuracy.

■ *Use appropriate timing.* Keep in mind that most people, particularly at the managerial level in an organization, are flooded with messages every day. An important memo or e-mail may get no attention simply because it is competing with more pressing problems facing the receiver. Appropriately timing the delivery of your message will help ensure that it is accepted and acted on.

## ■ Develop Listening Skills

In addition to sending clearer messages, we need to practice listening. Most of us are born with the ability to hear, but we have to learn how to listen. Tom Peters, in his book *Thriving on Chaos: Handbook for a Management Revolution,* entitles an entire chapter "Become Obsessed with Listening." Psychologist Carl Rogers has said, "Listening is such an incredible and magical thing." Peters, Rogers, and others agree: We need to accept listening as a skill that can be learned.

Many of the misunderstandings in life are due to poor listening. Most people never learn to listen. This helps explain why people listen at a 25 percent efficiency rate in typical situations. They miss about 75 percent of the messages spoken by other people.[22] All too frequently, most of us hear the message but do not take the time to really listen and blend the messages we hear with critical thinking and human understanding.

## ■ Active Listening

Many people believe that listening is passive, something that does not require any response. Actually, **active listening** requires an intense involvement as you

## HUMAN RELATIONS *in* ACTION

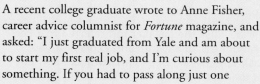

### Career Advice

A recent college graduate wrote to Anne Fisher, career advice columnist for *Fortune* magazine, and asked: "I just graduated from Yale and am about to start my first real job, and I'm curious about something. If you had to pass along just one piece of advice on which to build a career, what would it be?"

Anne answered, "I've always liked Albert Einstein's dictum: 'If *A* equals success, then the formula is $A = X + Y + Z$. *X* is work. *Y* is play. And *Z* is, Keep your mouth shut.' Or as my dad used to say, 'Nobody ever learns anything while they're talking.' If you make it a habit to listen more than you speak, you can't go too far wrong."

## Good listening is fueled by curiosity.

concentrate on what you are hearing, exhibit your listening attitude through your body language, and feed back to the speaker what you think he or she meant. When you learn how to become an active listener—sometimes referred to as "generous" listening—you have the opportunity to:

- *Gain stronger relationships.* One of the highest compliments you can pay anyone is to really listen. This communicates respect, and people will be more likely to listen receptively to you in return.[23]

- *Learn new information.* "Nobody ever learns anything while they're talking." Good listening is fueled by curiosity.

- *Make fewer mistakes.* You are acting on more accurate information.

---

**TOTAL PERSON INSIGHT**

*GERRY MITCHELL*

Chairman, Dana Corporation

*"Listening, really listening, is tough and grinding work, often humbling, sometimes distasteful. It's a fairly sure bet that you won't like the lion's share of what you hear."*

---

Active listening doesn't just happen. It isn't easy and rarely comes naturally. However, active listening is a *skill* that can be learned. Carefully examine Table 2.1, Active Listening Skills. Implement these ideas the next time you want to improve a relationship. You may be surprised by the impact you make.

**TABLE 2.1**

**Active Listening Skills**

1. *Develop a listening attitude.* Regard the speaker as worthy of your respect and attention. Drop your expectations as to what you are going to hear or would like to hear. Maintain good eye contact and lean slightly forward. Don't rush the speaker. Be patient and refrain from planning what to say in response until the speaker has finished talking.

2. *Give the speaker your full attention.* This is not easy because the messages you hear are often spoken at a much slower rate than you are able to absorb them. This allows your mind to roam. Your senses are constantly receiving extraneous information that may divert your attention. To stay focused, you may want to take notes, if it is appropriate to do so.

3. *Clarify by asking questions.* If something is not clear because the speaker has referred to a person or an event that you are not familiar with, ask him or her to back up and explain. If you want the speaker to expand on a particular point, ask open-ended questions such as "How do you feel about that?" or "Can you tell us some ways to improve?"

4. *Feed back your understanding of the speaker's message.* Paraphrase, in your own words, your understanding of what the speaker has just said: for example, *"Do you mean . . . ?" "Am I right in assuming that we should . . . ?" "What I hear you saying is . . ."* or *"In other words, we. . . ."*

**Critical Listening** **Critical listening** is the organized, cognitive process you use to carefully examine the thinking of others, in order to clarify and improve your understanding.[24] It is the attempt to see the topic of discussion from the *speaker's* point of view, and to consider how the speaker's perception of the situation may be different from your own. To improve your ability to critically view the new information, be sure to listen for evidence that confirms as well as challenges your own point of view. William Isaacs, director of the Dialogue Project at the Massachusetts Institute of Technology, states:

> Whenever we face a tough problem, we tend to think about our own position and how others are responding to it. . . . Dialogue involves listening and thinking beyond my position . . . there's something new here, a sense of curiosity, of possibility. The challenge is to listen to what it really might be.[25]

It is especially important to implement your critical listening skills when emotions are involved. The active listening skills you use when trying to learn something new (giving your full attention, asking questions, repeating your understanding of the new idea) and those you use in arguing with another person *should* be similar. However, emotions tend to distort your ability and/or willingness to listen. To activate your critical listening skills, ask yourself, Does the speaker's reasoning make sense? What evidence is being offered as part of each reason? Do I know each reason to be true, valid, or from my own experience? Is each reason based on a source that can be trusted?[26]

Software entrepreneur John Lauer can't stand to be cut off from his work, so he is constantly plugged in. Lauer tells friends, "I cannot be disconnected." Planning his honeymoon with fiancée Erin Ribiat turned out to be a real challenge because he wanted to stay connected to his work every hour of every day.

**Empathic Listening**   Many people today face serious personal problems and feel the need to talk about them with someone. They do not expect specific advice or guidance; they just want to spend some time with an empathic listener. Stephen Covey, the noted author and consultant, described **empathic listening** as listening with the intent to understand how the person feels. Empathic listening, according to Covey, requires listening with your ears, your eyes, and your heart.[27] If you want to practice empathic listening, adopt the following practices:

- *Avoid being judgmental.* Objectivity is the heart and soul of empathic listening. The person is communicating for emotional release and does not seek a specific response.

- *Accept what is said.* You do not have to agree with what is being said, but you should let the person know you are able to understand his or her viewpoint.

- *Be patient.* If you are unable or unwilling to take the time to hear what the person has to say, say so immediately. Signs of impatience send a negative message to the person needing to talk.[28]

---

### THINKING / LEARNING STARTERS

1. Think of some people you know who are active listeners. How can you tell? Describe an instance when their active listening improved their relations with you or another person.

2. Have you recently been approached by someone who wanted to talk to an empathic listener? Were you able to respond in the manner recommended? Explain.

---

### ■ *Use Constructive Self-Disclosure*

**Self-disclosure** is the process of letting another person know what you think, feel, or want. It is one of the important ways you let yourself be known by others. The primary goal of self-disclosure is to build strong and healthy interpersonal relationships.

It is important to note the difference between self-disclosure and self-description. **Self-description** involves disclosure of nonthreatening information, such as your age, your favorite food, or where you went to school. This is information that others could acquire in some way other than by your telling them. Self-disclosure, by contrast, usually involves some risk. When you practice self-disclosure, you reveal private, personal information that cannot be acquired from another source. Examples include your feelings about being a member of a minority group or your thoughts on new policies and procedures.

The importance of self-disclosure, in contrast to self-description, is shown by the following situation. You work at a distribution center and are extremely conscious of safety. You take every precaution to avoid work-related accidents. But another employee has a much more casual attitude toward safety rules and often "forgets" to observe the proper procedures, endangering you and other workers. You can choose to disclose your feelings to this person or hide your concerns. If you choose to stay silent, the problem will likely persist.

> **As a general rule, relationships grow stronger when people are willing to reveal more about themselves.**

**Benefits of Self-Disclosure**    There are a number of benefits you gain from openly sharing what you think, feel, or want. As a general rule, relationships grow stronger when people are willing to reveal more about themselves. When two people engage in an open, authentic dialogue, they often develop a high regard for each other's views. Often they discover they share common interests and concerns, and these serve as a foundation for a deeper relationship.

Self-disclosure often results in increased accuracy in communication. It takes the guesswork out of the communication process. No one is a mind reader; if people conceal how they really feel, it is very difficult for others to know how to respond to them appropriately. People who are frustrated by a heavy workload but mask their true feelings may never see the problem resolved.

In many cases, constructive self-disclosure can reduce stress. Sidney Jourard, a noted psychologist who has written extensively about self-disclosure, states that too much emphasis on privacy and concealment of feelings creates stress within an individual.[29] To the extent that persons can share with others their inner thoughts and feelings, they experience less stress. Constructive self-disclosure can be a very important dimension of a stress management program. Too many people keep their feelings bottled up inside, which can result in considerable inner tension.

**Guidelines for Appropriate Self-Disclosure**    In the search for criteria to determine appropriate self-disclosure, many factors must be considered. How much information should be disclosed? How intimate should the information be? Under what conditions should the disclosures be made? The following guidelines will help you develop your self-disclosure skills.

---

### TOTAL PERSON INSIGHT

*AARON LAZARE*

Doctor of Medicine

"*A genuine apology offered and accepted is one of the most profound interactions of civilized people. It has the power to restore damaged relationships, be they on a small scale, between two people, such as intimates, or on a grand scale, between groups of people, even nations. If done correctly, an apology can heal humiliation and generate forgiveness.*"

1. *Use self-disclosure to repair damaged relationships.* Many relationships are unnecessarily strained. The strain often exists because people refuse to talk about real or imagined problems. Self-disclosure can be an excellent method of repairing a damaged relationship.

   If your actions have caused hurt feelings, anger, or deep-seated ill will, an apology may be in order. A sincere apology can have a tremendous amount of healing power. In addition, it may set the stage for improved communications in the future.

2. *Discuss disturbing situations as they happen.* Your reactions to a work-related problem or issue should be shared as soon after the incident as possible. It is often difficult to recapture a feeling once it has passed, and you may distort the incident if you let too much time go by. Your memory is not infallible. The person who caused the hurt feelings is also likely to forget details about the situation.

3. *Select the right time and place.* Remarks that otherwise might be offered and accepted in a positive way can be rendered ineffective, not because of what we say but because of when and where we say it.[30] When possible, select a time when you feel the other person is not preoccupied and will be able to give you his or her full attention. Also, select a setting free of distractions.

4. *Avoid overwhelming others with your self-disclosure.* Although you should be open, do not go too far too fast. Many strong relationships are built slowly. The abrupt disclosure of highly emotional or intimate information may actually distance you from the other person. Your behavior may be considered threatening.

---

### THINKING / LEARNING STARTER

Mentally review your previous work or volunteer experience. Identify at least one occasion when you felt great frustration over some incident but avoided disclosing your feelings to the person who could have solved the problem. What factors motivated you not to self-disclose? In retrospect, do you now perceive any benefits you might have gained by choosing to self-disclose?

---

 ## Communicating via Technology

The traditional memos, letters, phone calls, and face-to-face conversations seem to be the exception rather than the rule in today's high-tech communications environment. Many people now maintain **virtual offices,** networks of coworkers connected by the latest technology. These workers can "set up shop" wherever they are—at home, on an airplane, in a motel room—and communicate with colleagues via e-mail, cellular phone, fax modem, or some other method. **Telecommuting,** an arrangement that allows employees to work from their homes, enables people scattered all over the world to work as one office staff. The Labor Department estimates that up to 19 million Americans now work online from home or from other locations outside the office.[31]

Today information can be shared by **voice mail;** recorded telephone messages can be sent or retrieved from anywhere in the world. Of course e-mail has become part of every computer owner's daily life. **Scanners** take pictures of documents and transmit them electronically. Documents can be sent via **fax modems** (transmission of information directly from a computer screen) to a fax machine or photocopier in another office, building, state, or country. Copiers receiving the electronic fax of multiple-page documents can reproduce, collate, and staple multiple copies of the information, often before the receiver is notified that the material is being sent.

The advantages of using these technology-based communication alternatives are obvious. Time efficiency is unsurpassed because people can transmit simple or detailed information across all time zones, and receivers can retrieve the information at their convenience. Cost effectiveness is unsurpassed as fiber-optic and satellite transmissions cost the consumer virtually pennies, compared to traditional transworld phone calls. Though some workers believe technology has produced more stress, others appreciate the freedom it offers. When asked how technology has changed the way he does his job, Jim McCann, president of 800-FLOWERS, explains:

> . . . it used to be a real burden to take a week off. But this past summer my family and I rented a place out on Long Island. I was able to exercise with my kids in the morning, go to the beach and be back in by 11; from

Advances in technology allow Joanna Dapkevich to stay at home with her family while effectively managing fifty IBM software sales representatives who work from the office in Raleigh, North Carolina.

11–2:30 I had my portable [laptop computer] plugged in, and I'd return phone calls on my cellular phone. I'd answer my e-mail. I'd be in touch with my secretary, who would have updated my calendar on line. So I'd work for three and a half concentrated hours. I'd play golf with my son in the afternoon, and when I'd get paged, I'd use my cellular phone to return the call. I'd come back in the afternoon, look at my e-mail, answer everything. The kids would go to bed around 10, and I'd spend 45 minutes just going through stuff on my computer, even making a couple of appointments for the next day.[32]

In all the frantic speed with which communication now flows, many people forget that communication still must be carefully created before it is transmitted. Voice mail can be frustrating and time-consuming if it is not handled properly, and poorly written e-mails can leave the impression that the sender is either uneducated or not very intelligent.

## ▪ *Voice Mail*

Now that everyone is adjusting to the opportunities that immediate communication systems offer, nothing is more dismaying than playing voice mail tag (the exchange of several voice mails without successful transmission of the message). Whether you are on the sending or the receiving end, though, there are ways to avoid this counterproductive exercise in frustration.

For incoming calls, be sure you keep your recorded message updated; daily, if necessary. It is a good idea to practice your greeting before recording it, so that you will sound more natural. Include your first and last names, the date, and when you will be retrieving your messages. If you are going on an extended business trip or vacation, your retrieval date will prevent repeat calls from colleagues or customers who might get angrier with each unanswered message. Forward your calls to another person's extension, if possible. Always explain how the caller can reach a live person if the call is urgent.

When retrieving your voice mail, keep a notepad beside your phone. Write down the essential information you need for calls you want to return; then delete them. And even in our high-tech environment, the Golden Rule still applies: "Do unto others as you would have them do unto you." Return calls promptly!

When you are leaving someone a voice mail message, be courteous. For example, give your name at the beginning of the message and leave your phone number at the end. Speak clearly and slowly, and do not smoke, drink, or eat while talking. Avoid rambling and repeating; keep your message short and simple. If possible, let the receiver know when you will be available or set a time when you will call again.[33] One of the best ways to avoid voice mail tag is to state *why* you are calling. Then, if the receiver reaches *your* voice mail when calling back, he or she can simply give you the information you wanted and get back to business.

**When you are leaving someone a voice mail message, be courteous.**

### ■ *E-mail*

Sending information electronically has become the standard operating procedure for most business and personal communications because it offers many advantages over the traditional phone call/letter/memo process. Not only is e-mail faster, it also provides a wonderful alternative for those painfully shy individuals who find it difficult to express themselves face to face. It has become the great equalizer: Lower-level employees can now send messages to executives without anyone in between misinterpreting, sabotaging, or blocking the message.

## HUMAN RELATIONS *in* ACTION

### E-mail Tips

■ Do not send e-mail when you are angry or exhausted.

■ When a face-to-face meeting is necessary, do not use e-mail as a substitute.

■ When receiving large amounts of e-mail, you may selectively choose which ones you want to read, by scanning the subject lines and deleting those of no interest.

■ Make every attempt to create e-mail messages that are error-free. Messages that contain errors may misrepresent your competence and give the wrong impression.

■ Don't send messages in all capital letters: People may feel they are being yelled at.

■ Do not use e-mail to share rumors or innuendos about real people, your company, or any other company.

■ Avoid using unprofessional abbreviations such as BCNU for "Be seeing you," GG for "Got to go," or J/K for "Just kidding."

Even though e-mail offers some advantages, it has some drawbacks. Many e-mail users dash off notes to friends and coworkers without stopping to think about how a message might be perceived. In the past, people who had poor writing skills *could* communicate in person, but that is no longer the case. It may take practice to effectively adjust your communication style to this electronic medium.

E-mail etiquette takes careful planning and new writing skills, since those who read your e-mail will make judgments about your competence. Therefore, you need to guide your readers' assumptions. Watch not only what you write, but also how you word it: that is, the way you "say" it. Here are some guidelines to follow.

**Know your company's e-mail policies.** Most organizations monitor their employees' e-mail carefully. Keep in mind that even deleted messages live on indefinitely in the company's hard drives and may resurface. E-mail that might be sexually offensive could be considered sexual harassment and have serious ramifications. (See the Case Problem, Cybersurveillance, at the end of this chapter.) Keep work-related messages professional and avoid sending personal e-mail messages on company time. Ask your coworkers and supervisors what e-mail rules you should be aware of.

**Create an appropriate e-mail address and signature.**   Carefully design your e-mail address to give the impression you want to convey. Addresses such as Crazylady@_____.com or Buddyboy@_____.com may be acceptable for personal e-mail but should never be used in a business setting.

Although this may seem obvious, *always* make sure you are sending an e-mail to the correct address. This quick double-check will prevent delays and embarrassment for everyone involved if your message contains negative or potentially libelous comments about colleagues, or semiprivate information.

**Use the *Subject:* line.**   One of the best ways to set the stage for effective communications is to learn how to appropriately use the *Subject:* line available on all e-mail messages. It usually appears next to the sender's name on the receiver's screen. This brief introduction to your message will cue the receiver as to the probable content of your message. If your message is time-critical, use *Urgent* on the subject line. If you merely want to share information and don't expect a response, insert *FYI* ("For Your Information") on the subject line. If you are placing an order, announcing a baby's birth, or responding to an e-mail, give the receiver an abbreviated clue as to your intent.

**Watch your language.**   The biggest clue to your competence will be through the words you use. Be sure they are all spelled correctly and that there are no typographical errors. (E-mails filled with typing errors convey an attitude of disrespect toward the reader, which may come right back at the sender.) Be sure that you have selected the appropriate word—when choosing, for example, from *there/their/they're; sight/site/cite; then/than; which/witch,* and so on. Do your verbs agree with their subjects? If your writing skills are limited, use software that includes grammar- and spelling-checkers.

Keep your messages brief by summarizing your main points, indicate the action or response you are seeking, and be sure you provide all the details the receiver needs. Be very careful about the *tone* of your messages. Remove any potentially offending words and phrasing from your documents. Some people feel that they have to use stronger language to get a message across because the receiver cannot "hear" them. If you use solid capital letters in your e-mail, though, readers may perceive a nonverbal message that indicates you are shouting at them.[34]

*Warning:* e-mail does not easily convey emotions, because you cannot hear voice inflections or see body language. Neither the sender not the receiver can assume anything about the correspondent's frame of mind. Readers will not be able to tell if you are serious or being sarcastic, prying or simply curious, angry or merely frustrated. After creating your message, reread it as a stranger might. If words or phrases might be misconstrued, rewrite it so as to make clear *exactly* what you mean to say.

**Avoid forwarding junk mail.** Advertisements, jokes, funny photographs, and so forth should be left for personal e-mail opportunities and sent from your private home computer only. Do *not* send them through your organization's system. Many such attachments include viruses that can shut down an entire operating system when someone views the contents. Often the people receiving your "junk" classify you as a "junky" and will merely delete future messages from you.

## HUMAN RELATIONS *in* ACTION

### Selected Telephone Tips

- Identify yourself and the company you represent.
- Set yourself apart from others by using a friendly tone and impeccable phone manners.
- Never smoke, drink, eat, click a retractable pen, or tap on the desk while talking on the phone.
- Keep brief customer profiles near your phone. Details might include personal details (hobbies, birthday, family members' names), contact dates, and business history.
- Smile when you speak; your telephone listener can hear it in your voice.

- When completing the call, briefly summarize whatever action that will be taken and thank the caller for his or her time.
- If you are using a speakerphone, let the caller know it. Don't use a speakerphone if you share office space with other people.
- Never talk on a cellular phone while you are in a meeting or at a restaurant. If you receive a call, excuse yourself and talk with the caller only when you reach a private area.

## Summary

The age of information has generated rapid advances in communications technology. But technology needs people to make it work. No longer is there a need to communicate more; instead, we need to sort through the mounds of information that bombard us daily and learn to communicate more effectively. This becomes possible when we understand the communication process.

Impersonal, one-way communication methods can be effectively used to share basic facts, policies, instructions, and other such information that requires no feedback from the receiver. Interpersonal communication involves a two-way exchange in which the receiver understands the message in the same way the sender intended it.

Communication is often filtered through semantics, language and cultural barriers, emotions, attitudes, role expectations, and nonverbal messages. Often, too, men and women view conversations through their gender-specific focus. Body language conveys information about a person's thoughts and feelings through eye contact, facial expressions, gestures, and use of personal space.

Individuals can make their messages clearer by choosing words carefully, using repetition, and timing the message so that the receiver can focus on what is being said. They can also learn active, critical, and empathic listening skills. Cell phones, voice mail, and e-mail require new skills and appropriate business etiquette.

## Career Corner

Q: The company I work for discourages personal phone calls during working hours. I am a single parent with two young children. How can I convince my supervisor that some personal calls are very important?

A: Placing personal phone calls during working hours is an issue that often divides employers and employees. From the employer's point of view, an employee who spends time on nonwork calls is wasting time, a valuable resource. Also, many organizations want to keep telephone lines clear for business calls. From your point of view, you need to know about changes in child-care arrangements, serious health concerns of family members, and similar problems. In fact, you will probably perform better knowing that family members are secure. Explain to your supervisor that some personal calls will be inevitable. It is very important that you and your supervisor reach an agreement regarding this issue. When possible, make most of your personal calls during your lunch hour or during work breaks. Encourage friends to call you at home.

To improve communications with your supervisor, become familiar with this person's strengths, weaknesses, work habits, needs, and communication preferences. Then begin thinking of how to communicate in a manner that will build rapport and prevent conflict.

## Key Terms

e-commerce
impersonal communication
interpersonal communication
feedback
semantics
nonverbal messages
active listening
critical listening

empathic listening
self-disclosure
self-description
virtual offices
telecommuting
voice mail
scanners
fax modems

## Review Questions

1. Describe the difference between impersonal and interpersonal communication. Explain the communication process in your own words.
2. Why is feedback essential to good communication?

3. What are the responsibilities of both sender and receiver in the communication process?
4. What are communication filters? How can they be stumbling blocks to effective communication?
5. What techniques can be used to send clear messages? How can you know if you have been successful?
6. What happens when a sender's nonverbal cues do not agree with the verbal message being sent?
7. What is the major difference between self-disclosure and self-description?
8. How can self-disclosure contribute to improved teamwork?
9. What steps can you take to avoid voice mail tag?
10. List the advantages and disadvantages of using e-mail.

## Application Exercises

1. Carefully examine Table 2.1, Active Listening Skills. Select a partner from your class and explain your favorite hobbies to each other. As your partner is speaking, follow the four guidelines in the table. When both have completed this exercise, discuss whether or not each felt the partner was really listening. Did either of you find that the other person was distracted and not really paying attention? Be prepared to share your insights with your instructor and other class members.
2. Print out the most recent e-mails (if you have an account) that you have sent and received and bring them to class. Analyze their effectiveness in terms of the e-mail tips in this chapter. Did the messages violate any of the tips? If so, which ones? How could these messages be improved?

## Internet Exercise

As noted in this chapter, we spend more time listening than we spend speaking, reading, or writing. However, most of us are not good listeners. To learn more about listening and how to improve your listening skills, access Amazon.com and search for "active listening" and "empathic listening." Examine the information available on these topics. Could this information be useful as you attempt to improve your listening skills? Explain.

## Self-Assessment Excercise

The purpose of this application exercise is to help you assess those attitudes and skills that contribute to effective human relations. A similar exercise will appear at the end of each subsequent chapter. Your honest response to each item will help you determine your areas of strength and those areas that need improvement. Completion of this self-assessment will provide you with information needed to develop goals for self-improvement.

Circle the number from 1 to 5 that best represents your response to each statement: (1) strongly disagree (never do this); (2) disagree (rarely do this); (3) moderately agree (sometimes do this); (4) agree (frequently do this); (5) strongly agree (almost always do this).

A.  I am an effective communicator who sends clear, concise verbal messages.  1  2  3  4  5

B.  When people talk, I listen attentively and frequently use active listening skills.  1  2  3  4  5

C.  I am conscious of how I express nonverbal messages (facial expression, tone of voice, body language, and so on) when communicating with others.  1  2  3  4  5

D.  I engage in appropriate self-disclosure in order to achieve improved communication and increased self-awareness and to build stronger relationships.  1  2  3  4  5

E.  I am able to share information about myself in appropriate ways, avoiding the extremes of complete concealment and complete openness.  1  2  3  4  5

F.  When using voice mail, e-mail, the telephone, and other communication technologies, I follow appropriate etiquette guidelines.  1  2  3  4  5

After recording your response to each item, select an appropriate attitude or skill you would like to improve. Write your goal in the space provided. Then describe the steps you will take to achieve this goal.

GOAL: _____

_____

_____

_____

## Case Problem   *Cybersurveillance: Big Brother Is Watching!*

One of the most combustible issues in today's organizations is cybersurveillance, the electronic eavesdropping employers can do when organizations' computers are connected to the Internet. Nearly three-quarters of U.S. companies say they actively monitor their workers' communications. Computer programs such as LittleBrother and MIMEsweeper alert employers when individual employees are ordering a new wardrobe, planning a vacation, participating in cyberaffairs, or day-trading stocks. Software like Investigator tracks every keystroke and mouseclick, churning out reports as specific as desired.

Originally companies used cybersurveillance to root out wasted time, stop sexual harassment, and keep networks free of viruses. UPS caught an employee running a personal business during working hours. Some Edward Jones & Co. brokers in St. Louis and twenty *New York Times* employees were fired by their firms for circulating "inappropriate and offensive" (pornographic) e-mails in clear violation of company policy. The Melissa virus and the Love Bug virus creators, among others, were tracked through cybersurveillance. "Cyberstings" have, in fact, become the corporate norm, with their focus expanded to catch employees who are disloyal or dishonest—in many cases, with good cause. Wolverton & Associates, a civil engineering company, discovered that 4 percent of its Internet capacity was being consumed by employees downloading music. At Lockheed Martin Corp., a single e-mail celebrating a religious holiday was sent to all 60,000 employees, disabling the company network for more than six hours and costing Lockheed hundreds of thousands of dollars in lost productivity. A Chevron Corp. intranet e-mail posting that listed "25 reasons why beer is better than women" cost that company $2.2 million to compensate employees who were offended.

The courts have consistently ruled that communications written on company-provided computers and e-mail systems belong to the company and are not private. Privacy proponents argue that Internet transmissions—largely accessed via phone lines—should fall under the federal laws about listening to phone conversations. (It takes a court order and tight supervision to listen legally over a telephone link.) In an attempt to control potential invasion of privacy, the California State Assembly passed legislation that would allow companies to monitor but would require them to notify employees when their computer-based communications were being monitored. However, the governor vetoed it.

As this issue becomes more volatile, some organizations have made adjustments. Boeing Co. allows employees to use faxes, e-mail, and the Internet for personal reasons, but sets guidelines for such use. The policy contains phrases like "reasonable duration and frequency" and "embarrassment to the company." The National Labor Relations Board recently ordered Pride and Whitney to back off on a blanket policy barring employees' use of e-mail for nonbusiness purposes. Some workers have successfully argued that they deserve to take care of personal business during work hours, since "personal" hours are severely limited due to the virtual office trend and the resultant blurring of lines between work life and personal life.[35]

## Questions

1. Do you believe that computers at work should be used only to provide service to customers and for other business purposes? Explain.
2. Proponents of cybersurveillance suggest that evaluating managers' integrity is just as important as evaluating their managerial skills. Opponents suggest

that employers have the capability to "set up" or "entrap" employees already targeted for dismissal. Do you agree with the proponents or the opponents? Explain your reasoning.

3. When Microsoft was being investigated for violation of antitrust laws, prosecutors unveiled a rich trail of electronic communications among Microsoft employees that indicated that there was collaboration to create a business monopoly. The defendants spent countless hours, and lost face with the public, in attempting to explain these electronic messages.[36] Do you agree or disagree that the courts should allow this type of information to be introduced as evidence? Explain your opinion.

# Building High Self-Esteem

Dennis Kalup, a college senior, vividly remembers the ridicule he suffered as an overweight child. He remembers his sister's taunts of "Fatty, Fatty, Boobalatty" every time he ate anything fattening, the humiliation of having to go to the special store to buy "husky" clothes, and the nickname *Jabba Jr.* that followed him after he and his friends watched *Return of the Jedi.* As he grew older, he blamed his mother for feeding him the wrong food, and society for stigmatizing fat people. Dennis was delighted whenever he saw someone on television who was overweight and *not* the butt of jokes. Then he realized his problem wasn't about blame; it was about being happy. He accepted the idea that he couldn't change society, but *could* try to change the way he felt about himself.[1]

Another chubby little boy, Keith Zucker, went at age 7 to Camp Kingsmont in Massachusetts, where he was taught to eat right and get plenty of exercise. Today, he owns the camp. Photos in his camp office show him as a child and as he is now, his lean, powerlifting body serving as an inspiration to his campers. Children attending the camp look up to him as a role model: someone who was where they are, yet overcame the stigma of being "fat." Camp Kingsmont is one of about fifteen American Camping Association's accredited camps that serve as a haven for overweight kids by teaching them the new eating and exercise habits that could change their lives forever. These kids often are teased by their peers and suffer a poor self-image. As Zucker remembers, ". . . you just don't want to do anything. You close yourself off from everything. It's a wasted youth."

A recent nationwide survey of several thousand young workers found that their self-esteem was improved by increasing their education and gaining more work experience. But it also found that low self-esteem can stifle the motivation to obtain more education and more work experience. If they felt themselves worthy and capable, they pursued additional training opportunities and expanded work experiences. If they felt they were not capable of achieving success, they didn't even try to improve their performance. This study indicates that there is a direct correlation between workers' self-esteem and their professional success and income potential.[2]

## The Power of Self-Esteem

Nathaniel Branden, author of *The Six Pillars of Self-Esteem* and *Self-Esteem at Work,* has spent the past three decades studying the psychology of self-esteem. In countless speeches, articles, and books, he has attempted to describe the connection between self-esteem and many of the human problems common to our society today. He notes that high self-esteem enhances our ability to build effective relationships with others:

> The healthier our self-esteem, the more inclined we are to treat others with respect, benevolence, goodwill, and fairness—since we do not tend to perceive them as a threat, and since self-respect is the foundation of respect for others.[3]

The importance of self-esteem as a guiding force in our lives cannot be overstated. It is very difficult for people to act beyond their deepest vision of who and what they believe themselves to be.[4] Many business owners, managers, and team leaders recognize the importance of self-esteem. During orientation new employees at Starbucks are introduced to guidelines for on-the-job interpersonal relations. The first guideline is to maintain and enhance self-esteem. Starbucks has discovered that when employees feel respected, they are less likely to leave the company.[5]

## HUMAN RELATIONS *in* ACTION

### The Power of Strong Self-Efficacy

Over the years many people we now know to be extremely intelligent and talented have had to develop a strong belief in themselves. If they had relied on others' opinions of their capabilities and potential, who knows where this world would be!

**Walt Disney** was fired by a newspaper editor for lack of ideas. He went bankrupt several times before he built Disneyland. In fact, the proposed park was rejected by the city of Anaheim on the grounds that it would only attract riffraff.

**Thomas Edison's** teacher said he was "too stupid to learn anything."

**Charles Darwin,** father of the theory of evolution, wrote in his autobiography, "I was considered by all my masters and my father, a very ordinary boy, rather below the common standard of intellect."

**Fred Astaire** recalls the 1933 memo from the MGM testing director that stated, "Can't act. Can't sing. Slightly bald. Can dance a little."

**Vince Lombardi,** famous football coach and motivational speaker and writer, recalls an expert's description of his talents: "He possesses minimal football knowledge and lacks motivation."

**Albert Einstein** did not speak until he was 4 years old and did not read until he was 7. His teacher described him as "mentally slow, unsociable, and adrift forever in foolish dreams."

## ■ *Self-Esteem = Self-Efficacy + Self-Respect*

Nathaniel Branden states that the ultimate source of **self-esteem** can only be internal: It is the relationship between a person's self-efficacy and self-respect. **Self-efficacy** is the belief that you can achieve what you set out to do.[6] When your self-efficacy is high, you believe you have the ability to act appropriately. When your self-efficacy is low, you worry that you might not be able to do the task, that it is beyond your abilities. Your perception of your self-efficacy can influence which tasks you take on and which ones you avoid. Albert Bandura, a professor at Stanford University and one of the foremost self-efficacy researchers, views this component of self-esteem as a resilient belief in your own abilities. According to Bandura, a major source of self-efficacy is the experience of mastery, in which success in one area builds your confidence to succeed in other areas.[7] For example, an administrative assistant who masters a sophisticated computerized accounting system is more likely to master future complicated computer programs than is a person who feels computer illiterate and may not even try to figure out the new program, regardless of how well he or she *could* do it.

**Self-respect,** the second component of self-esteem, is what you think and feel about yourself. Your judgment of your own value is a primary factor in achieving career success. People who respect themselves tend to act in ways that confirm and reinforce this respect. People who lack self-respect may put up with verbal or physical abuse from others because they feel they are unworthy of praise and deserve the abuse.[8] If you don't treat yourself with respect, no one else will treat you that way either. One of the great tragedies in life is that people look for respect in every direction except within.

Self-esteem includes your feelings about your adequacy in the roles you play in life, such as that of friend, brother or sister, daughter or son, employee or employer, student or teacher, researcher, leader, and so on. Often your self-esteem derives from your physical characteristics and your skills and abilities. Are you tall, slender, short, or heavy? Do you like what you see in the mirror? Are you good at writing, fixing appliances, researching topics, playing the piano, or engaging in some other skill?

Although high self-esteem is the basis for a healthy personality, it does not mean becoming egotistical—that is, thinking and acting with only your own interests in mind. Genuine self-esteem is not expressed by self-glorification at the expense of others or by the attempt to diminish others so as to elevate yourself. Arrogance, boastfulness, and the overestimation of your abilities reflect inadequate self-esteem rather than, as it might appear, too much self-esteem. Someone with an egotistical orientation to the world sees everything and everyone in terms of their usefulness to her or his own aims and goals. This attitude undermines good human relations.

> **The importance of self-esteem as a guiding force in our lives cannot be overstated.**

## How Self-Esteem Develops

A Sunday school teacher once asked her class of small children, "Who made you?" Instead of giving the expected reply, an insightful child responded, "I'm not finished yet!" You are not born knowing who and what you are. You acquire your image of yourself over time by realizing your natural abilities and by constantly receiving messages about yourself from the people closest to you and from your environment.

**Childhood**    Researchers have discovered that a child's potential is determined in the early years. The neurons of the brain—those long wiry cells that carry electrical messages through the nervous system and the brain—literally make their

connections during the birth-to-preschool period. If these connections are not made, the child may suffer later in life. For example, emotional stability, which directly affects how individuals feel about themselves, is greatly affected by how the brain develops in the first two years of life. Your potential adult vocabulary is determined by the words filtered through your brain before you were 3, and the foundations for math and logic were set before you were 4.[9] This early development can serve as the basis for your success or failure at various endeavors throughout your life.

Do you remember that when you started school your childhood friends, siblings, teachers, and various authority figures began sending you messages such as these:

- Bad boy! Bad girl!
- You're so lazy!
- You'll never learn.
- What's wrong with you?
- Why can't you be more like . . . ?

- You're great!
- You can do anything!
- You're a fast learner.
- Next time you'll do better.
- I like you just the way you are.

In most cases, you probably did not stop and analyze these messages; you simply accepted them as true and recorded them in your memory. As a result, you gradually developed a picture of yourself, whether accurate or distorted, that you came to believe as real. The authors of *Staying OK* describe this subconscious level of activity:

> Everyone was once a child. Our experience today is filtered through the events and feelings of childhood, recorded in detail. We cannot have a feeling today that is "disconnected" from similar feelings recorded in the past, the most intense of which occurred to us in the first five years of life. This does not mean that today's feelings are not real, or that we are to

*OPRAH WINFREY*

**Founder and Editorial Director,
O, The Oprah Magazine**

*"Feeling good about who you are and what you're here
on earth to do—that is the real work of your life. And it's
ongoing. Each of us arrives with all we need to feel valued
and unique, but slowly that gets chipped away."*

discount them by claiming "they're just an old recording." We are today
who we once were.[10]

**Adolescence**    The years from age 12 to age 18 are very crucial in developing
and consolidating your feelings about yourself. During these years, you are moving away from the close bond between parent and child and are attempting to establish ideals of independence and achievement.[11] You fluctuate between determi-
nation to reach your goals and self-doubt about whether or not you are capable.
You must also deal with physical changes, relationships with your peers, the loss of
a carefree childhood, and the assumption of some adult responsibilities.

Society today, however, unlike previous generations when teens had to help
out on the farm or in family business or care for siblings, does not "need" adolescents, and this lack of importance and direction can lead to feelings of insecurity
and uncertainty. Teens often feel vulnerable as the media and real life expose them
to more violence in the form of schoolroom and drive-by shootings, date rape,
sexual abuse, and drug-induced behaviors than ever before. To compensate, they
frequently adopt an attitude of not caring.[12] When you do not care about
anything or anyone, you do not care about yourself, and the result is low self-esteem.

Teens with low self-esteem are more vulnerable to peer pressure. They are
more likely to look at *Chic, Seventeen, GQ,* and "ezines" (electronic magazines)
and attempt to emulate the unrealistic body images and fashions their peers
deem worthwhile. They are more likely to have eating disorders, experience alcohol and drug abuse, and take risks such as driving dangerously, so that they will
feel accepted as "one of the gang." They often lack the confidence to resist impulses and negative peer pressure.

Even though peers can have tremendous impact, parents too can have a powerful effect on their teenagers' self-esteem. When parents offer encouragement, support, enthusiasm, and commendation, they enable their teens to learn how to take
healthy risks, tolerate frustration, and feel proud of their accomplishments. Those
teens whose parents offer unconditional acceptance of their child as a person with
limitations and imperfections will grow up understanding that they are worthwhile, regardless of any particular ability or attribute. They will believe that they
deserve good relationships and positive experiences. As they learn to recognize and
appreciate the impact of their choices and behaviors, teens will be more likely to
view themselves as competent rather than as victims of circumstance and fate.[13]

**Adulthood**   When you reach adulthood, your mind has a time-reinforced picture of who you are, molded by people and events from all your past experiences. You have been bombarded over the years with positive and negative messages from your family, friends, teachers, strangers, and the media. You may compare yourself to others, as was so common in adolescence, or you may focus on your own inner sense of self-worth. Emmett Miller, a noted authority on self-esteem, says that as adults we tend to define ourselves in terms of:[14]

1. *The things we possess.* Miller says this is the most primitive source of self-worth. If we define ourselves in terms of what we have, the result may be an effort to accumulate more and more material things to achieve a greater feeling of self-worth. People who define themselves in terms of what they have may have difficulty deciding "what is enough" and may spend their life in search of more material possessions.

2. *What we do for a living.* Miller points out that too often our self-worth and identity depend on something as arbitrary as a job title. Amy Saltzman, author of *Downshifting*, a book on ways to reinvent (or redefine) success, says, "We have allowed our professional identities to define us and control us."[15] She points out that we have looked to outside forces such as the corporation, the university, the media, counselors, or our parents to provide us with a script for leading a satisfying, worthwhile life.

3. *Our internal value system and emotional makeup.* Miller says this is the healthiest way for people to identify themselves:

   > If you don't give yourself credit for excellence in other areas of life, besides your job and material possessions, you've got nothing to keep your identity afloat in emotionally troubled waters. People who are in touch with their real identity weather the storm better because they have a more varied and richer sense of themselves, owing to the importance they attach to their personal lives and activities.[16]

As an adult, you will be constantly adjusting the level of your self-esteem as you get in touch with your identity. Wally Amos is a prime example of a person who literally lost his identity. He started the gourmet-cookie craze with his Famous Amos Chocolate Chip Cookies, built an extremely successful company, then mismanaged it and lost everything, including two wives and the affections of his children. A court injunction denied him the use of his name and likeness in connection with any food-related venture. He was left without his family, his money, his company, or his name. In typical Wally fashion, however, he realized that there was only *one* name he could not use, and millions more names to choose from, and so the Uncle Noname Cookie Company was born.[17]

---

**TOTAL PERSON INSIGHT**

*WALLY AMOS*

Founder, Uncle Noname
Cookie Company

*"If you keep on thinking what you've always thought, you'll keep on getting what you've always got."*

---

**THINKING / LEARNING STARTERS**

1. Can you recall two or three people from your childhood or adolescence who had a positive effect on your self-esteem? What did these people say or do? Were there any who had a negative effect on you? What did they say or do?

2. Identify at least two people who exhibit the characteristics of people with high self-esteem. What behaviors helped you identify them?

---

## Self-Esteem Influences Your Behavior

Your self-esteem has a powerful impact on your behavior at work and in your personal life. In general, people with low self-esteem tend to have more trouble with interpersonal relationships and to be less productive than people with high self-esteem.[18]

### ■ Characteristics of People with Low Self-Esteem

1. *They tend to maintain an* **external locus of control.** Psychologists believe that a person's general outlook on life influences self-esteem. People who think they are masters of their own fates and believe they are responsible for what happens to them maintain an *internal locus of control*. Individuals who maintain an *external locus of control* believe their life is controlled by outside forces

and that they bear little responsibility for what happens to them.[19] Even when they succeed, they tend to attribute their success to luck rather than to their own expertise and hard work. This often results in reliance on the approval of others. This seeking of others' approval often pressures us into behaving contrary to our deepest convictions. When we rely too heavily on validation from external sources, we can lose control over our lives.[20]

2. *They tend to participate in self-destructive behaviors.* If you do not like yourself, there is no apparent reason to take care of yourself. Therefore, people with low self-esteem tend to drink too much, smoke too much, and eat too much. Some may develop an eating disorder such as bulimia or anorexia, often with devastating results.

3. *They exhibit poor human relations skills.* Individuals with low self-esteem are more likely to feel hostile, show a lack of respect for others, and attempt to retaliate against others to save face in difficult situations. They tend to blame others for everything that goes wrong. Workers with low self-esteem can reduce the efficiency and productivity of a group: They tend to exercise less initiative, hesitate to accept responsibility or make independent decisions, and refuse to ask for help, fearing that others might think them incompetent.

4. *They may experience the failure syndrome.* As noted previously in this chapter, you form a mental picture of yourself at a very early age. Your subconscious mind was, and continues to be, "programmed" by other people's negative and positive comments. If your subconscious mind has been saturated with thoughts of past failures, these thoughts will continue to undermine your efforts to achieve your goals. If you see yourself as a failure, you will usually find some way to fail. William Glasser, author of *Reality Therapy* and other books on human behavior, calls this the **failure syndrome.** Individuals with a failure syndrome think, "I always fail. . . . Why try?" They have a fear of taking action because they expect to fail . . . again.

**If you do not like yourself, there is no apparent reason to take care of yourself.**

## ◼ *Characteristics of People with High Self-Esteem*

1. *People with high self-esteem are future oriented and not overly concerned with past mistakes or failures.* They learn from their errors but are not immobilized by them. They believe every experience has something to teach—if they are willing to learn. A mistake can show you what does not work, what not to do. One consultant, when asked whether he had obtained any results in trying to solve a difficult problem, replied, "Results? Why, I've had lots of results. I know a hundred things that won't work!" The same principle applies to your own progress. Falling down does not mean failure. Staying down does.

2. *People with high self-esteem are able to cope with life's problems and disappointments.* Successful people have come to realize that problems need not

depress them or make them anxious. It is their attitude toward problems that makes all the difference. In his book *They All Laughed: From Lightbulbs to Lasers,* Ira Flatow examines the lives of successful, innovative people who had to overcome major obstacles to achieve their goals. He discovered that the common thread among these creative people was their ability to overcome disappointing events and press on toward their goals.

3. ***People with high self-esteem are able to feel all dimensions of emotion without letting those emotions affect their behavior in a negative way.*** This characteristic is one of the major reasons people with high self-esteem are able to establish and maintain effective human relations with the people around them. They realize emotions cannot be handled either by repressing them or by giving them free rein. Although you may not be able to stop feeling the emotions of anger, envy, and jealousy, you can control your thoughts and actions when you are under the influence of these strong emotions. Say to yourself, "I may not be able to control the way I feel right now, but I can control the way I behave."

4. ***People with high self-esteem are able to accept other people as unique, talented individuals.*** They learn to accept others for who they are and what they can do. Our multicultural work force makes this attitude especially important. Individuals who cannot tolerate other people who are "different" may find themselves out of a job. People with high self-esteem build mutual trust based on each individual's uniqueness. These trusting relationships do not limit or confine either person because of group attributes such as skin color, religion, gender, lifestyle, or sexual orientation. Accepting others is a good indication that you accept yourself.

5. ***People with high self-esteem exhibit a variety of self-confident behaviors.*** They accept compliments or gifts by saying, "Thank you," without making self-critical excuses and without feeling obligated to return the favor. They can laugh at their situation without self-ridicule. They let others be right or wrong without attempting to correct or ridicule them. They feel free to express opinions even if they differ from those of their peers or parents. They are able to maintain an **internal locus of control**—that is, they make decisions for their own reasons based on their standards of what is right and wrong, and they are not likely to comply with the inappropriate demands of others. This internal control helps raise self-esteem every time it is applied.

## THINKING / LEARNING STARTERS

1. Have you ever felt envious of another person's possessions, relationships, or lifestyle? How did this feeling affect your relationship with that person?

2. When you make decisions in your personal life, do you operate from an internal or external locus of control? Give an example.

## How to Build Self-Esteem

"The level of our self-esteem is not set once and for all in childhood," says Nathaniel Branden. It can grow throughout our lives or it can deteriorate.[21] Examining your present self-image is the first step in understanding who you are, what you can do, and where you are going.

The person you will be tomorrow has yet to be created. Too often people continue to shape that future person in the image of the past, repeating the old limitations and negative patterns without realizing what they are doing. The development of a new level of self-esteem will not happen overnight, but it can happen. Such a change is the result of a slow evolution that begins with the desire to overcome low self-esteem.

### ■ Search for the Source of Low Self-Esteem

Many people live with deep personal doubts about themselves, but have difficulty determining the source of those feelings. They even have difficulty finding the right words to describe those negative feelings. People with low self-esteem do not see themselves with great clarity. The self-image they possess is like a reflection in a warped funhouse mirror; the image magnifies their weaknesses and minimizes their strengths. To raise your self-esteem requires achieving a higher level of self-awareness and learning to accurately perceive your particular balance of strengths and weaknesses.[22]

To build self-esteem, you must examine the negative thoughts you have about yourself and try to discover their origins. If you are having doubts about your chances of succeeding in your career, try to determine why. A college freshman had doubts about her ability to succeed in a major requiring several math courses. After reflecting on these thoughts, she remembered her mother's comment that no one in her family was good at math. Negative ideas we encountered in childhood and adolescence live on within us. In some cases, our "memories" of past events may be distortions of what really happened.

The negative thoughts that surface throughout your life are referred to as your **inner critic.** The critic keeps a record of your failures, but never reminds you of your strengths and accomplishments. Your inner critic was formed during the early years of your life. Your parents taught you which behaviors were lovable, acceptable, annoying, wrong, or dangerous.[23] Throughout childhood, you retained conscious and subconscious memories of those experiences, along with the emotional feelings of being wrong or bad. These memories continue to influence how you feel about your behavior and yourself today. A major step toward improving your self-esteem is to understand how to respond to attacks from your inner critic, so that you have a clear, conscious path toward improving your self-esteem.

### ■ Identify and Accept Your Limitations

To raise your self-esteem, it is absolutely necessary to identify and accept your limitations. Become realistic about who you are and what you can and cannot do. Demanding perfection of yourself is unrealistic because no one is perfect. The past cannot be changed: Acknowledge your mistakes; learn from them; then move on. Your future, however, can be effectively shaped by how you think and act from this day forward.

> Accepting ourselves begins with an honest look at who we are. We don't need to like everything we find. We can just say, for example, "Oh, yes, I can recognize that I sometimes feel impatient. This is a human feeling, and I don't need to deny it or dislike myself for feeling it."[24]

Acting as an observer and detaching yourself from negative thoughts and actions can help you break the habit of rating yourself according to some scale of perfection and can enable you to substitute more positive and helpful thoughts. A good first step is learning to dislike a behavior you may indulge in, rather than condemning yourself. Criticizing yourself tends to make the behavior worse. If you condemn yourself for being weak, for example, how can you muster the strength to change? But if you become an "observer" and view the activity as separate from yourself, you leave your self-esteem intact, while you work on changing the behavior.

### ■ *Take Responsibility for Your Decisions*

Psychologists have found that children who were encouraged to make their own decisions early in their lives have higher self-esteem than those who were kept dependent on their parents for a longer period of time. Making decisions helps you develop confidence in your own judgment and enables you to explore options. Take every opportunity you can to make decisions both in setting your goals and in devising ways to achieve them. As you make your decisions, be willing to accept the consequences of your actions, positive or negative.

---

**TOTAL PERSON INSIGHT**

FRAN COX AND LOUIS COX

Authors, *A Conscious Life*

*"There is little understanding in our culture that being an adult is an ongoing process of learning and self-correcting. Life is always changing, revealing what was previously unknown and unplanned for."*

---

When Jim Burke became head of a new products division at Johnson & Johnson, one of his first projects was the development of a children's chest rub. The product failed miserably, and Burke expected that he would be fired. When he was called in to see the Chairman of the Board, however, he met a surprising reception. "Are you the one who just cost us all that money?" asked Robert Wood Johnson. "Well, I just want to congratulate you. If you are making mistakes, that means you are taking risks, and we won't grow unless you take risks." Some years later, Burke became the chairman of J&J.[25]

The attitude that you must be right all the time is a barrier to personal growth. With this attitude you will avoid doing things that might result in mistakes. Much unhappiness comes from the widespread and regrettable belief that it is important to avoid making mistakes at all costs.[26]

### ■ *Develop Expertise in Some Area*

Developing "expert power" not only builds your self-esteem but also increases the value of your contribution to an organization. Identify and cultivate a skill or talent you have, whether it is a knack for interviewing people, a facility with math, or good verbal skills. Developing expertise may involve continuing your studies after completing your formal education. Some institutions offer professional courses to enable people to advance in their careers. For example, the Institute of Financial Education conducts courses for persons employed by financial institutions, and the Certified Medical Representatives Institute offers a series of professional development courses for pharmaceutical representatives.

## HUMAN RELATIONS *in* ACTION

### Know Your Stuff

Esther Dyson, chair of EDventure Holdings, a New York City–based venture capital firm, urges the new employees to learn everything about the new job: "Your best guarantee of credibility is to know your stuff, even if it means staying up all night reading trade journals, product manuals, anything you can get your hands on." Dyson also encourages new employees to take chances. She says, "A failure can be the best learning experience you'll ever have."

### ■ *Seek the Support and Guidance of Mentors*

Chip Bell, author of *Managers as Mentors: Building Partnerships for Learning*, defines a **mentor** as "someone who helps someone else learn something the learner would otherwise have learned less well, more slowly, or not at all."[27] Although mentoring is most often a one-on-one partnership, a mentor will sometimes guide a group of protégés through the process of developing their organizational savvy and their careers. In most organizations mentoring is carried out informally, but formal programs that systematically match mentors and protégés are common.

General Electric has traditionally used mentoring programs pairing veteran employees with young new workers who need to learn how things are done at GE. When upper management decided to aggressively pursue e-commerce, so as to reduce costs and open new markets, CEO John F. Welch, Jr., turned the tables. He ordered his top 600 managers to search their rank-and-file employees for Internet-savvy "youngsters" who could serve as their mentors and teach them how to surf the Internet. Lloyd Trotter, 57, an industrial systems operations manager who had rarely used the Net, selected Rachel Dorman, 27. The one-to-one rapport that developed over the biweekly hour-long meetings helped Trotter get a fast start in understanding the power of the Internet and how to use it effectively. And Dorman learned, through her relationship with Trotter, the skills managers need in order to run a big operation, skills such as the ability to communicate with different people.[28]

Most people who have had a mentoring experience say it was an effective development tool. However, many surveys indicate that only a small percentage of employees say they have had a mentor. In today's fast-paced work environment, where most people have a heavy workload, you must be willing to take the initiative and build a mentor relationship. Here are some tips to keep in mind.

1. *Multiple mentors are recommended.* Some people feel the need for both internal and external mentors. An internal mentor, an experienced associate or supervisor, can provide guidance as you navigate the organizational bumps and potholes. An external mentor, someone who does not work for your company, can provide an objective, independent view of your skills and talents.[29] Many people benefit from short-term "learning partners" who will coach them on specific skills.

2. *Search for a mentor who has the qualities of a good coach.* Mentors need to be accomplished in their own right, but success alone does not make someone a good mentor. Look for someone whom you would like to emulate, both in business savvy and in operating style. Be sure it is someone you trust enough to talk about touchy issues.[30] A good mentor is someone who will give you feedback in a straightforward manner.

3. *Market yourself to a prospective mentor.* The best mentor for you may be someone who is very busy. Sell the benefits of a mentoring partnership. For example, point out that mentoring can be a mutually rewarding experience such as the Lloyd Trotter and Rachel Dorman relationship at GE. Describe specific steps you will take to avoid wasting the time of a busy person. You might suggest that meetings be held during lunch.

Although mentors are not mandatory for success, they certainly help. Indeed, there will always be days when you feel nothing you do is right. Your mentor can help repair damaged self-esteem and encourage you to go on. With the power of another person's positive expectations reinforcing your own native abilities, it is hard to fail.

Carolyn Robinson had a secure job with a national bank when she was bitten by the entrepreneurial bug. Confident in her ability to establish a successful business, she quit her job and began researching two start-up ideas. Robinson is someone who believes in setting goals; she plans to start two businesses and retire by age 50.

### ■ *Set Goals*

Research points to a direct link between self-esteem and the achievement of personal and professional goals. People who consistently set goals are more likely to maintain high self-esteem. People who fail to set goals tend to wander aimlessly through life with no purpose, and they are more likely to suffer from low self-esteem. The key is to set realistic goals and then figure out what steps are necessary to get there. It's a good idea to mentally rehearse these steps frequently. Goals can be an important part of your plan to break old habits and form new ones.

### ■ *Practice Visualization*

To **visualize** means to form a mental image of something. The power to visualize (sometimes called guided imagery) is in a very real sense the power to create. If you really want to succeed at something, picture yourself doing it successfully over and over again. Simulate every step in your brain before you ever attempt to make the goal a reality. Visualize yourself overcoming any obstacles that might interfere with your success.[31]

Shakti Gawain, author of *Creative Visualization,* states that when we create something, we always create it first in the form of a thought:

Imagination is the ability to create an idea or mental picture in your mind. In creative visualization you use your imagination to create a clear image of something you wish to manifest. Then you continue to focus on the idea or picture regularly, giving it positive energy until it becomes objective reality . . . in other words, until you actually achieve what you have been visualizing.[32]

Many famous athletes choreograph their moves in their imagination before going into action. For example, champion skiers imagine themselves negotiating almost every inch of a slope, champion tennis players picture themselves executing successful shots, and gymnasts practice their moves as much in their imagination as in actual rehearsal. World famous golfer Tiger Woods says, "I think about every shot in every round in every practice every time."[33]

This mental rehearsal can be a powerful step toward improving your self-image. Review the "Characteristics of People with High Self-Esteem" listed earlier in this chapter. If you would like to make them part of your behavior pattern, mentally rehearse these self-confident behaviors. See yourself walking with your chin up and your shoulders straight and speaking with a strong, confident voice. Picture yourself making appropriate eye contact with other people. As you gain confidence, practice these new skills by actually performing them when you are with your friends, family, and coworkers.

### ■ Use Positive Self-Talk

People with a strong inner critic will receive frequent negative messages that can erode their self-esteem. It helps to refute and reject those negative messages with positive self-talk. **Self-talk** takes place silently in the privacy of your mind. It is the series of personal conversations you have with yourself almost continually throughout the day. Just like statements from other people, your self-talk can affect your behavior and self-esteem.[34] Talking back to your inner critic may take the form of words and phrases that are designed to disarm the critic. If you are preparing for a job interview and the messages you hear are "You don't measure up" or "You are incompetent," respond with the message "These are lies" or "Stop this garbage."[35] Figure 3.1 indicates how self-talk is part of the cycle of self-esteem, whether that talk is negative or positive.

If you want to develop and achieve a specific goal, positive self-talk can help. Create self-talk statements for each of your goals by using the following guidelines:

1. Be *specific* about the behavior you want to change. What do you want to do to increase your effectiveness? You should firmly believe that what you want is truly possible.

2. Begin each self-talk statement with a first-person pronoun, such as *I* or *my.* Use a present-tense verb, such as *am, have, feel, create, approve, do,* or *choose.* Don't say "My ability to remember the names of other people *will* improve." Instead, focus on the present: "I *have* an excellent memory for the names of other people."

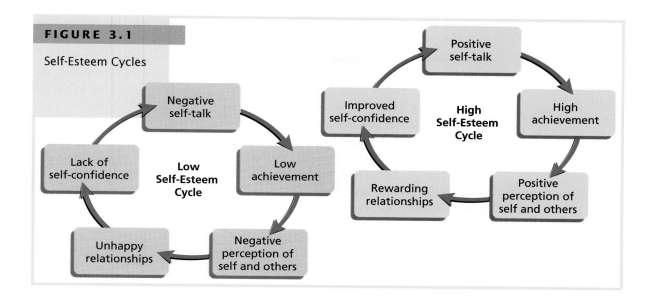

**FIGURE 3.1**

Self-Esteem Cycles

3. Describe the results you want to achieve. Be sure to phrase the statement as though you have already achieved what you want. Table 3.1 offers several general self-talk statements that might help you improve your self-esteem.[36]

This last step is critical. Because your brain is merely a computer filled with various data from all your past experiences, you need to use, literally, the correct words. When you think of the words *spider, tornado,* or *blue,* your brain develops

**Table 3.1**

**Creating Semantically Correct Self-Talk**

| *Wrong* | *Right* |
|---------|---------|
| I can quit smoking. | I am in control of my habits. |
| I will lose twenty pounds. | I weigh a trim _____ pounds. |
| I won't worry anymore. | I am confident and optimistic. |
| Next time I won't be late. | I am prompt and efficient. |
| I will avoid negative self-talk. | I talk to myself, with all due respect. |
| I will not procrastinate. | I do it now. |
| I'm not going to let people walk all over me anymore. | I care enough to assert myself when necessary. |

an automatic understanding of the word and a response or image based on years of conditioning and training. If you are attempting to quit smoking, don't mention the word *smoke* in your self-talk because your brain will react to the word. "I will not smoke after dinner" conjures an image in your subconscious mind, and your behavior follows accordingly. Say instead, "I am in control of my habits" or "My lungs are clean."

Write positive self-talk statements for different facets of your personal and professional life. Put them on 3-by-5-inch index cards, and attach them to your bathroom mirror, refrigerator, car dashboard, desk blotter, and so on, and review them often. Barbara Grogan, a successful entrepreneur who founded Western Industrial Contractors, has a placard on the dashboard of her car that reads, "I am powerful, beautiful, creative, and I can handle it!"[37] This positive message helps her through the tough times.

## HUMAN RELATIONS *in* ACTION

### Positive Self-Talk That Builds Self-Esteem

I am unique and talented.

I'm a winner!

I am responsible for the choices I make.

As my self-esteem grows, I am more effective.

My future depends on the goals I set *now*.

I may not be able to control my emotions, but I *can* control my actions.

Only I decide what success means to me.

I fuel my body with healthy foods and thoughts.

My mistakes offer me an opportunity to learn.

I am at peace, even when I am surrounded by chaos.

## Organizations Can Help

Even though each of us ultimately is responsible for raising or lowering our own self-esteem, we can make that task easier or more difficult for others. We can either support or damage the self-efficacy and self-respect of the people we work with, just as they have that option in their interactions with us. Organizations are beginning to include self-esteem modules in their employee- and management-training programs.

When employees do not feel good about themselves, the result will often be poor job performance. This view is shared by many human resource professionals and managers. Many organizations realize that low self-esteem affects their workers' ability to learn new skills, to be effective team members, and to be productive. Research has identified five factors that can enhance the self-esteem of employees in any organization[38] (see Figure 3.2).

- *Workers need to feel valuable.* A major source of worker satisfaction is the feeling that one is valued as a unique person. Self-esteem grows when an organization makes an effort to accommodate individual differences and to recognize individual accomplishments.

- *Workers need to feel competent.* Earlier in this chapter we noted that self-efficacy grows when people feel confident in their ability to perform job-related tasks. One of the best ways organizations can build employee confidence is to involve employees in well-designed training programs. Effective training programs give employees plenty of opportunities to practice newly acquired job skills.

- *Workers need to feel secure.* Employees are more likely to feel secure when they are well informed and know what is expected of them. Managers need to clarify their expectations and provide employees with frequent feedback regarding their performance.

- *Workers need to feel empowered.* Progressive organizations such as Corning Incorporated and Federal Express Corporation are demonstrating to employees that their opinions and views matter and that their ideas are being implemented in significant ways. These companies make sure that each person has a voice in helping the organization achieve its goals.

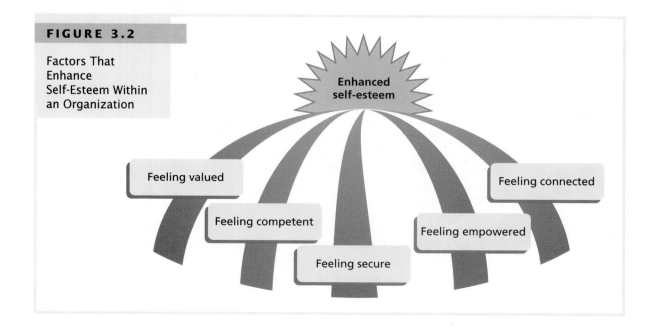

**FIGURE 3.2**

Factors That Enhance Self-Esteem Within an Organization

■ *Workers need to feel connected.* People are likely to achieve high self-esteem when they feel their coworkers accept, appreciate, and respect them. Many companies are fostering these feelings by placing greater emphasis on teamwork. Team-building efforts help promote acceptance and cooperation.

## Summary

Self-esteem is a combination of self-respect and self-efficacy. If you have high self-esteem, you are more likely to feel competent and worthy. If you have low self-esteem, you are more likely to feel incompetent, unworthy, and insecure. Self-esteem reflects your feelings of adequacy about the roles you play, your personality traits, your physical appearance, your skills, and your abilities. High self-esteem is the foundation for a successful personal life and professional life.

A person starts acquiring and building self-esteem from birth. Parents, friends, associates, the media, and professional colleagues all influence the development of that person's self-esteem. As an adult, a person often defines herself or himself in terms of possessions, jobs, and/or internal values. People with high self-esteem tend to be future oriented, cope with problems creatively, handle their emotions, and give as well as receive help. They also accept others as unique, talented individuals and exhibit self-confident behaviors.

To build high self-esteem, individuals must accept the past and build for the future. They have to accept their limitations and develop expertise in some area. Making decisions and living with the consequences, positive or negative, can also help build self-esteem. Individuals need to set goals by visualizing the person they want to be and monitoring their self-talk.

Many organizations now realize that they need to help build employees' self-esteem and are doing so through training sessions, clear statements of expectations and feedback, giving greater respect to individuals in the workplace, and fostering teamwork.

## Career Corner

Q: As a teenager, I was involved in a major car accident in which several bones in my face were broken. I was left with a large scar on my chin. Although I have had several operations to correct the visible damage, I still feel self-conscious whenever I meet new people. It is affecting my career opportunities. What can I do to gain more confidence?

A: In his book *Psycho-Cybernetics,* plastic surgeon Maxwell Maltz demonstrates that what your mind has been conditioned to believe about yourself can override or undermine what you actually see in the mirror. Throughout his twenty-five-year practice, Maltz operated on wounded soldiers, accident victims, and children with birth defects. Many of these individuals saw only their defects and doubted that they could ever be successful. Even after their corrective surgery, these patients' deformities continued to exist in their minds. Their inner self-images had not been changed.

You can learn to use the creative power of your subconscious mind. Even though your external image has been improved, you still need to change the inner self-image you carry within your mind. When you are successful in changing your mental image of yourself, your self-confidence will increase.

## Key Terms

self-esteem

self-efficacy

self-respect

external locus of control

failure syndrome

internal locus of control

inner critic

mentor

visualize

self-talk

## Review Questions

1. What is self-esteem? Why is the development of high self-esteem important in a person's life?
2. What influences help shape a person's self-esteem?
3. What characteristics do people with high self-esteem exhibit?
4. Describe the behaviors of people with low self-esteem.
5. List the steps you can take to build high self-esteem. Which two do you feel are the most important? Why?
6. Explain how a person with an internal locus of control differs from a person with an external locus of control. Which of these two people is more likely to have high self-esteem and therefore greater human relations skills?
7. What influence does self-talk have on a person's self-esteem? How can this influence be controlled?
8. In your own words, explain the two cycles portrayed in Figure 3.1.
9. List the three elements necessary for the construction of positive self-talk statements. Give three examples of such statements.
10. How can organizations help raise the self-esteem of workers?

## Application Exercises

1. Describe a situation in which you achieved a goal you had set for yourself. Did any outside positive or negative forces influence your progress toward the goal? If there were negative forces, how did you overcome them? Did you visualize or mentally simulate the completed goal? If so, how did this simulation help?
2. Think about people you know at school, at work, or in your social environment who seem to exhibit low self-esteem. Describe the qualities that give you this impression. Now think about people you know who exhibit high

self-esteem. List their qualities. Often these two lists will reflect direct opposites, such as "has a sloppy appearance/keeps a neat appearance," "slumps down the hall/walks tall," or "avoids eye contact during conversations with others/makes eye contact." What steps might the people you identified as having low self-esteem take to enhance their images? How might these steps improve their self-esteem? Could you take any similar steps to improve your own self-esteem? Explain.

3. Identify a quality that you would like to experience more frequently in your life. Examples might be the ability to develop rapport quickly with new acquaintances, the patience to enjoy leisure time, or the perseverance to maintain a daily exercise program. Once you select a specific quality, create in your mind a very detailed mental picture of this behavior. Now develop positive self-talk statements that will guide you toward the desired change in behavior. Use the guidelines on pages 70 and 71 to ensure that you achieve your goal.

## Internet Exercise

As noted in this chapter, self-esteem has two interrelated components: self-respect and self-efficacy. Self-efficacy can be thought of as the confidence you have in your ability to do specific things. Your confidence level can influence which tasks you take on and which ones you avoid. To learn more about self-efficacy and how it can influence your career, visit the Internet and determine what types of resources (such as books, articles, and training programs) are available on this topic. Using your search engine, type in "self efficacy" and "self esteem," and then study the available information. Pay special attention to information on how one achieves high self-efficacy. Prepare a written report of your findings.

## Self-Assessment Exercise

For each statement circle the number from 1 to 5 that best represents your response: (1) strongly disagree (never do this); (2) disagree (rarely do this); (3) moderately agree (sometimes do this); (4) agree (frequently do this); (5) strongly agree (almost always do this).

A. I tend to be future oriented and not overly concerned with past mistakes or failures.

    1   2   3   4   5

B. I have developed and maintained high expectations of myself.

    1   2   3   4   5

C. I accept myself as a changing, growing person capable of improvement.

    1   2   3   4   5

D. I have the strength to cope with life's problems and disappointments.

    1   2   3   4   5

E. I am able to maintain an internal   1   2   3   4   5
    locus of control.

F. My goals are clearly defined, attainable,   1   2   3   4   5
    and supported by a plan for achieving
    each goal.

G. I constantly monitor my self-talk in   1   2   3   4   5
    order to maintain high self-esteem.

Select an appropriate attitude or skill you would like to improve. Write your goal in the space provided and then describe the steps you will take to achieve this goal.

GOAL: _____

_____

_____

_____

**Case Problem**     *Altering Your Body Image*

A growing number of people seem to be unhappy with how they look. Specifically, they are dissatisfied with the appearance of their body. *Psychology Today* uses the term "body image" to describe the perceptions people have of their physical appearance, attractiveness, and beauty. Body image is our mental representation of ourselves. The image we see in the mirror influences much of our behavior and self-esteem.

A negative body image can begin to take shape early in life. Teasing during childhood can have a crushing effect on body image. Memories of being teased haunt many people for years. Through adolescence the pressure to achieve an attractive body image is intense, especially among women. According to a recent National Health and Nutrition Examination Survey, half of all white adolescent girls think they are overweight when, in fact, their weight is normal. An astute teenage girl said, "A lot of what makes me mad is a society that idealizes the perfect woman."[39]

Appearance is more important today than it was in the past, according to Mary Pipher, author of *Reviving Ophelia.* She notes that we have moved from communities of primary relationships in which people know each other to cities where secondary relationships are much more common:

> In a community of primary relationships, appearance is only one of many dimensions that define people. Everyone knows everyone else in different ways over time. In a city of strangers, appearance is the only dimension available for the rapid assessment of others. Thus it becomes incredibly important in defining value.[40]

Preoccupation with body image follows many people throughout adulthood. Large numbers of people wish to conform to the body-size ideals projected in the media. They have learned to judge themselves, in many cases, by the standards of physical attractiveness that appear in fashion magazines and television commercials. The motivation to be thinner helps support a $50-billion-a-year diet industry.

Some people have found ways to remake their self-image and move away from a preoccupation with body image. One approach is to develop criteria for self-esteem that go beyond appearance. To make appearance less significant in your life, you develop other benchmarks for self-evaluation. These might include succeeding at work, forming new friendships, or achieving a greater feeling of self-worth through volunteer work. Another approach is to engage in exercise that makes you feel good about yourself. Exercise for strength, fitness, and health, not just for weight loss. You can also identify and change habitual negative thoughts about your body. When you look in the mirror, try to say nice things about your body.[41]

### Questions

1. Professionals in the field of psychology say that people with low self-esteem rely too much on the views of others for a sense of self-worth. Is this a problem you currently face in your life? Explain.
2. Mary Pipher says that in large communities appearance is the only dimension available for rapid assessment of others. Do you find yourself placing a heavy emphasis on appearance when assessing the worth of others?
3. Joan Borysenko, director of the Mind/Body Clinic at Harvard Medical School, says you need to accept yourself as you are. Acceptance, she says, means actually honoring yourself as you are now. Is this good advice? Is it realistic advice? Explain.
4. If you currently have a negative body image, what other criteria could you use to help enhance your self-esteem?

# 4 Personal Values Influence Ethical Choices

CHAPTER PREVIEW

After studying this chapter, you will be able to

■ Explain the advantage of developing a strong sense of character.

■ Understand how personal values are formed.

■ Understand value conflicts and how to resolve them.

■ Identify ways to resolve value conflicts.

■ Learn how to make the right ethical decisions based on your personal value system.

■ Understand the danger of corporate crime and the steps being taken to eliminate it.

Tomorrow's leaders will have reached adulthood during the early part of the twenty-first century. They are often referred to as the D-Generation (i.e., raised in the age of digital technology) or the Net Generation (raised with access to the Internet). How do they differ from people already on the job, many of whom are the same age as these younger workers' parents and grandparents? How well will the mixed generations get along when they work for and with each other in the same organization? Let's take a quick look at what the new generation values.

The first-year college students of 2001 were the target of a national opinion survey conducted by Northwestern Mutual Life Insurance Company. The survey suggests that parents, family, religion, and generosity are at the center of their lives. Their mothers and fathers are often identified as people they most respect and admire. Deanna L. Tillisch, director of the study, says, "[This generation] appears to be alive with idealism, optimism and a vision of a better world."[1] The survey results have indicated that

- 89 percent believe in God, nearly 70 percent attend religious services, and 75 percent believe in life after death.

- 90 percent agree that helping others is more important than helping oneself.

- 73 percent report having volunteered services to schools, charities, and church.

A similar poll conducted by *Newsweek* pointed out that the D-Generation is coming of age during a time of interracial marriages, cross-cultural neighborhoods and schools, instant worldwide communications, relative peace, thriving economic conditions, and low unemployment. It showed that they are the most occupationally and educationally ambitious generation ever.

Perhaps the most disturbing information discovered in these surveys is that this generation believes that lying and cheating are standard behavior,[2] and the young people do not necessarily find these two practices unacceptable. Perhaps the Clinton/Lewinsky affair, the 2002 Olympics scandal, and the tobacco industry cover-ups have provided role models different from those of previous generations. How will the Net Generation respond when it must deal with ethical dilemmas? Will it choose to do the right thing?

Whether you are a member of this new generation or not, this chapter will help you handle the human relations challenges that arise when individuals' values differ.

## Character, Integrity, and Moral Development

Many social observers believe that our nation is in moral decline. They cite research indicating that millions of students from middle school to medical school cheat. After graduation, some misrepresent their educational background and lie when asked to provide salary information about a previous job. Many employees report that they have been pressured by their bosses to do things that they felt were unethical or illegal.[3] Some critics of our current moral climate feel that

Ron Hemelgarn (left) has proven that honesty and integrity make up the winning formula at the famed Indianapolis 500. Years ago, Hemelgarn made a list of rules to guide him in business and racing. Rule 1: Be honest. He is pictured here with Buddy Lazier, the winning driver.

the moral decline began when society's focus shifted from "what is right" to "what is right for me."

When individuals or organizations experience an erosion of moral and ethical values, there are penalties. Employees who are weak in the area of ethical decision making are often terminated. Leaders who lack moral fortitude and integrity seldom enjoy long-term success. Organizations that engage in dishonest practices almost always fail.[4] Moral development takes place throughout life; therefore, the skills involved in making ethical decisions can be improved.

## ■ *Character and Integrity*

Former United States senator Al Simpson said, "If you have character, that's all that matters; and if you don't have character, that's all that matters, too."[5] **Character** is composed of personal standards of behavior, including honesty, integrity, and moral strength. It is the main ingredient we seek in our leaders and the quality that earns us respect in the workplace. In *The Corrosion of Character,* author Richard Sennett says that we have seen a decline of character which can be traced to conditions that have grown out of our fast-paced, high-stress, information-driven economy.[6] He notes that many people are no longer connected to their past, to their neighbors, and to themselves.

**If you have character, that's all that matters; and if you don't have character, that's all that matters, too.**

*HUMAN RELATIONS in ACTION*

### Liar, Liar

The percentage of executive-level candidates who misrepresent their educational credentials is nearly 17 percent, according to the *Liar's Index*. This index is published each year by Jude M. Werro & Associates, a Milwaukee-based executive search firm. The data used to develop the *Liar's Index* is collected during the process of checking résumé claims.

**Integrity** is the basic ingredient of character that is exhibited when you achieve congruence between what you know, what you say, and what you do.[7] When your behavior exhibits your beliefs, you have integrity. When you say one thing but do something else, you *lack* integrity. When your behavior is in tune with your professed standards and values—when you practice what you believe in—you have integrity.

How does a person "learn" integrity? One approach, recommended by author Stephen Covey, is to keep your commitments. "As we make and keep commitments, even small commitments, we begin to establish an inner integrity that gives us the awareness of self-control and courage and strength to accept more of the responsibility for our own lives."[8] Covey says that when we make and keep promises to ourselves and others, we are developing an important habit. We cannot expect to maintain our integrity if we consistently fail to keep our commitments.

Your character and integrity strongly influence your relationships with others. But where can you learn these qualities? College catalogs rarely list a course like "Character Building 101." The Josephson Institute of Ethics acknowledged this lack of character training by forming the Character Counts Coalition. The coalition is an alliance of organizations such as the American Federation of Teachers, the American Association of State Boards of Education, and the American Association of Community Colleges. Their mission is to address the issue of character development through educational institutions and organizations throughout the country. They have developed a variety of grassroots training activities involving what they refer to as the "six pillars of character": trustworthiness, respect, responsibility, fairness, caring, and citizenship.[9] Other organizations involved in this movement include the Center for the Advancement of Ethics and Character at Boston University; the Character Education Partnership in Washington, D.C.; the Center for the 4th and 5th Rs at the State University of New York at Cortland; and the Jefferson Center for Character Education in Pasadena, California. They all offer conferences, workshops, and publications to help individuals and organizations learn more about building character and integrity.[10]

**TOTAL PERSON INSIGHT**

*PETER SENGE*

Author, *The Fifth Discipline*

*"People working together with integrity and authenticity and collective intelligence are profoundly more effective as a business than people working together based on politics, game playing, and narrow self-interest."*

## How Personal Values Are Formed

Hyrum Smith, author of *The 10 Natural Laws of Successful Time and Life Management,* says that certain natural laws govern personal productivity and fulfillment. One of these laws focuses on personal beliefs: Your behavior is a reflection of what you truly believe.[11] **Values** are your deep personal beliefs and preferences that influence your behavior. They are deep-seated in your personality. To discover what really motivates you, carefully examine what it is you value.

Table 4.1 details the values clarification process. These five steps can help you determine whether or not you truly value something. Many times you are not consciously aware of what is really driving your behavior because values exist at different levels of awareness.[12] Unless you clarify your values, life events are likely to unfold in a haphazard manner. Once you are aware of your value priorities and consistently behave accordingly, your character and integrity are enhanced, and life in general is much more satisfying and rewarding. Hyrum Smith says that everything starts with your **core values,** those general statements of principles and beliefs that guide the development of your intermediate and long-range goals.

### Identifying Your Core Values

Core values influence the actions of both individuals and organizations. Anne Mulcahy, an executive at Xerox Corporation and mother of two sons, says she and her husband make decisions at home and work based on their core values: "Our kids are absolutely the center of our lives—and we never mess with that."[13] Maura FitzGerald, CFO of FitzGerald Communications, Inc., a public relations firm, asks all her employees to adhere to the "FitzGerald Family Values" before accepting a job with her company. All her workers carry with them a wallet-size card listing the organization's basic operating principles, one of which is "Never compromise our integrity—this is our hallmark."[14]

We often need to re-examine our core values when searching for a job. Joanne Ciulla, author of *The Working Life,* says taking a job today is a matter of choosing among four core values: high salary, security, meaningful work, and lots of time off.[15] Needless to say, most jobs would require putting at least one of these values on the back burner.

**Table 4.1**

**A Five-Part Valuing Process to Clarify and Develop Values**

### Thinking

We live in a confusing world where making choices about how to live our lives can be difficult. Of major importance is developing critical thinking skills that help distinguish fact from opinion and supported from unsupported arguments. Learn to think for yourself. Question what you are told. Engage in higher-level thinking that involves analysis, synthesis, and evaluation.

### Feeling

This dimension of the valuing process involves being open to your "gut level" feelings. If it doesn't "feel right," it probably isn't. Examine your distressful feelings such as anger, fear, or emotional hurt. Discover what you prize and cherish in life.

### Communicating

Values are clarified through an ongoing process of interaction with others. Be an active listener and hear what others are really saying. Be constantly alert to communication filters such as emotions, body language, and positive and negative attitudes. Learn to send clear messages regarding your own beliefs.

### Choosing

Your values must be freely selected with no outside pressure. In some situations, telling right from wrong is difficult. Therefore, you need to be well informed about alternatives and the consequences of various courses of action. Each choice you make reflects some aspect of your values system.

### Acting

Act repeatedly and consistently on your beliefs. One way to test whether or not something is of value to you is to ask yourself, "Do I find that this value is persistent throughout all aspects of my life?"

*Source:* Howard Kirschenbaum, *Advanced Values Clarification* (La Jolla, Calif.: University Associates, 1977).

As you engage in the values clarification process, it helps to reflect on those things that influence the development of your values. Let's look at some of the important factors that shape our values.

## Environmental Influences

Aristotle said, "If you would understand virtue, observe the conduct of virtuous men." But where are these "virtuous men," the role models we should observe? As a nation, we have witnessed many examples of shabby values. The daily news is filled with instances of fraud and deception such as the tobacco industry's cover-up of their intent to chemically addict millions of smokers throughout the world, sports heroes' greed, and religious leaders' moral failures. Even our political leaders often lack the moral courage to do the right thing.

Working parents today realize that they must take time to teach their children moral and ethical behaviors.

Many events and individuals have influenced the formation of values in the United States. Some of them are shown in Table 4.2. In general, the major environmental influences that shape our values are the family, religious groups, schools, the media, and people we admire.

**Influence of the Family**    Katherine Paterson, author of books for children, says being a parent these days is like riding a bicycle on a bumpy road—learning to keep your balance while zooming full speed ahead, veering around as many potholes as possible.[16] Parents must assume many roles, none more important than moral teacher. In many families in contemporary society, one parent must assume full responsibility for shaping children's values. Some single parents—those overwhelmed with responsibility for career, family, and rebuilding their own personal lives—may lack the stability necessary for the formation of the six pillars of character. And in two-parent families, both parents may work outside the home and at the end of the day may lack the time or energy to intentionally direct the development of their children's values. The same may be true for families experiencing financial pressures or the strains associated with caring for elderly parents.

**Influence of Religious Groups**    Many people learn their value priorities through religious training. This may be achieved through the accepted teachings of a church, through religious literature such as the Koran and the Bible, or through individuals in churches or synagogues who are positive role models.

**Table 4.2**

**People and events have influenced the formation of values for three groups of Americans: Matures, Baby Boomers, and Generation X. What will the next generation be called? Persons born between 1977 and 1997 have already been labeled Generation Y, Generation Next, D-Generation, Net Generation, Millennials, and Speeders. In the future, one of these names is likely to surface as the "official" label for this new generation.**

| Matures (born 1928–1945) | Baby Boomers (born 1946–1961) | Generation X (born 1962–1972) |
|---|---|---|
| Eisenhower | Television | AIDS |
| MacArthur | Beatniks | Wellness movement |
| A-bomb | Sputnik | Iran-Contra affair |
| Dr. Spock | Civil Rights Act | Operation Desert Storm |
| John Wayne | The pill | Glasnost |
| Mickey Mantle | Drug culture | Oklahoma City bombing |
| Doris Day | Women's movement | MTV |
| Frank Sinatra | Vietnam War | World Wide Web |
| The Waltons | Watergate | World Trade Center terrorist attack |
| Andy and Opie Taylor | JFK and MLK assassinations | Work/life balance concerns |

Some of the most powerful spiritual leaders do not have formal ties to a particular religion. John Templeton is one example. He is a successful investor and one of the greatest philanthropists of the modern age. Templeton says the only real wealth in our lives is spiritual wealth. Over the years, he has given over $800 million to fund forgiveness, conflict resolution, and character-building projects.[17]

Religious groups that want to define, instill, and perpetuate values may find an eager audience. Stephen Covey and other social observers say that many people are determinedly seeking spiritual and moral anchors in their lives and in their work. People who live in uncertain times seem to attach more importance to spirituality.[18] Healthy spirituality is discussed in Chapter 9.

**Influence of the Schools**   Many parents, concerned that their children are not learning enough about moral values and ethical behavior, want character education added to the curriculum.[19] Some have been influenced by William J. Bennett's *The Book of Virtues.* Bennett sees moral education as a fundamental purpose of education. In support of this practice, Thomas Lickona, professor of

## HUMAN RELATIONS *in* ACTION

### Terror Prompts Re-examination of Values

In the wake of the suicide hijackings that leveled the twin towers of Manhattan's World Trade Center and ripped apart the Pentagon complex, many Americans began to rethink their priorities. Values that were pre-eminent for many workers—career advancement, personal fulfillment, money, and status—are taking a back seat to more fundamental needs: family, friends, community and connectedness with others. A tragedy of this nature is likely to influence workers' decision-making for months, if not years. Soon after the terrorist attack a 28-year-old market research manager who describes herself as "very driven" and motivated to acquire things said, "Maybe I don't need all this stuff. Maybe I need to concentrate on enriching my life with my family."

education at the State University of New York, says many children have very little sense of right and wrong, so schools must help out.[20]

In the 1970s, many schools included values clarification in their curriculum. As various factions of society objected, fearing that values would be "imposed" on children, schools eliminated these classes, and teachers learned to be "value neutral." Today, however, there is a nationwide resurgence of the movement to teach moral values and ethics in the classrooms. Sanford McDonnell, chairman of the Character Education Partnership, says the schools have the greatest potential for overcoming what he describes as "the national crisis of character." The Character Education Partnership defines "good character" as understanding, caring about, and acting on core ethical values. McDonnell says our nation will not be strong if we graduate young people who are brilliant but dishonest or who have great intellectual knowledge but do not care about others.[21]

**Once you are aware of your value priorities and consistently behave accordingly, your character and integrity are enhanced, and life in general is much more satisfying and rewarding.**

**Influence of the Media**    Some social critics say that if you are searching for signs of civilization gone rotten, you can simply tune into the loud and often amoral voices of mass entertainment on television, radio, and the Internet. They point out that viewers too often see people abusing and degrading other people without any significant consequences. Mainstream television, seen by a large number of young viewers, continues to feature a great deal of violence and anti-social behavior. Children between the ages of 2 and 17 spend the equivalent of three years of their waking lives watching TV—an average of 15,000 to 18,000 hours (compared to 12,000 hours in school).[22]

Is there a connection between violence in the media and violence in real life? The American Academy of Pediatrics says media violence increases children's aggressiveness and antisocial behavior. However, it is not entirely clear if this aggression results in violence. Research has also found a connection between heavy television viewing and depressed children. More research is needed to help us fully understand the extent of the influence of media on our culture's values.

**Influence of People We Admire**    In addition to being influenced by the media, your values are likely to be influenced by **modeling**—shaping your behavior to resemble that of people you admire and embracing the qualities those people demonstrate. The heroes and heroines you discover in childhood and adolescence help you form a "dominant value direction."[23] Opie and Andy Taylor were positive role models for most children growing up in the 1950s and 1960s. Today Bart Simpson's unique family relationships teach children a new way of interacting with authority figures. We would be better served to point children and adolescents in the direction of humanitarian and tennis champion Arthur Ashe, who led an exemplary family and professional life until his untimely death from AIDS contracted after heart bypass surgery, or Oprah Winfrey, whose open and honest style can have a positive effect on girls and women of all ages. If we truly want to develop a more moral society, we need to keep track of the men and women our children are modeling and encourage our children to look for positive qualities such as Ashe's integrity and Winfrey's honesty. We would all be wise to focus on and emulate the positive qualities of those we admire.

## Avoiding Values Drift

Core values represent the starting point for personal and organizational success. As individuals, we need to reflect on our core values when making decisions related to important work/life issues. Write down your core values and then decide whether these values are reflected in the way you live.

Debbie and Randy Fields, cofounders of Mrs. Fields' Cookies, hold strong opinions about what it takes to successfully operate a large chain of retail stores. They are constantly looking for "drift." Drift is the slow erosion of the company's standards and values. When the company was expanding, they opened a new store in Hawaii and staffed it with capable employees. Over a period of five months, the people made tiny, infinitesimal changes in the cookie recipes. When

Debbie Fields visited the store, she discovered that her original chewy cookies had become spongy cakes.[24] Tiny changes in personal values can have a similar effect, steering a person slightly off course. That is why it is so important to constantly monitor your commitment to your values and make adjustments when necessary to get your life back on track. In his book *Conversations with God,* Neal Donald Walsch discusses the process of building a strong foundation for everything from your daily decisions to your long-range goals. He suggests: "Do not dismantle the house, but look at each brick, and replace those which appear broken, which no longer support the structure."[25] This careful examination of each of your values will help keep you on track toward your ideal future and help you avoid values drift.

---

### THINKING / LEARNING STARTERS

1. Identify the events and individuals that have been influential in forming your value system. Are those of your childhood and adolescence still important to you?

2. Based on the media's influence and the concept of modeling, what do you predict the next generation's values will be? The children of today will be your coworkers in the future. Will their attitudes and values be a potential problem for you?

##  Values Conflicts

One of the major causes of conflict between people is a clash between those individuals' personal values. There is no doubt about it, people are different. Everyone has been raised with different family backgrounds, religious experiences, education, role models, and media exposure. These differences can pop out anywhere and anytime people get together. Many observers suggest that organizations look for **values conflicts** when addressing such problems as declining quality, absenteeism, and poor customer service. The trouble may lie not so much in work schedules or production routines as in the mutual distrust and misunderstanding brought about by clashes in workers' and managers' value systems. Here are some examples of values conflicts:

ITEM: To improve profits, Ford Motor Company developed the oversized, gas-guzzling Expedition SUV. Critics quickly noted the contradiction between Ford's public position of working hard to manufacture vehicles that are less threatening to the environment. William Ford, Jr., chairman of Ford, publicly admitted that its popular SUVs contribute to greenhouse gas levels and global climate troubles.[26]

Following the site-selection corruption scandal of the 2002 winter Olympic games, Mitt Romney agreed to be the president of the Salt Lake City Olympic Committee. He was charged with the responsibility of restoring the integrity of the Olympic games and pledged that absolutely no bribes would be tolerated at the SLC 2002 games.

ITEM: Lionel Sosa, founder of one of the nation's largest Hispanic ad firms, says a web of traditional values sometimes keeps Latinos from rising to the top in corporate America. Latino values that promote humility, pessimism, and self-denial can conflict with the values that guide many organizations.[27]

ITEM: Herbert Lanese, former president of McDonnell Douglas Aerospace, was abruptly fired six months after he was hired because of a values clash with Chief Executive Harry Stonecipher. One problem became obvious during a 99-day machinists' strike at the St. Louis plant. Local newspapers quoted Lanese as saying that convenience store clerks with two weeks' training could do the machinists' jobs. Union members were elated when Lanese was removed.[28]

---

**TOTAL PERSON INSIGHT**

*ANDRÉ GIDE*

Twentieth-Century French Writer

*"It is better to be hated for what you are than to be loved for what you are not."*

---

■ **Internal Values Conflicts**

A person who is forced to choose between two or more strongly held values is experiencing an **internal values conflict.** As a manager, you may be torn between loyalty to your workers and loyalty to upper management. As an employee, you may find yourself in conflict between fulfilling family obligations and devoting the time and energy required to succeed at work. Trudy Desilets spent many years searching for a balance between her personal and professional life. Because travel demands left her exhausted, she gave up a fast-track sales job soon after the birth of her first child. When she asked to share her job with an equally qualified employee, her bosses turned her down. She loved her next job, but by the time her daughter was 3 she was facing burnout. The demands of being a good worker, a good mother, and a good wife were overwhelming.[29]

How you resolve internal values conflicts depends on how much time you are willing to invest in the values clarification process described in Table 4.1. Once you have completed the process and identified your core values, be sure to rank them in order of importance to you. This ranking process will help you make decisions when life gets complicated and you have to make difficult choices.[30] If one of your values is to be an outstanding parent and another is to maintain a healthy body, you should anticipate an internal values conflict when a busy schedule requires a choice between attending your daughter's soccer game and your weekly workout at the fitness center. However, when you rank which value is more important, the decision will be much easier.

### ■ *Values Conflicts with Others*

Some of the most common interpersonal values conflicts arise between people from different generations, races, cultures, ethnic backgrounds, or religions; between men and women; and between supervisors and workers. Individuals from diverse backgrounds may clash over different interpretations of the work ethic and the priorities of job and personal life. Unless such conflicts are handled skillfully, confrontation can make the situation worse, not better.

How will you handle a tense situation where it is obvious your values conflict with those of a colleague? You may discover your supervisor is a racist and you

 *HUMAN RELATIONS in ACTION*

### Values Clarification at Levi Strauss

At Levi Strauss & Co., values are considered a living element, an evolving foundation needed to guide employees in the decision-making process. In a meeting of 200 managers, each person was instructed to select key personal values from a deck of 50 "value cards." Each person arranged the cards according to his or her most important and least important values, then placed his or her name card on the piles. Next, everyone was encouraged to walk around the room and look at each array. Managers were surprised at the diversity of values and the range of values people selected as most important. Each table of participants then discussed how their values influenced the way they performed their duties at work.

strongly support the civil rights of all people. One option is to become indignant and take steps to reduce contact with your supervisor. The problem with being indignant is that it burns your bridges with someone who can influence your growth and development within the organization. The opposite extreme would be to do nothing. But when we ignore unethical or immoral behavior, we compromise our integrity, and the problem is likely to continue and grow.[31] With a little reflection, you may be able to find a response somewhere between these two extremes. If your supervisor tells a joke that is demeaning to members of a minority group, consider meeting with her and explaining how uncomfortable these comments make you feel. When we confront others' lapses in character, we are strengthening our own integrity.

## Personal Values and Ethical Choices

**Ethics** are the rules that direct your conduct and moral judgments.[32] They help translate your values into appropriate and effective behaviors in your day-to-day life. Personal ethics determine how you do business and with whom. Kickbacks and payoffs may be acceptable practices in some parts of the world yet may be viewed as unethical practices elsewhere. Where will you draw the line between right and wrong?

As competition in the global marketplace increases, moral and ethical issues can become cloudy. Although most organizations have adopted the point of view that "Good ethics is good business," exceptions do exist. Some organizations encourage, or at least condone, unethical behaviors. Surveys show many workers feel pressure to violate their ethical standards in order to meet business objectives.[33] Thus, you must develop your own personal code of ethics.

Every job you hold will present you with new ethical and moral dilemmas. These challenges can surface almost daily for people who direct and supervise the work of others. It may be tempting to tell employees to "do whatever is necessary" to get a job done on time, or to look the other way when employees engage in unethical or illegal acts. The authors of *Lessons from the Top,* a book that describes the characteristics of America's top business leaders, state that the person who doesn't live with integrity or lead by example will not be effective in a leadership role.[34]

As a laborer, salesperson, or office support worker, you too will be faced with ethical choices. Faced with the demands of overtime, balancing work and family, and layoffs due to downsizing, workers seem to feel more pressure to act unethically.[35] A survey sponsored by Professional Secretaries International discovered an alarming frequency of unethical behaviors including breaching confidentiality about hiring, firing, or layoffs, removing or destroying information, and falsifying documents.[36] Other studies indicate that underpaid employees who feel unappreciated are more prone to steal from their employers, with the price tag reaching billions of dollars each year—and climbing rapidly. According to the Association of Certified Fraud Examiners, unethical acts by workers cost U.S. businesses more than $400 billion a year.[37]

■  ### How to Make the Right Ethical Choices

In today's turbulent, fast-paced, highly competitive workplace, ethical dilemmas surface frequently, and telling right from wrong has never been more difficult. The following guidelines may help you avoid being part of this growing statistic.

**Learn to distinguish between right and wrong.**    Although selecting the right path can be difficult, a great deal of help is available today. Many current books and articles offer good advice. The book *The Measure of Our Success* by Marian Wright Edelman presents a collection of "lessons for life" that can offer guidance in making ethical choices. A few examples follow:

■  There is no free lunch. Don't feel entitled to anything you don't sweat and struggle for.

■  Never work just for money or for power. They won't save your soul or build a decent family or help you sleep at night.

■  Be honest. Struggle to live what you say and preach. Act with integrity.

■  Sell the shadow for the substance. Don't confuse style with substance; don't confuse political charm or rhetoric with decency or sound policy.[38]

Help in making the correct ethical choices at work may be as close as your employer's code of ethics, ethical guidelines published by your professional organization, or advice provided by an experienced and trusted colleague.

**Make certain your values are in harmony with those of your employer.**    You may find it easier to make the right ethical choices if your values are compatible with those of your employer. Many organizations have adopted a set of beliefs, customs, values, and practices that attract a certain type of employee (see Figure 4.1). Harmony between personal and organizational values usually leads to success for the individual as well as the organization. These **shared values** provide a strong bond among all members of the work force.

ITEM:  When selling their long-distance telephone service, employees of Working Assets assure their customers that 1 percent of every phone bill will be donated to liberal causes such as Greenpeace, the American Civil Liberties Union, gun control, abortion rights, and protection of redwoods. One marketing campaign read, "Be Socially Responsible: Talk on the Phone." Chief Executive Officer Laura Sure says that people are looking for other reasons to make a choice beyond the cost of services rendered.[39]

ITEM:  BMS Software in Houston, Texas, provides a work environment where you can find sustenance for the whole self—mind, body, and spirit. Employees can pump iron in the gym, enjoy a gourmet meal, or participate in massage therapy. The self-contained community offers an array of services (banking, dry cleaning, hair salon, etc.), and there is a large kitchen with free fruit, popcorn, soda, and coffee on each floor of the company's two glass towers. You live comfortably at BMS, but you also work long hours. Many employees work ten- to twelve-hour days.[40]

**FIGURE 4.1**

GEAR For Sports®
Vision and Values
Statement

*Source:* "GEAR For
Sports® Vision and
Values Statement."
Reprinted by permission
of GEAR For Sports.

# GEAR For Sports® Vision

*Guided by our GEAR values, we strive to be the leader in
quality and delivery of our customer's image through
marketing innovative sportswear, accessories and services.*

# GEAR Values

*GEAR For Sports' business is predicated on
respect for, and attention to, all of our customers,
business partners, employees, government
and community. We value:*

**Customers**
*by exceeding their expectations.*

**Excellence**
*by taking pride and responsibility in everything we do.*

**Employees**
*by demonstrating respect and consideration for each other.*

**Teamwork**
*by fostering trust and recognition
among all stakeholders.*

**Professionalism**
*by exhibiting integrity and proficiency.*

**Innovation**
*by embracing creativity and change.*

**Social Responsibility**
*by caring for and sharing with each other
and our community.*

ITEM: Research conducted by the Families and Work Institute indicates that
work/family decisions continue to be a battlefield for clashing values.
Increasingly, employees want the opportunity to openly discuss family issues
such as child care, requests for a flexible schedule, or care for an ailing parent.
Johnson & Johnson is one of several companies that is training managers to
sensitize them to values priorities that are different from their own.[41]

---

**TOTAL PERSON INSIGHT**

*DAN RICE AND
CRAIG DREILINGER*

Management Consultants;
Authors, "Rights and Wrongs
of Ethics Training"

*"Nothing is more powerful for employees than seeing their
managers behave according to their expressed values and
standards; nothing is more devastating to the development
of an ethical environment than a manager who violates the
organization's ethical standards."*

**Don't let your life be driven by the desire for immediate gratification.** Progress and prosperity have almost identical meanings to many people. They equate progress with the acquisition of material things. One explanation is that young business leaders entering the corporate world are under a great deal of pressure to show the trappings of success. This is the view expressed by John Delaney, who is a professor at the University of Iowa and has done extensive research on ethics. He says, "You're expected to have the requisite car and summer house to show you're a contributor to society, and many people do whatever it takes to get them."[42] Many people are trapped in a vicious cycle: They work more so that they can buy more consumer goods; then, as they buy more, they must work more.

To achieve immediate gratification often means taking shortcuts. It involves pushing hard, cutting corners, and emphasizing short-term gains over the achievement of long-term goals. The Internet has created an "ethical gray zone," according to *Fortune* magazine. Greed has motivated many high-tech companies to promise investors, customers, and employees things they cannot deliver. Some dot.com companies have discovered clever ways to recycle their balance sheets—ways that mislead current and potential investors. The "get-the-deal-done-today" mentality seems to leave little time for ethical deliberation.[43]

> **The "get-the-deal-done-today" mentality seems to leave little time for ethical deliberation.**

Why do so many people seek immediate gratification? The answer to this question is somewhat complex. Some people feel pressure from friends and family members to climb the ladder of success as quickly as possible and display the trappings of success such as a new car, boat, or house. They fail to realize that the road to peace of mind and happiness is not paved with Rolex watches, Brooks Brothers suits, and a Lexus. In Chapter 9 we describe a new definition of success and discuss the nonfinancial resources that make the biggest contribution to a happy and fulfilling life.

---

### THINKING / LEARNING STARTERS

1. Think about the last time you felt guilty about something you did. Did you hurt someone's feelings? Did you take credit for something someone else accomplished? Which of your basic values did your actions violate?

2. When was the last time you broke off a friendship or relationship with another person in your personal or professional life? Does the reason for the breakup reflect back to a values conflict between the two of you? Explain.

---

## Corporate Values and Ethical Choices

When organizations consistently make ethical decisions that are in the best interest of their stakeholders—employees, customers, stockholders, and the community—they are considered good corporate citizens because they are socially responsible. The list "The 100 Best Corporate Citizens" published by *Business Ethics* magazine reminds us that a company can be socially responsible and still achieve excellent earnings. In her *Business Week* article "A Conscience Doesn't Have to Make You Poor," Susan Scherreik interviewed stockholders that invest only in companies that are good corporate citizens. One stated, "I see the damage that many companies do to people's health and the environment by polluting or creating dangerous products. Investing in them makes no sense because these companies won't flourish in the long run."[44] Figures from The Social Investment Forum, a nonprofit group in Washington, D.C., show that the total amount of money invested in socially responsible organizations stands at $2.16 trillion.[45] Many people want their money to help others and will support organizations that do, too.

## ■ *Corporate Crime*

Many organizations have gotten into serious trouble by ignoring ethical principles. In recent years, the media have carried headlines concerning organizations involved in corporate crime.

ITEM: Eighteen former Honda Motor Co. executives pleaded guilty to bribery-related charges. The executives admitted that they accepted over $50 million in bribes from dealers in exchange for generous supplies of fast-selling Honda cars. Most of the executives went to prison.[46]

**"Welcome stockholders, I'd love to be there in person, but as you may have read, I am under house arrest."**

ITEM: Royal Caribbean Cruises agreed to pay a record $18 million fine for routinely dumping oil and dangerous chemicals in U.S. coastal waters.[47]

Those items represent only a small fraction of the corporate crime that goes on today. Many offenders are not caught or brought to trial. But on the positive side, recent surveys indicate that a large majority of America's major corporations are actively trying to build ethics into their organizations.

ITEM: Minnesota Mutual Life Insurance Company has been able to steer clear of scandal for more than one hundred years by adopting a values-based management philosophy that rewards integrity and honesty. Success at the management level requires commitment to the company's core values. Managers must demonstrate their ability to infuse ethical values in their subordinates.[48]

ITEM: At Harley-Davidson the soul of the "Hog" can be traced to values that emphasize strong working relationships. The company's idea of a healthy working relationship is embedded in five formal values that constitute a code of behavior for everyone:[49]

- Tell the truth.

- Be fair.

- Keep your promises.

- Respect the individual.

- Encourage intellectual curiosity.

Many say they have difficulty determining the right course of action in complex "gray-area" situations. And even when the right ethical course of action is clear, competitive pressures sometimes lead well-intentioned managers astray.[50] Tom Chappell, author of *The Soul of a Business* and founder of Tom's of Maine, explains why organizations often have difficulty doing what is morally right and socially responsible: "It's harder to manage for ethical pursuits than it is to simply manage for profits."[51]

### Help Prevent Corporate Crime

**Honor Ethics Codes**    Mark Twain once wrote, "To be good is noble. To tell people how to be good is even nobler, and much less trouble." Many corporate leaders have decided that it is time to put their views on ethics in writing and have developed written codes of ethics. A written code, highly publicized throughout the company and enforced without exception, can be a powerful force in preventing unethical behavior. A Tulane University study, however, discovered that the drive for a "comfortable life" and "pleasure" controlled the decisions of many managers even though their organizations had codes of ethics in place. Researchers say organizations need to do more to create an overall "ethical climate" that includes a system that recognizes acts of moral courage.[52]

Sears, Roebuck and Company's Office of Ethics and Business Policy offers support to other individuals and organizations that are seeking ways to promote ethical business behaviors.

Our associates *know* there is an "I" *in* ETHICS.

Sears is proud to sponsor the 2000 Business Ethics Awards.

To obtain copies of Sears' ethics and business practices materials, please write to the **Sears Office of Ethics and Business Policy,** 3333 Beverly Road, C3135B, Hoffman Estates, IL 60179.

SEARS

© 2000 Sears, Roebuck and Co.

**Seek Honorable Coworkers**    Thomas Melohn, president of North American Tool & Die Inc., located in San Leandro, California, says the key to operating a successful company is to first identify a guiding set of values and then "make sure you find people who have those values and can work together."[53] He says the hiring process should be given a very high priority. Melohn never hires any employee without checking references and conducting a lengthy job interview.

If you work for a company that has organized workers into self-managed teams, you may be involved in hiring new team members. This traditional management task is often delegated to employees.

Some companies use integrity tests (also called honesty tests) to screen out dishonest people and drug users. The first honesty test was developed more than 40 years ago by Reid Psychological Systems. Many people question the accuracy of these tests and the fairness of using them to hire or turn away applicants. Some states have made it illegal to deny someone a job on the basis of low integrity-test scores. Testing companies admit that these tests are not foolproof.

**Participate in Ethics Training** Many ethical issues are complex and cannot be considered in black-and-white moral terms. It is for this and other reasons that ethics training has become quite common in the business community. In some cases, the training involves little more than a careful study of your company's ethics code and its implications for day-to-day decision making. You will be notified where the code of ethics is displayed in the building and asked to sign a document verifying that you have read, understand, and agree to abide by the code of ethics. In other cases, you may be asked to participate in in-depth discussions of ethical decisions. At Martin Marietta Corp., ethics training includes the use of a game called Gray Matters, in which a game leader presents minicases to teams of players. Each team also receives a list of potential responses to an ethical dilemma presented in the minicase. After discussing the responses, each team selects what it thinks is the best answer. The team leader then discloses the point value of each answer. Learning takes place as team members debate the pros and cons of each possible response.[54] Sears, Roebuck and Company provides its employees with a booklet entitled *Code of Business Conduct*. It outlines the company's position on a wide range of issues such as receiving gifts, employee discounts, care of company assets, and foreign business dealings. It also includes guidelines for making ethical decisions (see Table 4.3).

Is it possible to instill ethical values in employees through the use of training programs? Some critics say ethics training programs prepare employees to make the right decision only when actions are covered by specific rules. They see more merit in providing guidelines that employees can use to resolve many ethical issues. Almost everyone agrees that ethics training must start at the top of the organization.

**TABLE 4.3**

**Sears's Guidelines for Ethical Decision Making**

**Guidelines for Making Ethical Decisions:**

1. Is it legal?

2. Is it within Sears's shared beliefs and policies?

3. Is it right/fair/appropriate?

4. Would I want everyone to know about this?

5. How will I feel about myself?

*Source:* From Sears's *Code of Business Conduct*. Reprinted by permission of Sears, Roebuck and Co.

**Support Whistle-Blowing**    When you discover your employer or a colleague is behaving illegally or unethically, you have three choices. You can keep quiet and keep working. You can decide you can't be party to the situation and leave. Or you can report the situation in the hope of putting a stop to it. When you reveal wrongdoing within an organization to the public or to those in positions of authority, you are a **whistle blower.**

Jeffrey Wigand, a former chief researcher for Brown and Williamson Tobacco, testified that his company had misled the public about the danger of nicotine. The result was a record-breaking $145-billion judgment against the tobacco industry for years of tobacco-related health hazards.

All government-funded medical research grant money was jeopardized at the University of Oklahoma after nurse Cherlynn Mathias informed federal officials that research personnel had violated safety procedures during a major cancer study. Even after Mathias's warning, the site's Institutional Review Board, charged with the responsibility of keeping test patients safe, refused to stop human testing of a melanoma vaccine that had not yet been tested on animals and allowed patients to self-inject drugs that were shipped to their homes.

When FMC Corporation began producing the Bradley Fighting Vehicle, a tanklike troop carrier ordered by the U.S. Army, employee Henry Boisvert questioned its viability in water, in a report to his supervisors. When his report was quashed by his employer, he filed a lawsuit under the Federal False Claims Act, which had been written to reward people who report wrongdoing by federal contractors. His allegations took 12 years to prove and a grueling four months in court, but he won $171.6 million. Boisvert planned to give away most of his share of the award. Following the verdict, he said, "This wasn't about the money. They were sending false materials to the government and were telling me to cover up everything. They didn't care about the troops."[55]

In each of these cases and in hundreds like them, someone had to come forward with information, even though the informant knew he or she might be subject to harassment from the employer. Whistle-blowing is not an easy path to take. You may be right, win your case, and still lose friends and perhaps your job. However, taking steps to get rid of unethical practices is often your responsibility.

**TOTAL PERSON INSIGHT**

*EDMUND BURKE*

Nineteenth-Century English Political Philosopher

*"All that is necessary for evil to triumph is for good men to do nothing."*

## HUMAN RELATIONS *in* ACTION

### Bible Study in the Boardroom

Throughout the past few years, Burton Visotzky has been leading nondenominational Bible study groups in boardrooms. The participants have been CEOs in both large and small companies. Jews, Christians, Muslims, and even atheists sit around the table discussing stories from Genesis and Exodus. The first two books of the Bible present numerous stories illustrating the moral questions that business leaders face on a daily basis.

Will Bible study groups replace the ethics officer or the need for a code of ethics? Visotzky believes the most effective moral education takes place when people study ethical questions in a group setting and learn from one another. He may be right. Today, Bible study groups can be found at over 1,000 business firms throughout the nation. Torah and Koran study groups are growing in popularity.

## Values and Ethics in International Business

If the situation is complex on the domestic scene, values and ethical issues become even more complicated at the international level. The subject is too broad to treat in detail in this chapter, but we can provide an overview of some problem areas that exist in international business. Here are some examples.

1. *Bribery used to secure foreign contracts.* Most industrial nations have signed a multinational treaty outlawing corporate bribery. Nevertheless, many corporate employees and government officials still seek payments for favors. In 1977 the U.S. Congress passed the Foreign Corrupt Practices Act, which bars companies from bribing government officials.

2. *Human rights violations.* American business firms are under great pressure to avoid doing business with overseas contractors that permit human rights violations in their factories. Starbucks Coffee, Levi Strauss, and many other companies have developed codes of conduct that focus on such problem areas as child labor, low wages, and long hours.

3. *Lack of sensitivity to foreign customs.* The need to be aware of foreign business etiquette is very important if you are conducting international business. You must avoid unwittingly offending people from foreign countries. If you are doing business in Central or South America, don't be alarmed if the person you are meeting is late for an appointment. In Germany there is a strong emphasis on punctuality. In Israel it is not impolite to discuss business during the evening meal. In England it would be poor manners to talk about business after the end of the workday.[56]

Now that trade relations have been resumed with countries such as Vietnam, South Africa, and China, it is important for all parties to recognize value differences and to spend time and effort building mutual respect and understanding.

## Summary

A strong sense of character grows out of your personal standards of behavior. When you consistently behave in accordance with your values, you maintain your integrity. Your values are the personal worth or importance you give to an object or idea. People's values serve as the foundation for their attitudes, preferences, opinions, and behaviors. Personal values are largely formed early in life and are influenced by family, religious upbringing, schools, the media, and role models.

Internal values conflicts arise when we must choose between strongly held personal values. Values conflicts with others, often based on age, racial, religious, gender, or ethnic differences, require skilled intervention before they can be resolved.

Once you have clarified your personal values, your ethical decisions will be easier. You must learn to distinguish right from wrong, choose an employer whose values you share, and avoid the pursuit of immediate gratification. Shared values unify employees in an organization by providing guidelines for behavior and decisions.

Corporate values and ethics on both the domestic and the international levels are receiving increasing attention because of the devastating effect and expense of corporate crime. Many organizations are developing ethics codes to help guide employee behavior, hiring only those individuals who share their corporate values, and offering ethics training opportunities to all employees. As transnational organizations increase in number, the individuals involved will need to consciously examine their values and ethical standards to deal effectively with differing value structures in each country.

## Career Corner

Q: I will soon graduate from college and would like to begin my career with an organization that shares my values. I have carefully examined what is most important to me and believe I know the type of organizational culture in which I can thrive. But how do I discover the "real" values of an organization when my interviews are permeated with buzzwords such as "family-friendly" and "teamwork-oriented"? How can I determine whether or not they truly mean what they seem to say?

A: Direct questions about an organization's values often result in well-rehearsed answers from the interviewer. Try using *critical incident* questions such as "How did you handle the recent downsizing of your middle managers?" or "Tell me about the heroes in your organization." And don't depend solely on the interviewer's answers. Ask current and former employees as well as the organization's customers or clients. Listen carefully to the language used during your interviews. Do you hear a lot of talk about "love," "caring," and "intuition," or do you hear statements like "We had to send in the SWAT team," "They beat their brains out," and "We really nailed them"? If possible, sit in on a team meeting with your potential coworkers. A perfect match between your values and your potential employers' is hard to find, so be patient. You may need to compromise.

## Key Terms

character

integrity

values

core values

modeling

values conflict

internal values conflict

ethics

shared values

whistle blower

## Review Questions

1. How do values differ from attitudes, opinions, or behavior?
2. How are our values formed? How have the sources of our values changed in recent years?
3. Differentiate between internal values conflicts and values conflicts with others.
4. Explain the five dimensions of Kirschenbaum's valuing process (see Table 4.1).
5. Describe the advantages and disadvantages of employees sharing the same values as their organization.
6. Explain the negative effects of the pursuit of immediate gratification.
7. How do top management values affect the purpose and direction of an organization?
8. List some of the steps corporations are taking to eliminate crime in their organizations.
9. How might an ethics code help organizations be more productive?
10. How do seemingly accepted unethical business practices in foreign countries affect Americans' ability to compete for business contracts in those countries?

## Application Exercises

1. Guilt and loss of self-respect can result when you say or do things that conflict with what you believe. One way to feel better about yourself is to "clean up" your integrity. Make a list of what you are doing that you think is wrong. Once the list is complete, look it over and determine if you can stop these behaviors. Consider making amends for things you have done in the past that you feel guilty about.[57]
2. In groups of four, discuss how you would react if your manager asked you to participate in some sort of corporate crime. For example, the manager could

ask you to help launder money from the company, give a customer misleading information, or cover up a budget inaccuracy and keep this information from reaching upper management. You might want to role-play the situation with your group. Follow up with class discussion.

3. One of the great challenges in life is the clarification of our values. The five-part valuing process described in Table 4.1 can be very helpful as you attempt to identify your core values. Select one personal or professional value from the following list, and clarify this value by applying the five-step process.

    a. Respect the rights and privileges of people who may be in the minority due to race, gender, ethnicity, age, physical or mental abilities, or sexual orientation.

    b. Conserve the assets of my employer.

    c. Utilize leisure time in order to add balance to my life.

    d. Maintain a healthy lifestyle.

    e. Balance the demands of my work and personal life.

## Internet Exercise

Visit the Web site of the Josephson Institute: www.josephsoninstitute.org. Navigate through the various icons available. Take notes on those items you consider relevant to your life at work, home, or school. Report your discoveries to your class members.

## Self-Assessment Exercise

For each of the following statements, circle the number from 1 to 5 that best represents your response: (1) strongly disagree (never do this); (2) disagree (rarely do this); (3) moderately agree (sometimes do this); (4) agree (frequently do this); (5) strongly agree (almost always do this).

A. I base my personal and professional decisons on clearly defined personal values.　　1　2　3　4　5

B. I accept the fact that others' values may differ from mine, and I respect their right to maintain a value system that differs from my own.　　1　2　3　4　5

C. I have a clear sense of what is right and wrong, and my character reflects the fundamental strengths of honesty, fairness, service, humility, and modesty.　　1　2　3　4　5

D. I maintain my integrity by practicing what I believe in and keeping my commitments.　　1　2　3　4　5

E. When I observe unethical practices, I will report them to the appropriate person(s).　　1　2　3　4　5

Select an appropriate attitude or skill you would like to improve. Write your goal in the space provided, and describe the steps you will take to achieve this goal.

GOAL: _____

_____

_____

_____

## Case Problem    *Disney Versus the Southern Baptist Convention*

If you look up *wholesome* in the dictionary, you might very well discover the Walt Disney Company logo beside it because Disney has become *the* family-entertainment giant known for its theme parks and G-rated movies. The Walt Disney Company has been functioning on the family-oriented values passed on by its revered founder and is now the largest entertainment company in the world since purchasing the American Broadcasting Company. Recently, however, Disney's organizational culture has been changing to reflect new company initiatives and to value the diversity of its work force as well as its customers. Disney has extended health care benefits to all company employees with same-sex partners, allowed gays and lesbians to gather annually at Disney parks, and contracted with film producers that make R-rated movies.

In response, leaders of the 16-million-member Southern Baptist Convention voted to boycott Disney to protest what they see as its drift away from commitment to traditional family and Christian values. The Southern Baptists believe that same-sex relationships do not qualify as "family," that Disney should stop the annual gay/lesbian get-togethers, and that Disney should refuse to participate in the creation or marketing of R-rated movies. Their nonbinding resolution specifically requests members to cancel plans to visit Disney theme parks, refuse to pay to see Disney movies, and cut Disney product purchases by $100 each year. Sixteen million members times $100 can equal a devastating blow to any corporation's bottom line.

A Disney spokesperson called the boycott "misguided" because it targets the most family-friendly media company in the world.[58]

### Questions

1. Do you agree or disagree with the decision to launch a boycott? Explain.
2. If you were a Southern Baptist Convention member who did not vote at the convention and who had children who had saved money for their trip to Disney World, would you go on the trip? Explain.
3. If you were a Southern Baptist minister who did not vote at the convention and did not agree with the vote, how would you guide your church's membership?
4. What steps should Disney take to reduce the potentially destructive effect of the boycott? Would these actions violate the values of any other groups?

# 5

# Attitudes Can Shape Your Life

**CHAPTER PREVIEW**

After studying this chapter, you will be able to

- Understand the impact of employee attitudes on the success of individuals as well as organizations.

- List and explain the ways people acquire attitudes.

- Describe attitudes that employers value.

- Learn how to change your attitudes.

- Learn how to help others change their attitudes.

- Understand what adjustments organizations are making to develop positive employee attitudes.

In recent years several companies have expanded their work force. When Southwest Airlines needed 4,500 new employees, there were more than 150,000 applications. When Bellagio, a Las Vegas luxury resort, needed 9,600 workers, 75,000 applied. When Toyota Motors wanted to staff a new truck factory in Princeton, Indiana, over 55,000 applications were received. IBM hired 35,000 people in one year, but received 850,000 applications. The four companies compete in a wide range of industries, yet interviews with their human resource managers revealed a common focus. Hiring is not about finding people with the right experience; it is about finding people with the right mind-set. These four companies hire for attitude and train for skill.[1] This does *not* mean that technical skills are insignificant when someone is looking for a new job or career advancement. But is does tell us that when the playing field is equal (applicants have similar education and work experience), it is a person's attitude that gets him or her the job or promotion.

In an era of low unemployment, some workers "job hop" and play the game of interviewing the interviewers. Many present a what's-in-it-for-me? attitude. While this may work for some who have highly specialized skills, most of these self-centered individuals soon discover that because of their attitude, they are not called back for a final interview. Eric Lane, director of worldwide staffing at Silicon Graphics Inc., says: "Technical virtuosity seldom determines who makes the grade. It's all about mind-set. . . . In interviews, I give people an opportunity to have fun, to show their sense of humor. We look for people's passions, what they've done with their lives."[2]

## What Is an Attitude?

An **attitude** is a relatively strong belief about or feeling toward a person, object, idea, or event. It is an "emotional readiness" to behave in a particular manner.[3] Values serve as a foundation for attitudes, and attitudes serve as a foundation for behavior (see Figure 5.1). Throughout life we form attitudes toward political movements, religions, national leaders, various occupations, government programs, laws, and other aspects of our daily lives. They become deeply ingrained

**FIGURE 5.1**

The Relationship Between Values, Attitudes, and Behaviors

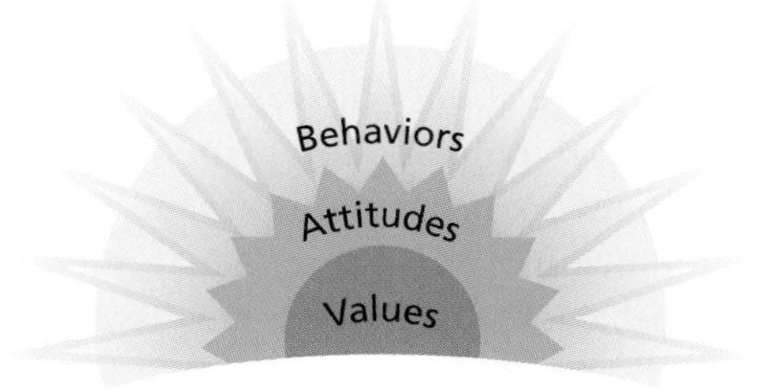

Behaviors
Attitudes
Values

At job fairs such as this one in Mission Viejo, California, employers can find prospective employees with the right skills and knowledge, but they often make hiring decisions based on the applicant's attitude.

in our personalities as we learn and grow. We tend to have a positive attitude toward things we like or enjoy—and a negative attitude toward things we are very much against. Some of our attitudes are so strong that we encourage others to adopt our views and copy our behaviors. When others hold strong contrasting attitudes, based on their values and past experiences, a potential human relations challenge exists.

Some attitudes, such as job satisfaction, are multidimensional. The feelings we have about our work, for example, are made up of attitudes toward the company's compensation plan, opportunities for promotion, coworkers, supervision, the work itself, and other factors. Job satisfaction is usually of major concern to an employer because management knows there is a link between attitudes and behavior. Persons who are dissatisfied with their jobs are more likely to be late or absent from work, become unproductive, or quit.

**TOTAL PERSON INSIGHT**

*PRICE PRITCHETT*

Chairman, EPS Solutions

*"The biggest career challenges these days are perceptual . . . psychological. Not technical. Not even skills-based. The major adjustments we need to make are mental. For example, how we frame things at work. The way we process events in our head. Our attitudes and outlook about how our jobs and organizations now have to operate."*

## ■ The Powerful Influence of Attitudes

Charles Swindoll is credited with saying, "The longer I live, the more I realize the impact of attitude on life." He is convinced that attitude is more important than appearance, giftedness, or skill.[4] For example, people who go through life with a positive mental attitude see daily obstacles as opportunities rather than road-blocks and are therefore more likely to achieve their personal and professional goals. People who filter their daily experiences through a negative attitude tend to focus on what is going wrong and find it difficult to achieve contentment or satisfaction in any aspect of their lives. It makes no difference how attractive, intelligent, or skilled they are; their attitude holds them back.

Attitudes represent a powerful force in any organization. An attitude of trust, for example, can pave the way for improved communication and greater cooperation between an employee and a supervisor. A sincere effort by management to improve working conditions, when filtered through attitudes of suspicion and cynicism, may have a negative impact on employee-management relations. These same actions by management, filtered through attitudes of trust and hope, may result in improved worker morale. As another example, a caring attitude displayed by an employee can increase customer loyalty and set the stage for repeat business.

## ■ The Age of Information Mandates Attitude Changes

The rapidly changing economic, social, and cultural environment in the age of information requires us to take a look at our attitudes toward traditional versus new practices and policies at work. Here are just a few examples of the workplace changes that are taking place.

**Teamwork**  A growing number of organizations are structured around teams rather than the traditional boss/subordinates hierarchy. As a team member, you can expect occasional conflict between your own self-interests and what is best for the team. The temptation to take credit for success and place the blame for mistakes on others will always be present. Perhaps you will have to make personal sacrifice part of the price you pay for winning your team's support.[5]

**Loyalty**   In the industrial economy, people tended to give their loyalty and commitment in exchange for a lifetime of job security. The shift from an economy based on production to an economy based on information has displaced millions of such workers. Workers today are likely to leave a company for better pay or a more flexible work schedule, or to acquire more skills. Employers today are less likely to view anyone who quits as a traitor. In fact, progressive organizations have found that hiring those who have quit stagnant jobs is an effective recruiting technique.[6]

**Privacy**   In Chapter 2, we noted that one hazard of using e-mail is the loss of privacy. With a small investment in software, your employer can monitor every stroke on your keyboard. Background checks are another threat to privacy. Many new employees are asked to sign a document that gives the company permission to conduct a detailed, ongoing investigative report on their character, general reputation, and personal characteristics.

What will be your attitude when you are faced with these situations? As change continues to accelerate, you may need to reinvent yourself and change some of your behavior. As the world evolves, so must you.

## How Attitudes Are Formed

Throughout life you are constantly making decisions and judgments that help formulate your attitudes. These attitude decisions are often based on behaviors your childhood authority figures told you were right or wrong, childhood and adult behaviors for which you were rewarded or punished, role models you selected, and the various environmental and corporate cultures you chose to embrace.

### ■ Socialization

The process through which people are integrated into a society by exposure to the actions and opinions of others is called **socialization.**[7] As a child, you interacted with your parents, family, teachers, and friends. Children often feel that statements made by these authority figures are the "proper" things to believe. For example, if a parent declares, "People who live in big, expensive houses either are born rich or are crooked," the child may hold this attitude for many years.

Children learn a great deal by watching and listening to family members, teachers, and other authority figures. In some cases, the influence is quite subtle. Children who observe their parents recycling, using public transportation instead of a car to get to work, and turning off the lights to save electricity may develop a strong concern for protection of the environment.

## ■ *Peer and Reference Groups*

As children reach adolescence and begin to break away psychologically from their parents, the **peer group** (people their own age) can have a powerful influence on attitude formation. In fact, peer-group influence can sometimes be stronger than the influence of parents, teachers, and other adult figures. With the passing of years, reference groups replace peer groups as sources of attitude formation in young adults. A **reference group** consists of several people who share a common interest and tend to influence one another's attitudes and behaviors. The reference group may act as a point of comparison and a source of information for the individual member. In the business community a chapter of the American Society for Training and Development or of Sales & Marketing Executives International may provide a reference group for its members.

## ■ *Rewards and Punishment*

Attitude formation is often related to rewards and punishment. People in authority generally encourage certain attitudes and discourage others. Naturally, individuals tend to develop attitudes that minimize punishments and maximize rewards. A child who is praised for sharing toys with playmates is likely to develop positive attitudes toward caring about other people's needs. Likewise, a child who receives a weekly allowance in exchange for performing basic housekeeping tasks learns an attitude of responsibility.

As an adult, you will discover that your employers will continue to attempt to shape your attitudes through rewards and punishment at work. Many organizations are rewarding employees who take steps to stay healthy, avoid accidents, increase sales, or reduce expenses.

 *HUMAN RELATIONS in ACTION*

### Attitude Is Everything

Keith Harrell was captain of the Seattle University basketball team for three years in a row. He fully expected to be drafted by the National Basketball Association after graduation, but the call never came. Harrell walked away from that dream and later spent fourteen years with IBM. When he made presentations as a trainer for IBM, audiences were always receptive to his comments because he had the ability to combine humor and wisdom. Soon he started dreaming of a new career as a professional speaker. He developed a presentation entitled "Attitude Is Everything" and started knocking on doors. Before long, he was presenting his thoughts on attitudes to audiences across the United States. He always tells his listeners that "the only difference between a bad day and a good day is attitude." Today he receives $10,000 each time he reminds an audience that "Attitude Is Everything."

## ■ *Role Model Identification*

Most young people would like to have more influence, status, and popularity. These goals are often achieved through identification with an authority figure or a role model. A **role model** is that person you most admire or are likely to emulate. Preschoolers are most likely to identify their parents as their role models. Later they search for other role models—perhaps a popular athlete, a rock star, or an actor. During later stages of development, new role models are adopted. As you might expect, role models can exert considerable influence—for better or for worse—on developing attitudes.

The media have a tremendous influence on people's selection of role models. Many of the television programs they watch are dominated by crime, violence, and stereotyped or deviant characters and life situations. At the other extreme, other programs present positive superheroes with superhuman abilities. With this constant reinforcement from fictional negative and positive role models, young people sometimes have difficulty sorting out which behaviors and attitudes are acceptable in the real world.

**Role models can exert considerable influence—for better or for worse—on developing attitudes.**

Role models at work can have a major influence on employee attitude development. The new salesperson in the menswear department naturally wants help in adjusting to the job. So does the new dental hygienist and the recently hired auto mechanic. These people will pay special attention to the behavior of coworkers and managers. If a senior employee is rude to customers and suffers no negative consequences, new employees may imitate this attitude and behavior.

## ■ *Cultural Influences*

Our attitudes are influenced by the culture that surrounds us. **Culture** is the sum total of knowledge, beliefs, values, objects, and customs that we use to adapt to our environment. It includes tangible items, such as foods, clothing, and furniture, as well as intangible concepts, such as education and laws.[8] Our personal identity may be influenced by our ethnic identity. This part of our identity reflects the religious, racial, or cultural group to which we belong.

Today's organizations are striving to create corporate cultures that attract and keep workers in these volatile times. When employees feel comfortable in their work environment, they do tend to stay.

ITEM: When it comes to providing a strong, "fun," corporate culture, Icarian Inc., a provider of online software that helps companies hire and manage their work forces, is a prime example of going the extra mile. Balloons and roller-hockey gear are everywhere, and pet dogs frolic in the hallways. Employees work hard, and at break time they play hard with chess, Ping-Pong, and other games in the lunchroom. If someone pops in a music CD, everyone gets up to dance. Employees are encouraged to work at home, and

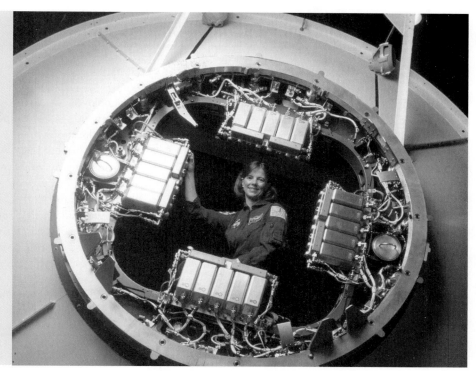

Role models such as astronaut Bonnie Dunbar can have a major influence on the attitudes of those who work with her and admire her tenacity.

community volunteerism is rewarded with time off to participate. After-hours events include wine tasting and barbecues. Happy workers, CEO Doug Merritt believes, are bound to be productive.[9]

ITEM: When Amy Miller started her first ice cream store, her market niche was safe from competition. However, it was not long before national companies such as Baskin-Robbins and Steve's were setting up shop nearby. Miller decided the best way to differentiate her store from the others was to provide some entertainment along with each purchase. When you visit an Amy's Ice Creams store, you may see an employee dance on the freezer top or juggle serving spades. Employees might be wearing pajamas (because it's Sleep-Over Night) or masks (because it's Star Wars Night). Employees are likely to do anything to create fun, including contests that involve the customers. Miller communicates her cultural message to prospective employees the day they show up looking for a job. Instead of a formal application form, they are given a white paper bag along with instructions to do anything they want with it and bring it back in a week. Applicants use the bag to create masks, cartoons, and works of art.[10]

ITEM: The U.S. Marines have developed an eleven-week basic training program that has a dramatic impact on those who complete it. Recruits emerge as self-disciplined Marines who are physically fit, courteous to their elders, and

## *HUMAN RELATIONS in ACTION*

### Avoiding the Things That Annoy

Harry Griendling, creator of the Staffing Solutions Group, called together his team of recruiting consultants, who work from their home offices helping corporate clients find employees, and asked them to create the kind of company benefits they'd always wanted but could not find in any other organization. They started by creating a list of all the practices that had irked them in previous jobs. Using the list as a "Don't go there" guideline, the team developed the following plan.

■ An open book policy allows all employees to access any financial information about the company they need in order to do their job.

■ All employees and spouses (not just the sales staff) attend yearly training seminars in exotic vacation locations.

■ Employees submit their own annual assessment of their strengths, weaknesses, and goals in place of the traditional performance review conducted by a supervisor.

■ Salary guidelines were created according to a mutually agreed-upon formula for assessing overhead and splitting profits.

In turn, the happy employees made the company number 251 on *Inc.* magazine's 500 list of top performers and increased annual sales from $255,000 to more than $3 million in five years.

drug-free. Many have had to overcome deep differences of class and race and have learned to live and work as a team. They live in an organizational culture where a hint of racism can end a career and the use of illegal drugs is minimized by a "zero tolerance" policy.[11]

### THINKING / LEARNING STARTERS

1. Identify at least one matter you feel strongly about. Do you know how you acquired this attitude? Is it shared by any particular group of people? Do you spend time with these people?

2. Think of an attitude that a friend or coworker holds but that you strongly disagree with. What factors do you believe contributed to the formation of this person's attitude?

## *Attitudes Valued by Employers*

As this chapter's opening vignette indicates, employers are looking for new employees with those unique characteristics that go beyond the basic job skills. At the same time, entire companies are being purchased so that the buyers can close

Hundreds of organizations each year hire motivational speaker Keith Harrell to present his "Attitude Is Everything" speech to their employees. Why is his topic so popular?

their competitors' doors, and giant corporations are merging with other giant corporations, resulting in massive duplication of human resources. Employees and managers alike who have had attitudinal problems during their job tenure find themselves on the outside looking in. Whether you are looking for your first career position, anticipating a career change, or in the process of being retrained for new opportunities, the following discussion may be helpful as you discover what attitudes employers want in their employees.

### ■ Be Self-Motivated

Dawn Overstreet, a lecturer associated with the Americana Leadership College, once said, "People need to be leaders of themselves." In her presentations she emphasizes the importance of self-sufficiency—the ability to handle life despite difficulties.[12] People who are self-motivated are inclined to set their own goals and monitor their own progress toward those goals. They do not need a supervisor hovering around them making sure they are on task and accomplishing what they are supposed to be doing. Many find ways to administer their own rewards after they achieve their goals. Employers often retain and promote those employees who are capable of making their own decisions and following through. They want their employees to feel driven to find better ways of doing old jobs and curious about

> **People who are self-motivated are inclined to set their own goals and monitor their own progress toward those goals. They do not need a supervisor hovering around them making sure they are on task. . . .**

learning new ones. Workers who read professional journals and monitor news media for research and technology advances will always get their employers' attention.

## ■ *Be Accepting of Change*

The new economy challenges us to accept and embrace change. The biggest challenge for many workers is adjusting to the rapidly accelerating rate of change itself. Some resistance to change is normal because change often poses a threat to our self-esteem.

When an organization is going through a period of intense change, three "bad" attitudes may surface:[13]

1. *Stubbornness* Some workers refuse to be influenced by someone else's point of view. When changes are announced, don't be too quick to criticize or find fault.

2. *Arrogance* Employees who reject advice, or who give the impression that they do not want retraining or other forms of assistance, send the wrong message to their employer.

3. *Inflexibility* Displaying a closed mind to new ideas and practices can only undermine your career advancement opportunities.

## ■ *Be a Team Player*

In sports, the person who is a "team player" receives a great deal of praise and recognition. A team player is someone who is willing to step out of the spotlight, give up a little personal glory, and help the team achieve a victory. Team players are no less important in organizations. Employers are increasingly organizing employees into teams (health teams, sales teams, product development teams) that build products, solve problems, and make decisions.

## ■ *Be Concerned About Your Health and Wellness*

The ever-growing cost of health care is one of the most serious problems facing companies today. Many organizations are promoting wellness programs for all employees as a way to keep costs in line. These programs include tips on healthy eating, physical-fitness exercises, stress management practices, and other forms of assistance that contribute to a healthy lifestyle. Employees who actively participate in these programs frequently take fewer sick days, file fewer medical claims, and bring a higher level of energy to work. Some companies even give cash awards to employees who lose weight, quit smoking, or lower their cholesterol levels. Employees who pay a great deal of attention to their health needs can be a real asset. In Chapter 9 we discuss health and wellness in greater detail.

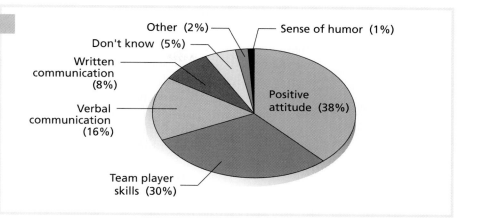

**FIGURE 5.2**

Interpersonal Skills
Necessary for Office
Personnel

*Source:* Press Release,
"Accentuate the Positive,"
*Accountemps,* January 4,
2000.

Other (2%) — Sense of humor (1%)
Don't know (5%)
Written
communication
(8%)
Verbal
communication
(16%)
Positive
attitude (38%)
Team player
skills (30%)

## ■ *Value Coworker Diversity*

To value diversity in the work setting means to make full use of the ideas, talents, experiences, and perspectives of all employees at all levels within the organization. People who differ from each other often add richness to the organization. An old adage states: If we both think alike, one of us is not necessary.

Development and utilization of a talented, diverse work force can be the key to success in a period of fierce global competition. Women and people of color make up a large majority of the new multicultural, global work force. Many people, however, carry prejudiced attitudes against those who differ from them. They tend to "prejudge" others' value based on the color of their skin, gender, age, religious preference, lifestyle, political affiliation, or economic status. Although deeply held prejudices that have developed over a long time are difficult to change, employers are demanding these changes. Wisconsin Power and Light Company is typical of many organizations that have made a strong commitment to valuing diversity. One of the company's expectations concerning diversity says, "Employees at all organizational levels must be intolerant of behaviors in the workplace that are inconsistent with the objectives of equal opportunity and the building of a diverse work force.[14] Chapter 7 contains specific guidance on how to develop positive attitudes toward joining a diverse work force.

 ## *How to Change Attitudes*

If you are having difficulty working with other team members, if you feel you were overlooked for a promotion you should have had, or if you go home from work depressed and a little angry at the world, you can almost always be sure you need an attitude adjustment. Unfortunately, people do not easily adopt new attitudes or discard old ones. It is difficult to break the attachment to emotionally laden beliefs. Yet attitudes *can* be changed. There may be times when you absolutely hate a job, but you can still develop a positive attitude toward it as a steppingstone to another job you actually do want. There will be times as well when you will need to help colleagues change their attitudes so that you can work with them more effectively. And, of course, when events, such as a layoff, are beyond your control, you must strive to maintain a positive attitude. It is often said that life is 10 percent what happens to you and 90 percent how you react to it. Knowing how to change attitudes in yourself and others can be essential to effective human relations—and your success—in life.

### ■ *Changing Your Own Attitude*

You are constantly placed in new situations with people from different backgrounds and cultures. Each time you go to a new school, take a new job, get a promotion, or move to a different neighborhood, you may need to alter your attitudes to cope effectively with the change. In all these situations, the events are out of your control. But you can control your attitude toward these events. If you allow yourself to dwell on the negative aspects of change, you can expect to exhibit negative, self-destructive behaviors. When you make an effort to focus on the positive, you will find your world a much pleasanter place in which to live.

Being able to control your attitudes is a powerful human relations skill that usually involves certain basic changes:

1. *Choose happiness.* In his best-selling book *The Art of Happiness,* the Dalai Lama presents happiness as the foundation of all other attitudes. He suggests that the pursuit of happiness is the purpose of our existence. Although many

 **HUMAN RELATIONS *in* ACTION**

### Look at the Bright Side

Researchers at Washington University in St. Louis, Missouri, discovered that those individuals who are able to look at the bright side following a traumatic event recover the best and grow the most as a result of the tragedy. The study involved interviews with the survivors of a tornado, a plane crash, and a mass shooting a few weeks after their respective traumatic event and then three years later. Some survivors were able to look at the "positives" that resulted from their tragedy, making statements such as "I realized how much I loved my family" or "I decided that life was too short not to follow my dreams." These optimistic survivors had made a better recovery at the time of the follow-up interviews than those who were unable to control their negative attitudes about the event. The lead author of the study, J. Curtis McMillen, Ph.D., suggests that even those whose lives are in the worst shape at the time of a tragedy may have the most to gain from adverse experiences. They can use the traumatic event as the motivation to reorganize their lives.

**"Where am I going? Straight to the top, Sir, and nothing's going to stop me!"**

Western thinkers from Aristotle to William James agree with this idea, it raises a question in the minds of many other people: After all, wouldn't a life based on seeking personal happiness be of its very nature self-centered, even self-indulgent? The Dalai Lama reminds us that survey after survey has shown it is unhappy people who tend to be most self-focused, socially withdrawn, and even antagonistic. He notes that "happy people, in contrast, are generally found to be more sociable, flexible, and creative and are able to tolerate life's daily frustrations more easily than unhappy people."[15]

Michael Crom, executive vice president of Dale Carnegie Training, believes that happiness is the state of mind that permits us to live life enthusiastically. He views enthusiasm as an energy builder and as the key to overcoming adversity and achieving goals.[16] But how can you become happy and enthusiastic when the world around you is filled with family, career, and financial crises on a daily basis? Most psychologists, in general, agree that happiness or unhappiness at any given moment has very little to do with the conditions around us, but rather with how we perceive our situation, how satisfied we are with what we have.[17] For example, if you are constantly comparing yourself to people who seem smarter, more attractive, or wealthier, you are likely to develop feelings of envy and frustration. By the same token, you can achieve a higher level of happiness by comparing yourself to those who are less fortunate and by reflecting on the good things you have received in life.[18]

2. *Become an optimist.* Optimistic thoughts give rise to positive attitudes and effective human relationships. When you are an optimist, your coworkers, managers, and—perhaps most important—your customers feel your energy and vitality and tend to mirror your behavior.

> **It is often said that life is 10 percent what happens to you and 90 percent how you react to it.**

It does not take long to identify people with an optimistic outlook. Optimists are more likely to bounce back after a demotion, layoff, or some other disappointment. According to Martin Seligman, author of *Learned Optimism,* optimists are more likely to view problems as merely temporary setbacks on their road to achieving their goals. They focus on their potential success rather than on their failures.[19]

Pessimists, in contrast, tend to believe bad events will last a long time, will undermine everything they do, and are their own fault. A pessimistic pattern of thinking can have unfortunate consequences. Pessimists give up more easily when faced with a challenge, are less likely to take personal control of their life, and are more likely to take personal blame for their misfortune.[20] Often pessimism leads to **cynicism,** which is a mistrusting attitude regarding the motives of people. When you are cynical, you are constantly on guard against the "misbehavior" of others.[21] If you begin to think that everyone is screwing up, acting inconsiderately, or otherwise behaving inappropriately, cynicism has taken control of your thought process, and it is time to change.

Fortunately, pessimism and optimism are both learned attitudes, so they can be changed. If you feel the need to become a more optimistic person, you can spend more time visualizing yourself succeeding, a process that is discussed in Chapter 3.

3. *Think for yourself.* One of the major deterrents to controlling your own attitude is the power of "group think," which surfaces when everyone shares the same opinion about what is going on in the organization. Individuals can lose their desire and ability to think for themselves as they strive to be accepted by the group. You are less likely to be drawn into group think if you understand that there are two overlapping relationships among coworkers. *Personal relationships* develop as you bond with your coworkers. When you share common interests and feel comfortable talking with someone, the bonds of friendship may grow very strong. *Professional relationships* exist for just one purpose: to get the job done.[22] Having two kinds of relationships with the same people can be confusing.

Let's assume you are a member of a project team working on a software application. The deadline for completion is rapidly approaching, yet the team

---

**TOTAL PERSON INSIGHT**

HIS HOLINESS THE DALAI LAMA
AND HOWARD C. CUTLER

Co-authors, *The Art of Happiness*

*"We don't need more money, we don't need greater success or fame, we don't need the perfect body or even the perfect mate—right now, at this very moment, we have a mind, which is all the basic equipment we need to achieve complete happiness."*

still needs to conduct one more reliability test. At a team meeting, one person suggests that the final test is not needed because the new product has passed all previous tests, and it's time to turn the product over to marketing. Another member of the team, a close friend of yours, enthusiastically supports this recommendation. You have serious concerns about taking this shortcut but hesitate to take a position that conflicts with that of your friend. What should you do? In a professional relationship, your personal feelings are not relevant.[23] You are obliged to do what is right for the organization.

4. ***Keep an open mind.*** We often make decisions and then refuse to consider any other point of view that might lead us to question our beliefs. Many times our attitudes persist even in the presence of overwhelming evidence to the contrary. If you have been raised in a family or community that supports racist views, it may seem foreign to you when your colleagues at work openly accept and enjoy healthy relationships with people whose skin color is different from your own. Pay attention. Expose yourself to new information and experiences beyond what you have been socialized to believe.

   We live in a world where generalizations are commonplace: Men are too competitive. Women are too emotional. People on welfare are lazy. These generalizations need to be assessed with an open mind if you want to advance in your chosen career. James Allen, the famous Harvard psychologist, discovered that you can change many of the outer aspects of your life by changing the inner attitudes of your mind. When you face things you cannot change, take a few moments to reflect on the Serenity Prayer.

## ■ *Helping Others Change Their Attitudes*

It is true that you are really in control of only your own attitudes. Although you can bend and flex and alter these as often as you find it beneficial, sometimes you need to stand firm and maintain your position. At that point, you may want to help other people change their attitudes. Unfortunately, you cannot hand your

**FIGURE 5.3**

Serenity Prayer

*Source:* "Serenity Prayer" by Dr. Reinhold Niebuhr.

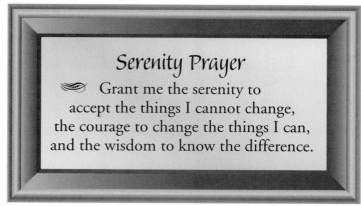

Serenity Prayer
≥ Grant me the serenity to
accept the things I cannot change,
the courage to change the things I can,
and the wisdom to know the difference.

colleagues "a ready-made box of attitudes." But often you can help produce an atmosphere in which they will want to change their thinking.

Some people attempt to beg, plead, intimidate, or even threaten others into adopting new attitudes. This process is similar to attempting to push a piece of yarn across the top of a table. When you *push* the yarn in the direction you want it to go, it gets all bent out of shape. When you gently *pull* the yarn with your fingertips, it follows you wherever you want it to go. Two powerful techniques can help you pull people in the direction you want them to go, often without their even realizing that you are attempting to change their attitudes:

1. Change the *conditions* that precede the behavior.

2. Change the *consequences* that follow the behavior.

**Change the Conditions**   If you want people to change their attitudes, identify the behaviors that represent the poor attitudes and alter the conditions that precede the behavior. Consider the following situation.

A new employee in a retail store is having a problem adjusting to her job. The manager needed her on the sales floor as soon as possible, so he rushed through her job training procedures without taking time to answer her questions. Now she finds there are many customers' questions she cannot answer, and she has trouble operating the computerized cash register. She wants to quit, and her negative attitudes are affecting her job performance and the way she handles her customers.

The manager could easily have prevented this employee's negative attitudes by answering all her questions *before* she was placed on the sales floor. Perhaps he could have asked an experienced salesperson to stay with her as she helped her first few customers. Above all, he could have displayed a caring attitude toward her and her success.

**Change the Consequences**   Another way to help other people change their attitudes is to alter what happens *after* they exhibit the behavior (attitudes in action) you are attempting to change. A simple rule applies: When an experience is followed by positive consequences, the person is likely to repeat the behavior. When an experience is followed by negative consequences, the person will soon learn to stop the behavior. For example, if you are a supervisor, and several of your employees are consistently late for work, you might provide some form of negative consequence each time they are tardy, such as a verbal reprimand. Keep in mind, however, that we tend to focus attention on the people who exhibit disruptive attitudes and to ignore the employees exhibiting the attitudes we want to encourage. Saying: "Thank you for being here on time. I really appreciate your commitment" can be an extremely effective reward for those who arrive at work on time. Behaviors rewarded will be repeated.

An attitude is nothing more than a personal thought process. We cannot control the thinking that takes place in someone else's mind, but we can mandate behavior. Some organizations have come to the conclusion that behavior that offends or threatens others must stop. It may be impossible to stop someone from thinking prejudicial thoughts, but you can establish a zero tolerance policy regarding acts that demean or threaten others.[25]

## Organizations' Efforts Toward Improving Employees' Attitudes

Most companies realize that an employee's attitude and performance cannot be separated. When employees have negative attitudes about their work, their job performance and productivity suffer. When they have positive attitudes, job performance and productivity are likely to improve. One CEO of a software company has stated, "The way you get superior performance is to get people's passionate loyalty and belief. That means being flexible and giving your people what they need to do a great job."[26] For generations, employers and labor unions focused on salaries and fringe benefits as the rewards that would keep workers producing at top efficiency. But gradually, both labor and management discovered that money was not always the primary ingredient of a satisfying job.

People who are asked what they most want from their job typically cite mutual respect among coworkers, interesting work, recognition for work well done, the chance to develop skills, and so forth. If employers want to maintain or improve the positive attitudes of their workers, and thereby maintain or improve productivity, they need to provide the benefits workers consider important. Of course, workers expect the pay to be competitive, but they want so much more. As author and management consultant Peter Drucker says, "To make a living is not enough. Work also has to make a life."[27] Organizations are finding creative

Southwest Airlines takes the position that happy employees are more likely to make the customer happy. These employees, assigned to the Communication Department, are participating in a company-sponsored Halloween party.

ways to influence worker attitudes. All these companies made *Fortune* magazine's list of the 100 best companies to work for.

ITEM: J. M. Smucker Company does not offer an outstanding benefits package, but it does offer a very positive work environment. The 103-year-old company has a history of treating each employee with respect.[28]

ITEM: W. L. Gore & Associates, maker of Gore-Tex fabrics and other high-tech products, offers employees a "bossless" style of management. They select their own projects to work on.[29]

ITEM: SAS Institute offers a 35-hour workweek, free on-site medical services, 12 holidays, and a paid one-week vacation between Christmas and New Year's Day. James Goodnight, who founded SAS in 1976, says, "If you do right by people, they'll do right by you."[30]

What do these organizations have in common? Each has given thought to the attitudes that are important for a healthy work environment and has taken steps to shape these attitudes. Many organizations are attempting to improve employee attitudes and productivity by enhancing the quality of their employees' work life.

## A Final Word

Viktor Frankl, a survivor of the Auschwitz concentration camp and author of *Man's Search for Meaning*, said, "The last of the human freedoms is to choose one's attitude in any given set of circumstances." We have noted throughout this chapter that attitudes have a major impact on our day-to-day lives. Given the importance of attitudes, you should regularly re-examine yours and choose the ones that will take you where you want to go in life. Changing an attitude that is detrimental to your personal or professional life can be a challenge, but the process can also be a critical step toward your continued growth and success. The happiest people don't necessarily *have* the best of everything; they just *make* the best of everything. It's all in their attitude.

## Summary

An attitude is any strong belief toward people and situations. It is a state of mind supported by feelings. People possess hundreds of attitudes about work, family life, friends, coworkers, and the like.

Attitudes represent a powerful force in every organization. If the persons employed by a service firm display a caring attitude toward customers, the business is likely to enjoy a high degree of customer loyalty and repeat business. If the employees of a manufacturing firm display a serious attitude toward safety rules and regulations, fewer accidents are likely to occur.

People acquire attitudes through early childhood socialization, peer and reference groups, rewards and punishment, role model identification, and cultural influences.

Employers hire and attempt to retain employees who are self-motivated, flexible, willing to be team players, concerned about health and wellness, and who value coworker diversity.

You can decide to change your attitude by choosing to be happy; becoming an optimist; thinking for yourself without undue pressure from others; and keeping an open mind. You can help others change their attitudes by altering the consequences and conditions that surround the situation. Positive consequences and conditions produce positive attitudes. Organizations are taking steps to improve employee attitudes by enhancing the quality of their work life.

## Career Corner

Q: I am a 24-year-old recent college graduate. Six months ago I accepted a job as assistant to the office manager of a small manufacturing plant. She is in her late 50s and has been with the company since she graduated from high school. She has made it perfectly clear that she never had the opportunity to go to college. Her attitudes about how work is to be done in our office seem so old-fashioned. I have so many creative ideas to improve our efficiency, but she seems to believe I am too young to know anything. Every time she says, "That's the way it has always been done; don't change it," my skin crawls and I feel very bitter for the rest of the day. What can I do to change her attitude toward my potential?

A: Begin by changing your attitude toward her traditional way of performing routine tasks in the office. Remember, she has had to adjust to many changes over the years to keep her organization running smoothly. Respect her past successes, and assure her that you are there to help with the changing demands of the future.

Second, begin to alter the conditions in the office so that they are conducive to your creative ideas. Bring your professional journals to work, and invite her to read various articles discussing innovative ideas that have been successfully implemented in other offices. Invite her to attend a seminar with you or to enroll in a class on some new software package that makes tedious office tasks easier. If she accepts a new idea, praise her intelligence and openness. When she receives positive feedback from you and others in the organization, she is likely to repeat the behavior and seek out additional ways to improve the efficiency of the office. Changing attitudes is not easy, so be patient.

## Key Terms

| | |
|---|---|
| attitude | role model |
| socialization | culture |
| peer group | cynicism |
| reference group | |

## Review Questions

1. It has been said that "attitudes represent a powerful force in any organization." What examples can you give to support this statement?
2. List five ways in which we form our attitudes.
3. Describe how rewards and punishment can shape the attitudes of employees in an organization. Give at least one example of each.
4. Why is happiness considered the foundation of all attitudes?
5. Describe the attitudes employers are looking for in their employees.
6. Explain how consequences can influence the shaping of attitudes in an organization.
7. Robert Mager says that the conditions that surround a subject can play an important role in shaping attitudes. Provide at least one example to support Mager's statement.
8. Identify the difference between a person with an optimistic attitude and one with a pessimistic viewpoint.
9. What are organizations doing to help improve the attitudes of their workers? Why do they bother to keep their workers happy?
10. Describe the impact your attitude has on your professional and personal relationships. Give an example.

## Application Exercises

1. Describe your attitudes concerning
   a. a teamwork environment
   b. health and wellness
   c. life and work
   d. learning new skills
   How do these attitudes affect you on a daily basis? Do you feel you have a positive attitude in most situations? Can you think of someone you have frequent contact with who displays negative attitudes toward these items? Do you find ways to avoid spending time with this person?

2. Identify an attitude held by a friend, coworker, or spouse that you would like to see changed. Do any conditions that precede this person's behavior fall under your control? If so, how could you change those conditions so the person might change his or her attitude? What positive consequences might you offer when the person behaves the way you want? What negative consequences might you impose when the person participates in the behavior you are attempting to stop?

3. For a period of one week, keep a diary or log of positive and negative events. Positive events might include the successful completion of a project, a compliment from a coworker, or just finding time for some leisure activities. Negative events might include forgetting an appointment, criticism from your boss, or simply looking in the mirror and seeing something you don't like. An unpleasant news story might also qualify as a negative event. At the end of one week, review your entries and determine what type of pattern exists. Also, reflect on the impact of these events. Did you quickly bounce back from the negative events, or did you dwell on them all week? Did the positive events enhance your optimism? Consider each negative event in relation to the Serenity Prayer (Figure 5.3). What did you discover?

## Internet Exercise

Every Friday, ABC News posts a new article called "Working Wounded," by Bob Rosner, author of the book with the same title. Each article discusses some aspect of the challenges people face in their life at work. Visit the Web site at www.go.com and scroll down until you find the Regular Features icon; click on Working Wounded to access this week's article. Write a brief paper explaining your reaction to the comments. If time allows, click on Working Wounded Archives and read earlier articles with titles that pique your interest. Report your findings to your classmates.

*Self-Assessment Exercise*

For each of the following statements, circle the number from 1 to 5 that best represents your response: (1) strongly disagree (never do this); (2) disagree (rarely do this); (3) moderately agree (sometimes do this); (4) agree (frequently do this); (5) strongly agree (almost always do this).

A. When forming attitudes about important matters, I maintain an open mind, listen to the views of others, but think for myself.　　1　2　3　4　5

B. I make every effort to maintain a positive mental attitude toward other people and the events in my life.　　1　2　3　4　5

C. I seek feedback and clarification on the influence of my attitudes and behaviors on others.　　1　2　3　4　5

D. I am willing to change my attitudes and behaviors in response to constructive feedback from others.　　1　2　3　4　5

E. I consistently monitor the way I shape the attitudes of others through my system of rewards and punishments.　　1　2　3　4　5

Select an appropriate attitude or skill you would like to improve. Write your goal in the space provided, and describe the steps you will take to achieve this goal.

GOAL: _____
_____
_____
_____

## Case Problem   *Where Is My Stability?*

Lewis Jenkle has worked for the past fourteen years as an accountant for Quest Electronics. He has always been happy and satisfied with his work environment, knowing exactly what was expected of him. During the past year, however, his entire department has been dismantled and all his accounting buddies are now assigned to various project teams. When a team's work is completed, the team members are assigned to another project. Sometimes Lewis is asked to participate in several team assignments at one time. He feels he is in constant chaos, with no one telling him what to do next because teams rarely have a designated boss; everyone just digs in and gets the job done. This autonomy and sense of responsibility make him nervous. His coworkers seem to enjoy the challenge and excitement of starting new projects and seeing their completion. However, Lewis misses the former stability of his once-traditional workplace. He has thought about changing jobs but has discovered that this project management approach is being used everywhere. Each day at work, his frustration and anger build. He is not a happy camper!

Many workers are experiencing this kind of trauma, and it is affecting their attitudes and productivity as well as their personal and professional relationships. It appears that the concept of project management is here to stay, but not everyone wants this kind of accountability. It seems obvious that if the unhappy workers want to have a satisfying life in this new atmosphere, they are going to have to change their attitudes.

In her book *Career Intelligence,* Dr. Barbara Moses offers support to those individuals who want or need to find satisfaction in their short-term work assignments and relationships. She suggests that they learn to connect with coworkers quickly through creative use of e-mails, faxes, videoconferences, phone calls, and one-to-one meetings. When handling more than one project at a time, developing a stable system that helps track various deadlines and individual team members' strengths and weaknesses may help prevent the feeling of chaos. She recommends that individuals conduct a personal strengths assessment by asking friends and colleagues to appraise specific talents the individual brings to specific projects. After receiving these appraisals, these individuals can try to position themselves to be assigned the projects of their choice. This will help strengthen their attitude that they *are* in control of *something.*[31]

## Questions

1. Dr. Jean Claude Kaufmann, a French sociologist, studied homemakers and their attitudes toward housework. While half of his subjects found the repetitive work drudgery, the other half described their tasks as pleasurable—even erotic! If the tasks were the same, what made the difference between drudgery and pleasure? What could Lewis Jenkle learn from this study?

2. What changes do you anticipate will happen in your career field over the next five to ten years? Will you have to adjust your attitude as time progresses? If so, why?

3. What steps identified in this chapter will you take to keep your personal and professional relationships productive as inevitable changes occur in your life?

# 6

# Developing a Professional Presence

## CHAPTER PREVIEW

After studying this chapter, you will be able to

- Explain the importance of professional presence.

- Discuss the factors that contribute to a favorable first impression.

- Distinguish between assumptions and facts.

- Define *image* and describe the factors that form the image you project to others.

- List and discuss factors that influence your choice of clothing for work.

- Understand how manners contribute to improved interpersonal relations in the workplace.

Kevin Wilkins, a sales executive with State Street Research & Management Company in Boston, believes that the clothing he wears on the job should help him make a good first impression. He recently started the day in khakis, a casual shirt, and boat shoes so as not to seem stuffy at an early morning meeting with rank-and-file employees. Later in the morning he had a meeting with a prospective client from a foundation, so he returned to his office and changed into a gray Hickey-Freeman suit, a white shirt, a tie, and black shoes. In the afternoon he met with a group of officers at a firm that had adopted semicasual dress. This time he changed into a blazer and loafers.[1]

Charles Goode, an environmental lobbyist who lives in Boise, Idaho, rides to work on his bike and usually wears cargo pants and sneakers. However, when the legislature is in session, he puts on a dark suit, white shirt, and tasseled loafers in a locker room near the capitol. Goode says, "You have to look like them and act like them. You have to blend in."[2]

Sometimes a quick change is difficult because many offices are not designed to serve as dressing rooms. Carreen Winters, a senior vice president at MWW Group, a New Jersey public relations firm, recalls an embarrassing moment. She was sitting at her desk, taking off her socks and sneakers and pulling on pantyhose. Suddenly she realized that a window washer with a big grin on his face was staring in at her.[3]

The clothing we wear, combined with a host of other things, helps us cultivate a professional presence. This "presence" helps us establish, build, and maintain relationships at work and in our personal life.

## Professional Presence—An Introduction

There are many personal and professional benefits to be gained from a study of the concepts in this chapter. You will acquire new insights regarding ways to communicate positive impressions during job interviews, business contacts, and social contacts made away from work. You will also learn how to shape an image that will help you achieve your fullest potential in the career of your choice.

This is not a chapter about ways to make positive impressions with superficial behavior and quick-fix techniques. We do not discuss the "power look" or the "power lunch." The material in this chapter will not help you become a more entertaining conversationalist or win new customers by pretending to be interested in their hobbies or families. Stephen Covey, author of *The 7 Habits of Highly Effective People,* says that the ability to build effective, long-term relationships is based on character strength, not quick-fix techniques. He notes that outward attitude and behavior changes do very little good in the long run *unless* they are based on solid principles governing human effectiveness. These principles include service (making a contribution), integrity and honesty (which serve as a foundation of trust), human dignity (every person has worth), and fairness.[4]

Few people can fake a sincere greeting or a caring attitude. If you really do not care about the other person's problem, that individual will probably sense your indifference. Your true feelings will be difficult to hide. Ralph Waldo Emerson was right on target when he said, "What you are shouts so loudly in my ears I cannot hear what you say."

## Professional Presence—A Definition

We are indebted to Susan Bixler, president of Professional Image, Inc., and author of *Professional Presence,* for giving us a better understanding of what it means to possess professional presence. **Professional presence** is a dynamic blend of poise, self-confidence, control, and style that empowers us to be able to command respect in any situation.[5] Once acquired, it permits us to be perceived as self-assured and thoroughly competent. We project a confidence that others can quickly perceive the first time they meet us.

Bixler points out that in most cases, the credentials we present during a job interview or when we are being considered for a promotion are not very different from those of other persons being considered. It is our professional presence that permits us to rise above the crowd. Debra Benton, a career consultant, says, "Any boss with a choice of two people with equal qualifications will choose the one with style as well as substance."[6] Learning to create a professional presence is one of the most valuable skills we can acquire.

## The Importance of Making a Good First Impression

As organizations experience increased competition for clients, patients, or customers, they are giving new attention to the old adage "First impressions are lasting ones." Research indicates that initial impressions do indeed tend to linger. Therefore, a positive first impression can be thought of as the first step in building a long-term relationship.

Of course, it is not just first contacts with clients, patients, customers, and others that are important. Positive impressions should be the objective of every contact. Many organizations have learned that in the age of information, high-tech without high-touch is not a winning formula.

## The Primacy Effect

The development of professional presence begins with a full appreciation of the power of first impressions. The tendency to form impressions quickly at the time of an initial meeting illustrates what social psychologists call a **primacy effect** in the way people perceive one another. The general principle is that first impressions establish the mental framework within which a person is viewed, and information acquired later is often ignored or reinterpreted to coincide with this framework.[7]

During his first term as president, Bill Clinton often appeared in brief jogging shorts and garish print shirts; his suits were loose fitting and in need of tailoring; and his military salute was viewed as half-hearted by many observers. Toby Fischer-Mirkin, fashion consultant

**The development of professional presence begins with a full appreciation of the power of first impressions.**

and author of *Dress Code,* said the president did not communicate a very commanding image.[8] Early in his first term, Clinton appeared vulnerable to many people, and this image had a negative influence on his popularity. Later in his first term, he communicated a more "presidential" image and went on to be re-elected to a second term. He discovered, or perhaps rediscovered, the power of the primacy effect.

## HUMAN RELATIONS *in* ACTION

### Director of First Impressions

Cathleen Jivoin is director of first impressions at Teltronics, a company based in Sarasota, Florida. She has held this title for six years and loves her work. Her primary responsibility is to establish the right mood for everyone who visits the company. Jivoin says, "I see as many as thirty-five to forty people a day, and no one leaves unhappy." Customers and vendors tell her that they enjoy doing business with people who care about them and their lives. Jivoin says the best way to make a good first impression is "Smile! Then smile again."

Lolenzo Poe, Multacah County (Oregon) Social Services Administrator, recognizes that the clothing we wear, combined with a host of other things, helps us cultivate a professional presence. People who work in administrative positions are more likely to wear clothing that is conservative, modest, and in good taste.

## ■ *The First Few Seconds*

When two people meet, their potential for building a relationship can be affected by many factors. Within a few moments, one person or the other may feel threatened, offended, or bored. Roger Ailes, communication adviser to three presidents and consultant to numerous Fortune 500 executives, says people begin forming an opinion of us in a matter of seconds. He believes that most people assess the other person very quickly and then settle on a general perception of that individual. Ailes says it is very difficult for us to reverse that first impression.[9] The following examples support his view of first impressions.

---

### THINKING / LEARNING STARTERS

To test the practical application of Roger Ailes's guideline in a real-life setting, examine it in the context of your past experiences. Review the following questions; then answer each with yes or no.

1. Have you ever entered a restaurant, hotel, or office and experienced an immediate feeling of being welcome after your first contact with an employee?

2. Have you ever met someone who immediately communicated to you the impression that he or she could be trusted and was interested in your welfare?

3. Have you ever placed a telephone call and known instinctively within seconds that the person did not welcome your call?

---

ITEM: Paula rushed into a restaurant for a quick lunch—she had to get back to her office for a 1:30 P.M. appointment. At the entrance of the main dining area was a sign reading "Please Wait to Be Seated." A few feet away, the hostess was discussing a popular movie with one of the waitresses. The hostess made eye contact with Paula but continued to visit with the waitress.

ITEM: When Sandy and Mike entered the showroom of a Mercedes-Benz dealer, they were approached by a salesperson wearing sport slacks (khaki color), a blue knit pullover shirt (short sleeve), and casual gum-soled shoes. The salesperson smiled and said, "Are you looking or buying?"

In each of these examples, a negative first impression was created in a matter of seconds. The anxiety level of the restaurant customer increased because she was forced to wait while two employees talked about a personal matter. And the potential customers made judgments about the automobile salesperson based solely on his appearance and casual greeting. Unfortunately, these employees were probably not fully aware of the impression they communicated to customers.

**TOTAL PERSON INSIGHT**

*SUSAN BIXLER AND NANCY NIX-RICE*

Authors, *The New Professional Image*

*"Books are judged by their covers, houses are appraised by their curb appeal, and people are initially evaluated on how they choose to dress and behave. In a perfect world this is not fair, moral, or just. What's inside should count a great deal more. And eventually it usually does, but not right away. In the meantime, a lot of opportunities can be lost."*

**Assumptions Versus Facts**    The impression you form of another person during the initial contact is made up of both assumptions and facts. Most people tend to rely more heavily on **assumptions** during the initial meeting. If a job applicant sits slumped in the chair, head bowed and shoulders slack, you might assume the person is not very interested in the position. If the postal clerk fails to make eye contact during the transaction and does not express appreciation for your purchase, you may assume this person treats everyone with indifference. Needless to say, the impression you form of another person during the initial contact can be misleading. The briefer the encounter with a new acquaintance, the greater the chance that misinformation will enter into your perception of the other person. The authors of a popular book on first impressions state that "Depending on assumptions is a one-way ticket to big surprises and perhaps disappointments."[10]

## ■ *Cultural Influence*

**Cultural influences,** often formed during the early years of our life, lead us to have impressions of some people even before we meet them. People often develop stereotypes of entire groups. Although differences between cultures are often subtle, they can lead to uncomfortable situations. We need to realize that the Korean shopkeeper is being polite, not hostile, when he puts change on the counter and not in your hand. Some Asian students do not speak up in class out of respect for the teacher, not boredom.[11]

Many American companies are attempting to create a new kind of workplace where cultural and ethnic differences are treated as assets, not annoyances. Yet some employees feel pressure to conform to dress and grooming standards that their employer considers "mainstream." When LaToya Rivers, a black college student, applied for a position at the Boston Harbor Hotel, she asked whether braids were allowed. She was told, "Yes, as long as they are neat and professional in appearance." Once hired, the policy seemed to change. A manager told her to restyle her braided hair or leave.[12]

Norine Dresser, author of *Multiculture Manners—New Rules of Etiquette for a Changing Society*, notes that it is becoming more difficult for organizations to develop policies that do not offend one ethnic group or another. She argues that it is the collective duty of the mainstream to learn the customs and practices of established minority groups as well as the ways of the latest arrivals from other countries.[13]

## The Image You Project

**Image** is a term used to describe how other people feel about you. In every business or social setting, your behaviors and appearance communicate a mental picture that others observe and remember. This picture determines how they react to you.

Think of image as a tool that can reveal your inherent qualities, your competence, your attitude, and your leadership potential. If you wish to communicate your professional capabilities, invest the time and energy needed to refine and enhance your personal image.

In many respects, the image you project is very much like a picture puzzle, as illustrated in Figure 6.1. It is formed by a variety of factors, including manners, self-confidence, voice quality, versatility, integrity (see Chapter 4), entrance and carriage, facial expression, surface language, competence, positive attitude, and handshake. Each of these image-shaping components is under your control.

### Surface Language

As noted earlier, we base opinions about other people on both facts and assumptions. Unfortunately, assumptions often carry a great deal of weight. Many of the assumptions you develop regarding other people are based on **surface language,**

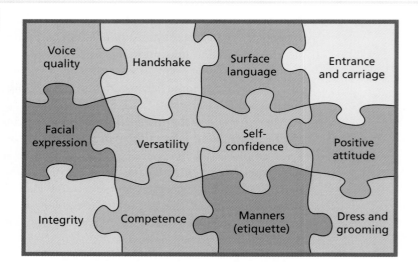

**FIGURE 6.1**

Major Factors That Form Your Image

a pattern of immediate impressions conveyed by appearance. The clothing you wear, your hairstyle, the fragrances you use, and the jewelry you display all combine to make a statement about you to others.

According to many writers familiar with image formation, clothing is particularly important. Although a more relaxed dress code has evolved in recent years, people judge your appearance long before they judge your talents. It would be a mistake not to take your career wardrobe seriously. Bixler suggests that those making career wardrobe decisions should keep in mind that three things haven't changed:[14]

> **A good rule to follow is to dress for the job you want, not the job you have.**

1. *If you want the job, you have to look the part.* Establish personal dress and grooming standards appropriate for the organization where you wish to work. Before you apply for a job, try to find out what the workers there are wearing. If in doubt, dress conservatively.

2. *If you want the promotion, you have to look promotable.* A good rule to follow is to dress for the job you want, not the job you have. If you are currently an office worker and want to become an office manager, identify the successful office managers and emulate their manner of dress.

3. *If you want respect, you have to dress as well as or better than your industry standards.* One would expect to find conservative dress standards in banking, insurance, accounting, and law, and more casual dress standards in advertising, sports entertainment, and agriculture. Spend time researching the dress and grooming standards in the industry in which you hope to find a job.

---

## THINKING / LEARNING STARTER

Do you recall a teacher, coworker, or supervisor whose surface language impressed you—either positively or negatively? What specific elements (such as dress or hairstyle) were evident in this person's surface language? What type of image do you think he or she was trying to project?

---

### ■ Selecting Your Career Apparel

Over 23 million American workers wear a uniform especially designed for a particular job. The judges on the U.S. Supreme Court and the technicians at the local Midas Muffler and Brake shop have one thing in common—both groups wear a special uniform to work. Today more and more people are donning uniforms to go to work. Companies that have initiated extensive career apparel programs rely on uniforms to project an image of consistent quality, good service, and uniqueness.

People who work in the service industry often wear a uniform at work. Many companies rely on uniforms to project an image of consistent quality, good service, and uniqueness.

Wells Fargo Bank adopted a custom line of clothing for employees working at banking centers located in Safeway and other supermarkets. The goal was to create a professional look that would define the bank's identity and build customers' confidence in the financial services that Wells Fargo offered. The bank also wanted to make sure that people distinguished its employees from supermarket workers.[15]

The uniforms worn by United Parcel Service employees, United Airlines reservation clerks, and the employees at your local restaurant might be classified as special-design **career apparel.** In addition to special-design uniforms, there is another type of career apparel, somewhat less predictable, worn by large numbers of people in the labor force. Here are some examples:

- A female lawyer representing a prestigious firm would be appropriately dressed in a gray or blue skirted suit. A dress with a suit jacket would also be acceptable. She should avoid clothing in brash colors or casual styles that might reduce her credibility.

- A male bank loan officer would be appropriately dressed in a tailored gray or blue suit, white shirt, and tie. This same person dressed in a colorful blazer, sport shirt, and plaid slacks would be seen as too casual in most bank settings.

- A technician employed by an auto dealership that sells new cars would be appropriately dressed in matching gray, tan, or blue shirt and pants. The technician would be inappropriately dressed in jeans and a T-shirt.

Many organizations seek advice about career apparel from image consultants. One source of image consultants is the Association of Image Consultants International.

## ■ *Wardrobe Engineering*

The term **wardrobe engineering** was first used by John Molloy, author of *Dress for Success*, to describe how clothing and accessories can be used to create a certain image. This concept was later refined by several other noted image consultants in hundreds of books and articles on dress and grooming. Although these authors are not in complete agreement on every aspect of dress, they do agree on a few basic points regarding wardrobe.

**The quality of your wardrobe will influence the image you project.** A wardrobe should be regarded as an investment, with each item carefully selected to look and fit well. Purchase a few basic items each year and you will soon have everything you need.

**The newest dress fad is often inappropriate in a business or professional setting.** In most cases, the world of work is more conservative than college, the arts, or the world of sports. If you are a fashion setter, you might be viewed as unstable or insincere. To be taken seriously, avoid clothing that is faddish or too flashy.

Women generally have more latitude than men in selecting appropriate attire, but they should still exercise some caution in choosing their wardrobe. In some cases, women are entering positions formerly dominated by men. They need to be taken seriously, and the wardrobe they select can contribute to this end.

**Your wardrobe should be appropriate for your field and for you.** Although you should consider the dress and grooming standards of others in your field, don't give in to blind conformity or duplication. As one image consultant noted, "Effective packaging is an individual matter based on the person's circumstances, age, weight, height, coloring, and objectives."[16] In addition to these personal factors, you need to consider what's appropriate for your career (see Table 6.1).

---

### THINKING / LEARNING STARTER

Assume you are planning to purchase (1) a life insurance policy, (2) a Lexus automobile, and (3) eyeglasses. What types of career apparel would you expect persons selling these products to wear? What grooming standards would you recommend?

**TABLE 6.1**

**Factors Influencing Your Choice of Clothing for Work**

Dress codes are undergoing major changes, and this complicates the selection of clothing for work. Business and professional people are image-conscious, so use the four factors described here for guidance.

1. *Products and services offered.* In some cases the organization's products and services more or less dictate a certain type of dress. For example, a receptionist employed by a well-established law firm is likely to wear clothing that is conservative, modest, and in good taste. These same dress standards would apply to a pharmaceutical sales representative who calls on medical doctors.

2. *Type of person served.* Research indicates that first impressions created by dress and grooming are greatly influenced by unconscious expectations. Throughout life we become acquainted with real estate salespeople, nurses, police officers, and others employed in a wide range of occupations. We form mental images of the apparel common to each of these occupations. When we encounter someone whose appearance does not conform to our past experiences, we often feel uncomfortable.

3. *Desired image projected by the organization.* Some companies establish dress codes that help shape the image they project to the public. Walt Disney Company, for example, maintains a strict dress and grooming code for all its theme-park employees. They are considered "cast members" and must adhere to dress and grooming standards that complement the image projected by Disney theme parks.

4. *Geographic region.* Dress in the South and Southwest tends to be more casual than dress in the Northeast. Climate is another factor that influences the clothing people wear at work.

## ■ *The Business Casual Look*

The term *business casual* is used to describe the movement toward dress standards that emphasize greater comfort and individuality. **Business casual** is clothing that allows you to feel comfortable at work but looks neat and professional. It usually means slacks, khaki pants, collared long-sleeved shirts and blouses, and shoes with socks or hosiery. It usually does not include jeans, T-shirts, shorts, sneakers, or sandals.[17]

Today's companies are relaxing dress codes and allowing workers to dress casually. Although no precise definition of business casual exists, most companies have developed a casual dress code. The following casual-dress guidelines are typical.

1. *Wear dressier business clothing when meeting with customers or clients.* Workers at Provox Technologies Corporation, based in Roanoke, Virginia, keep company-designed ProVox shirts and khakis in the office for client visits.[18] But the dressed-down look is not appropriate when doing business in a foreign country.

Many companies are relaxing dress codes and allowing workers to wear clothing that is more casual. These two workers are keeping the "business" in business casual. The clothing is clean and neat and it fits well.

2. *Respect the boundary between work and leisure clothing.* Victoria's Secret has sold body-hugging spandex tube tops as workplace wear, and Brooks Brothers has used tieless male models with shirts unbuttoned to reveal curly chest hair. Both companies are trying to make it big in the business casual market.[19] Anne Fisher of *Fortune* magazine's "Ask Annie" career advice column says, "As a rule, people should avoid wearing anything that shows so much skin that it distracts other people from their work." It is probably not a coincidence that the dress-down trend has been accompanied by an increase in flirtatious behavior.[20]

3. *Wear clothing that is clean and neat and that fits well.* Casual dress codes tend to emphasize the importance of this principle.

A number of companies have discovered creative ways to help employees select casual clothing. Chrysler Financial scheduled a fashion show that offered employees many examples of casual outfits appropriate for work. Sears, Roebuck and Company installed two mannequins in its cafeteria, one modeling "appropriate" dress, the other "inappropriate."[21]

## ■ *Your Facial Expression*

After your overall appearance, your face is the most visible part of you. Facial expressions are the cues most people rely on in initial interactions. They provide the clues by which others read your mood and personality.

**Facial expressions are the cues most people rely on in initial interactions.**

Studies conducted in nonverbal communication show that facial expressions strongly influence people's reactions to each other. The expression on your face can quickly trigger a positive or negative reaction from those you meet. How you rate in the "good-looks" department is not nearly as important as your ability to communicate positive impressions with a pleasant smile.

If you want to identify the inner feelings of another person, watch the individual's facial expressions closely. A frown may tell you "something is wrong." A smile generally communicates "things are OK." Everyone has encountered a "look of surprise" or a "look that could kill." These facial expressions usually reflect inner emotions more accurately than words. The smile is the most recognizable signal in the world. People everywhere tend to trust a smiling face.[22]

## ■ *Your Entrance and Carriage*

The way you enter someone's office or a business meeting can influence the image you project, says Susan Bixler. She notes that "your entrance and the way you carry yourself will set the stage for everything that comes afterward."[23] A nervous or apologetic entrance may ruin your chances of getting a job, closing a sale, or getting the raise you have earned. If you feel apprehensive, try not to let it show in your body language. Hold your head up, avoid slumping forward, and try to project self-assurance. To get off to the right start and make a favorable impression, follow these words of advice from Bixler: "The person who has confidence in himself or herself indicates this by a strong stride, a friendly smile, good posture, and a genuine sense of energy. This is a very effective way to set the stage for a productive meeting. When you ask for respect visually, you get it."[24] Bixler says the key to making a successful entrance is simply believing—and projecting—that you have a reason to be there and have something important to present or discuss.

## ■ *Your Voice*

The tone of your voice, the rate of speed at which you speak (tempo), the volume of your speech, and your ability to pronounce words clearly (diction) contribute greatly to the meaning attached to your verbal messages. In the case of telephone calls, voice quality is critical because the other person cannot see your facial expressions, hand gestures, and other body movements. You cannot trade in your current voice for a new one, but with a little practice you can make your voice more pleasing to other people and project a positive tone.

Although there is no ideal voice for all business contacts, your voice should reflect at least these four qualities: confidence, enthusiasm, optimism, and sincerity. Above all, try to avoid a speech pattern that is dull and colorless.

African Americans, Hispanics, Asians, Native Americans, and recent immigrants to America often face special challenges in verbal communication. New arrivals may have a unique accent because the phonetic habits of the speaker's native language are carried over to his or her new language. Many people born and

raised in America have a dialect that is unique. Should this uniqueness be viewed as a problem or an opportunity? Kim Radford, vice president of marketing at Wachovia Trust Company, had to answer this question soon after graduating from college. He took a position as a stockbroker in Charleston, West Virginia. Radford, a black man, conducted most of his business on the telephone and seldom met clients face to face. Early on, someone said, "Kim, you need to get that black accent out of your voice if you're going to be successful in this business." Radford faced a real dilemma: He wanted to be successful, but he did not want to compromise his personal integrity. He talked to several people, black and white, and the advice he received boiled down to this guideline:

> Stay honest to yourself, but communicate and be understood. There's no need to clean up the fact that you sound black as long as you're articulate and your diction's good and people can understand you.[25]

## ■ *Your Handshake*

When two people first meet, a handshake is usually the only physical contact between them. A handshake is a friendly and professional way to greet someone, or take leave, regardless of gender. The handshake can communicate warmth, genuine concern for the other person, and strength. It can also communicate aloofness, indifference, and weakness. The message you send the other party through your handshake depends on a combination of the following factors:

1. *Degree of firmness.* Generally speaking, a firm (but not viselike) grip communicates a caring attitude, whereas a weak grip communicates indifference.

2. *Degree of dryness of hands.* A moist palm is unpleasant to feel and can communicate the impression that you are nervous. A clammy hand is likely to repel most people.

3. *Duration of grip.* There are no specific guidelines for the ideal duration of a grip. Nevertheless, by extending the handshake just a little, you can often communicate a greater degree of interest in and concern for the other person.

4. *Depth of interlock.* A full, deep grip is more likely to convey friendship to the other person.

5. *Eye contact during handshake.* Visual communication can increase the positive impact of your handshake. Maintaining eye contact throughout the handshaking process is important when two people greet each other.[26]

Most individuals have shaken hands with hundreds of people but have little idea whether they are creating positive or negative impressions. It is a good idea to obtain this information from those coworkers or friends who are willing to provide you with candid feedback. Like all other human relations skills, the handshake can be improved with practice.

 *HUMAN RELATIONS in ACTION*

### Etiquette Book Presents a Code of Manners for Blacks

When Harriette Cole authored *How to Be: Contemporary Etiquette for African Americans,* she was often asked, "Why a book of manners just for blacks?"

Cole explains, "Our circles in corporate America and in our neighborhoods are broadening, and we need to better understand the rules and mores of Western culture." The book explains how to deal with stereotypes, celebrate cultural differences, and communicate with white coworkers. Cole offers guidance on a variety of topics:

■ Sticking together in the workplace does not mean you have to stay away from others. Build relationships with as many coworkers as you can.

■ It is rude not to take off your sunglasses when being introduced to someone. Keeping glasses on creates the impression that you are pretentious and untrustworthy.

■ Small hoops or studs for men at work are usually OK, but always check the dress code to see what's acceptable.

## ■ *Your Manners*

The study of manners (sometimes called etiquette) reveals a number of ways to enhance our professional presence. A knowledge of good manners permits us to perform our daily work with poise and confidence. Letitia Baldrige, author and business etiquette consultant, provides us with a basic definition of good manners: "It's consideration and kindness and thinking about somebody other than oneself."[27] The authors of the *Complete Business Etiquette Handbook* say, "It's a set of traditions, based on kindness, efficiency, and logic, that have evolved over time."[28]

In recent years we have seen an increase in etiquette training designed for employees. Thermo Information Solutions, a software developer in Charleston,

South Carolina, routinely sends new hires to etiquette classes offered by Eticon, Incorporated. Frank Williams, Thermo's finance director, believes that new college graduates need a manners update.[29]

As the world changes, our manners need updating. E-mail etiquette (introduced in Chapter 2) is today no less important than telephone etiquette. A diverse work force creates new challenges. To illustrate, what do you do if a client comes into your office in a wheelchair? Do you rise? Or suppose a man and a woman of equal status in an organization walk down a corridor and arrive at a door. If the woman reaches it first, should the man move ahead and open it for her?

Although it is not possible to do a complete review of this topic, some of the rules of etiquette that are particularly important in an organizational setting are covered here.

1. ***When you establish new relationships, avoid calling people by their first names too soon.*** Jacqueline Thompson, author of *Image Impact,* says assuming that all work-related associates prefer to be addressed informally by their first names is a serious breach of etiquette.[30] Use titles of respect—Ms., Miss, Mrs., Mr., or Dr.—until the relationship is well established. Too much familiarity can breed irritation. When the other party says, "Call me Susan," or "Call me Roy," it is all right to begin using the person's first name.

2. ***Avoid obscenities and offensive comments or stories.*** In recent years, standards for acceptable and unacceptable language have changed considerably. Obscenity is more permissible in everyday conversation than it was in the past. But it is still considered inappropriate to use foul language in front of a customer, a client, or, in many cases, a coworker. In addition, cursing is often viewed by others as showing a lack of maturity. According to Bob Greene, syndicated columnist, an obscenity communicates a negative message to most people:

   > What it probably all comes down to is an implied lack of respect for the people who hear you talk. If you use profanity among friends, that is a choice you make. But if you broadcast it to people in general, you're telling them that you don't care what their feelings might be.[31]

---

**TOTAL PERSON INSIGHT**

*JUDITH MARTIN*

Author

*"In a society as ridden as ours with expensive status symbols, where every purchase is considered a social statement, there is no easier or cheaper way to distinguish oneself than by the practice of gentle manners."*

Never assume that another person's value system is the same as your own. Foul language and off-color stories can do irreparable damage to interpersonal relations.

3. *Watch your table manners.* Business is frequently conducted at breakfast, lunch, or dinner these days, so be aware of your table manners. To illustrate decisions you might need to make during a business meal, let's eavesdrop on Tom Reed, a job candidate having a meal with several employees of the company he wants to work for. After introductions, the bread is passed to Tom. He places a roll on the small bread-and-butter plate to the right of his dinner plate. Soon, he picks up the roll, takes a bite, and returns it to the plate. Midway through the meal, Tom rises from his chair, places his napkin on the table, and says, "Excuse me; I need to make a potty run." So far, Tom has made four etiquette blunders: The bread-and-butter plate he used belongs to the person seated on his right; his own is to the left of his dinner plate. When eating a roll, he should break off one piece at a time and butter the piece as he is ready to eat it. The napkin should have been placed on his chair, indicating his plan to return. (When departing for good, leave it to the left of your plate.) And finally, the words *potty run* are too casual for a business meal. A simple statement such as, "Please excuse me; I'll be back in just a moment," would be adequate.

   There are some additional table manners to keep in mind. Do not begin eating until the people around you have their plates. If you have not been served, however, encourage others to go ahead. To prevent awkward moments during the meal, avoid ordering food that is not easily controlled, such as ribs, spaghetti, chicken with bones, or lobster.

4. *Express appreciation at appropriate times.* A simple thank-you can mean a lot. Failure to express appreciation can be a serious human relations blunder. The office worker who works hard to complete a rush job for the boss is likely to feel frustrated and angry if this extra effort is ignored. The customer who makes a purchase deserves a sincere thank-you. You want your customers to know that their business is appreciated.

5. *Be familiar with meeting etiquette.* Business meetings should start and end on time. When you attend a meeting, arrive on time and don't feel obligated to comment on each item on the agenda. Yes, sometimes silence is golden. In most cases, you should not bring up a topic unless it is related to an agenda item. If you are in charge of the meeting, end it by summarizing key points, reviewing the decisions made, and recapping the responsibilities assigned to individuals during the meeting. Always start and end the meeting on a positive note.[32]

6. *Be aware of personal habits that may offend others.* Sometimes an annoying habit can be a barrier to establishing a positive relationship with someone else. Chewing gum is a habit that bothers many people, particularly if you chew gum vigorously or "crack" it. Biting fingernails, cracking knuckles,

scratching your head, and combing your hair in public are additional habits to be avoided. If you wear a fragrance (cologne, perfume, or after-shave lotion), apply it in moderation when going to work. Do not risk causing a client or coworker discomfort with your fragrance.[33]

Letitia Baldrige says that in the field of manners, "Rules are based on kindness and efficiency." She also believes that good manners are those personal qualities that make life at work more livable.[34] Nancy Austin, co-author of *A Passion for Excellence,* says, "Real manners—a keen interest in and a regard for somebody else, a certain kindness and at-ease quality that add real value—can't be faked or finessed."[35] Real manners come from the heart.

## ■ *Incivility—The Ultimate Career Killer*

Civility in our society is under siege. In recent years we have witnessed an increase in coarse, rude, and obnoxious behavior. Unfortunately, some of the most outrageous behavior by athletes, coaches, politicians, and business leaders has been rewarded with wealth and influence.

As noted in Chapter 1, civility is the sum of the many sacrifices we are called to make for the sake of living together. At work, it may involve refilling the copier paper tray after using the machine, or making a new pot of coffee after you take the last cup. It may mean turning down your radio so workers nearby are not disturbed or sending a thank-you note to someone who has helped you complete a difficult project.

Small gestures such as saying "Please" and "Thank you," opening doors for others, or treating coworkers with dignity and respect can enhance your career. Learning to discipline your passions so as to avoid self-defeating behavior will demonstrate to others your maturity and self-control.

## ■ *Professional Presence at the Job Interview*

The guideline that says "You seldom get a second chance to make a good first impression" has special meaning when you are preparing for a job interview. In most cases you are competing against several other applicants, so you can't afford to make a mistake. A common mistake among job applicants is failure to acquire background information on the employer. Without this information, it's difficult to prepare questions to ask during the interview, and decisions about what to wear will be more difficult.

Keep in mind that regardless of the dress code of the organization, it's always appropriate to dress conservatively. If you arrive for an interview wearing torn jeans and a T-shirt, the person conducting the interview may think you are not serious about the job. The expectation of most employers is that the job applicant will be well groomed and dressed appropriately.

One of the most important objectives of a job interview is to communicate the image that you are someone who is conscientious, so be prepared. If possible, visit the place of business before your interview. Observe the people already working there; then dress one step up in terms of professional appearance. When in doubt about what to wear, opt for a more formal look. What's most important is that you show that you care enough to make a good impression.

## Summary

Professional presence permits us to be perceived as self-assured and competent. These qualities are quickly perceived the first time someone meets us. People tend to form impressions of others quickly at the time they first meet them, and these first impressions tend to be preserved. In an organizational setting, the time interval for projecting a positive or negative first impression is often reduced to seconds. Positive impressions are important because they contribute to repeat business and customer referrals.

The impression you form of another person during the initial contact is made up of assumptions and facts. When meeting someone for the first time, people tend to rely heavily on assumptions. Many of your assumptions can be traced to early cultural influences. Assumptions are also based on perceptions of surface language. Surface language is a pattern of immediate impressions conveyed by appearance. The clothing and jewelry you wear, your hairstyle, and the fragrances you use all combine to make a statement about you to others.

Image consultants contend that discrimination on the basis of appearance is still a fact of life. Clothing is an important part of the image you communicate to others. Four factors tend to influence your choice of clothing for work: (1) the products or services offered by the organization, (2) the type of person served, (3) the desired image projected by the organization, and (4) the region where you work.

In addition to clothing, research indicates that facial expressions strongly influence people's reactions to each other. The expression on your face can quickly trigger a positive or negative reaction. Similarly, your entrance and carriage, voice, handshake, and manners also contribute to the image you project when meeting others. All the factors that form your image should be given attention prior to a job interview or any other situation where a positive first impression is important.

## Career Corner

Q: In the near future I will begin my job search, and I want to work for a company that will respect my individuality. Some companies are enforcing strict dress codes and other policies that, in my opinion, infringe on the rights of their employees. How far can an employer go in dictating my lifestyle?

A: This is a good question, but one for which there is no easy answer. For example, most people feel they have a right to wear the fragrance of their choice, but many fragrances contain allergy-producing ingredients. In some employment settings, you will find "nonfragrance" zones. Secondhand smoke is another major issue in the workplace because some research indicates that it can be harmful to the health of workers. Rules regarding weight, hair length, and the type of clothing and jewelry that can be worn to work have also caused controversy. There is no doubt that many companies are trying to find a balance between their interests and the rights of workers. Blockbuster Entertainment Corporation has placed restrictions on the length of an employee's hair and the amount of jewelry that can be worn during work hours. The company believes employee appearance is crucial to the success of the company. The best advice I can give you is to become familiar with the employer's expectations before you accept a job. The company has a responsibility to explain its personnel policies to prospective employees, but sometimes this information is not covered until after a person is hired.

## Key Terms

professional presence
primacy effect
assumptions
cultural influences
image

surface language
career apparel
wardrobe engineering
business casual

## Review Questions

1. Image has been described as "more than exterior qualities such as dress and grooming." What other factors shape the image we project?
2. Define the term *primacy effect*. How would knowledge of the primacy effect help someone who works in patient care or customer service?
3. Why do people tend to rely more heavily on assumptions than on facts during the initial meeting?
4. Why should career-minded people be concerned about the image they project? Do we have control over the factors that shape the image we project? Explain.
5. What are the four factors that influence your choice of clothing for work?
6. Susan Bixler suggests that when making wardrobe decisions, you should keep in mind three things that have not changed. List and discuss these three factors.
7. What is meant by the term *business casual?* What factors should you consider when selecting casual clothing for work?
8. Describe the type of speaking voice that increases a person's effectiveness in dealing with others.
9. Provide a basic definition of good manners. Why is the study of manners important?
10. Stephen Covey says that changing outward attitudes and behaviors does very little good in the long run unless we base such changes on solid principles that govern human effectiveness. Do you agree or disagree with his views? Explain your answer.

## Application Exercises

1. Harvey Mackay, president of Mackay Envelope Corporation, has designed a sixty-six-question customer profile for his sales staff. Salespeople are encouraged to complete the form for each customer they call on. The profile includes such information as birth date, current position, marital status, professional memberships, and special interests. Mackay takes the position that a salesperson cannot build long-term relationships with customers unless she or he takes a personal interest in them.

   a. Do you support the use of a customer profile to build relationships with customers or clients? Explain.

   b. What type of organization would benefit most from use of a detailed customer profile similar to the one used at Mackay Envelope Corporation?

2. The first step toward improving your voice is to hear yourself as others do. Listen to several recordings of your voice on a dictation machine, tape recorder, or VCR, and then complete the following rating form. Place a checkmark in the appropriate space for each quality.

   | Quality | *Major Strength* | *Strength* | *Weakness* | *Major Weakness* |
   |---|---|---|---|---|
   | Projects confidence | _____ | _____ | _____ | _____ |
   | Projects enthusiasm | _____ | _____ | _____ | _____ |
   | Speaking rate is not too fast or too slow | _____ | _____ | _____ | _____ |
   | Projects optimism | _____ | _____ | _____ | _____ |
   | Voice is not too loud or too soft | _____ | _____ | _____ | _____ |
   | Projects sincerity | _____ | _____ | _____ | _____ |

3. To survive in today's competitive climate, organizations must provide good service. Employees who have direct contact with the customer, client, or patient play a key role in the area of service. Effective front-line employees are able to express a warm, sincere greeting, display a caring attitude, and provide competent service. During the next seven days keep a record of all contacts you have with front-line people. After each contact, record your impressions of the experience. Was it positive? Negative? Briefly describe what the person said or did that caused you to view the contact as either positive or negative.

## Internet Exercise

Throughout the past few years we have seen an increase in the number of etiquette consulting and training companies. These firms will help you develop and initiate dress codes, and conduct etiquette-training programs for employees. Contact two of the following companies and review the services offered. Then prepare a written summary of your findings.

Patricia Stephenson & Associates
West Palm Beach, FL
*etiquettepro.com*

The Protocol School of Washington
McLean, VA
*psow.com*

Brody Communications
Elkins Park, PA
*brodycomm.com*

Eticon Inc.
Columbia, SC
*eticon.com*

At Ease Inc.
Cincinnati, OH
*ateaseinc.com*

Professional Image
Atlanta, GA
*theprofessionalimage.net*

 **Self-Assessment Exercise**

For each of the following statements, circle the number from 1 to 5 that best represents your response: (1) strongly disagree (never do this); (2) disagree (rarely do this); (3) moderately agree (sometimes do this); (4) agree (frequently do this); (5) strongly agree (almost always do this).

A. I project to others an image that matches my talents and aspirations.  1  2  3  4  5

B. The clothes I wear to work and school are appropriate and project the image I want to exhibit to others.  1  2  3  4  5

C. My entrance and carriage project total confidence.  1  2  3  4  5

D. When I meet an acquaintance or someone new, I make eye contact and shake hands with a firm grip.  1  2  3  4  5

E. I believe that good manners are an important key to improved human relations.  1  2  3  4  5

F. My voice is pleasing to others and reflects the qualities of confidence, enthusiasm, optimism, and sincerity.  1  2  3  4  5

G. My handshake communicates warmth, genuine interest in the other person, and strength.  1  2  3  4  5

Select an appropriate attitude or skill you would like to improve. Write your goal in the space provided, and describe the steps you will take to achieve this goal.

GOAL: _____

_____

_____

_____

## Case Problem    *The Importance of Class*

The words *magnetism, charisma,* and *class* are used to describe persons who are admired and respected. These special individuals are also memorable. Some say class and charm are fading fast from the American scene, replaced by bad behavior displayed by professional athletes, movie stars, radio and TV commentators, and politicians. Many sports fans mourn the retirement of John Elway, Michael Jordan, and Wayne Gretzky, who were gracious in victory and gracious in defeat.

After Joe DiMaggio died in 1999, he was described in many articles as the classiest baseball player who ever lived. He displayed a unique combination of grace and class that captured the imagination of the nation. His career was marked by unflagging personal modesty, civility, and generosity. Off the field he was usually wearing a jacket and tie. The late Payne Stewart, killed in the bizarre crash of a Learjet, is remembered as a vicious competitor and a classy hero to many golf fans.

The authors of *Make Yourself Memorable* say that memorable people have style. They describe the four interlocking elements of style as *look, conduct, speech,* and *presentation.* Ann Landers, the noted advice columnist, says that if you have class, success will follow. She has described some of the elements of class:[36]

- Class never tries to build itself up by tearing others down.

- Class never makes excuses.

- Class knows that good manners are nothing more than a series of small, inconsequential sacrifices.

- Class is comfortable in its own skin. It never puts on airs.

- Class is real. It can't be faked.

### Questions

1. Some social critics say that too many people these days are rude, crude, and inconsiderate of others. Do you agree? Explain.

2. Make a list of prominent people who in your opinion have class. Also, make a list of friends or coworkers who have class. What personal qualities displayed by these individuals do you most admire?

3. Ann Landers says that if you have class, nothing else matters. Do you agree?

4. If you want to become a more memorable person—someone with class—what type of self-improvement program would you undertake? Explain.

# 7

# Valuing Work Force Diversity

CHAPTER PREVIEW

After studying this chapter, you will be able to

- Define the primary and secondary dimensions of diversity.

- Discuss how prejudiced attitudes are formed.

- Develop an awareness of the various forms of discrimination.

- Understand why organizations are striving to develop organizational cultures that value diversity.

- Identify ways in which individuals and organizations can enhance work force diversity.

- Discuss the current status of affirmative action programs.

Texaco's sprawling office headquarters north of New York City were the scene of an embarrassing and expensive class-action lawsuit charging racial discrimination. It was filed by some of the company's African American employees, who claimed they were victims of blatant acts of racism by Texaco managers and employees. The courts upheld the plaintiffs' claims, and Texaco paid the victims $140 million in damages and back wages and set aside another $35 million to establish an independent task force to monitor the company's diversity efforts for five years.

Bari-Ellen Roberts, a senior analyst for Texaco, was the lead plaintiff in the case. In her book detailing the corporatewide culture of discrimination, Roberts recalls that Texaco in the early 1990s was like "a Southern town after a lynching." She cites managers calling her a "little colored girl" behind her back and remembers when her performance rating was lowered by a white executive who said she was "uppity." When a white male with fewer qualifications was promoted above her and she was asked to train him, she organized the class-action suit. Soon other blatant discriminatory actions at Texaco were exposed: A division vice president told a black employee that if a white person and an African American were competing for a job, it was "only human nature to give it to the white person"; a white employee stopped outside a coveted two-window office occupied by an African American woman and said, ". . . I never thought I'd live to see the day when a black woman had an office at Texaco"; and hundreds of minority employees were being paid less than the minimum salary for their job category. The crowning blow, however, occurred when an audiotape of an executive meeting, released by a former Texaco executive, exposed plans to destroy incriminating documents surrounding the court case.

When Texaco CEO Peter Bijur discovered the extent of the discrimination, he ordered the attorneys to settle the case and acted quickly and decisively. Today Texaco is a model for ridding corporate corridors of discrimination.[1]

Organizations throughout the world are discovering the waste of valuable human resources that occurs when people are discriminated against not only because of race, but also because of gender, age, sexual orientation, or physical or mental disabilities. This chapter can help you understand the detrimental effects of prejudice and discrimination in the workplace and help you handle such behaviors if or when you are the victim.

## Work Force Diversity—A New Definition

*E Pluribus Unum*: "Out of many, one." No other country on earth is as multiracial and multicultural as the United States of America. The strength of most other nations lies in their homogeneity. Japan is made up mostly of people of Japanese descent, and their economy and business transactions reflect this common heritage. The People's Republic of China is populated mostly with people of Chinese ancestry, and their values and culture are a major part of their global

**FIGURE 7.1**

Foreign-Born Population Trend

*Source:* From "Immigrant Ranks are Swelling." Reprinted from April 24, 2000, issue of *Business Week* by special permission, copyright © 2000 by The McGraw-Hill Companies, Inc.

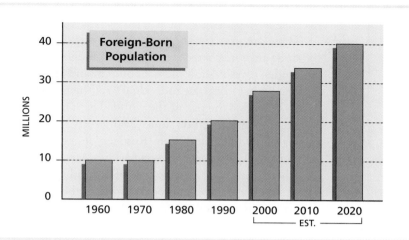

economic strength. But America has always served as host to a kaleidoscope of the world's cultures. Therefore, business practices must adjust accordingly. This trend toward **diversity**, the presence of a variety of races and cultures, is likely to continue. The foreign-born population in America now numbers about 30 million people and is projected to increase exponentially (see Figure 7.1).[2] Such diversity in the work force represents the country's biggest challenge as well as its greatest opportunity.

In the past, U.S. organizations attempted to assimilate everyone into one "American" way of doing things. Labor unions were formed so that everyone would be treated the same. The women's rights movement began when women wanted to be treated just like men in the workplace. The trend now, however, is to *value diversity*, which means appreciating everyone's uniqueness, respecting their differences, and encouraging every worker to make his or her full contribution to the organization. Organizations that foster the full participation of all workers are more likely to enjoy the sharpest competitive edge in the expanding global marketplace.

**In the past, U.S. organizations attempted to assimilate everyone into one "American" way of doing things.**

**TOTAL PERSON INSIGHT**

*J.T. "TED" CHILDS, JR.*

Vice President, IBM Global Workforce Diversity

*"No matter who you are, you're going to have to work with people who are different from you. You're going to have to sell to people who are different from you, and buy from people who are different from you, and manage people who are different from you."*

### ■ *Dimensions of Diversity*

There are primary and secondary dimensions of diversity. The **primary dimensions** are core characteristics of each individual that cannot be changed: age, race, gender, physical and mental abilities, and sexual orientation (see Figure 7.2). Together they form an individual's self-image and the filters through which each person views the rest of the world. These inborn elements are interdependent; no one dimension stands alone. Each exerts an important influence throughout life. Marilyn Loden and Judy Rosener describe individual primary dimensions in their book *Workforce America!* They say, "Like the interlocking segments of a sphere, they represent the core of our individual identities."[3]

The greater the number of primary differences between people, the more difficult it is to establish trust and mutual respect. When we add the secondary dimensions of diversity to the mix, effective human relations becomes even more difficult. The **secondary dimensions** of diversity are elements that can be changed or at least modified. They include a person's health habits, religious beliefs, education and training, general appearance, relationship status, ethnic customs, communication style, and income (see Figure 7.2). These factors all add a layer of complexity to the way we see ourselves and others and in some instances can exert a powerful impact on our core identities. A single mother who loses her job may be severely affected by her loss of income, whereas a married woman with no children may not be as affected by a similar loss. A vocational-technical school graduate may have expectations far different from those of a four-year-college graduate. A member of the Baptist church may feel she has little in common with a woman who follows Islamic teachings.

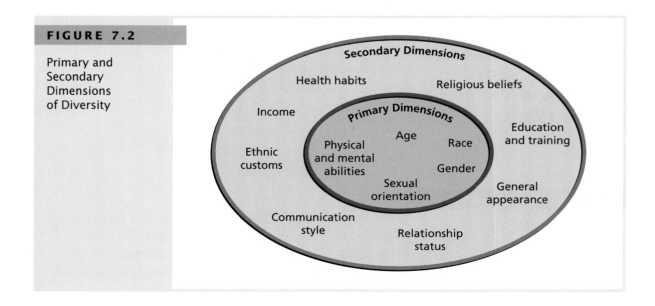

**FIGURE 7.2**

Primary and Secondary Dimensions of Diversity

General Motors has discovered the economic necessity of valuing diversity in its work force if it wants to stay competitive.

Even though differences like these intensify the impact of particular secondary dimensions, they do not diminish the impact of primary dimensions. Instead, they add depth to the individual. This interaction of primary and secondary dimensions shapes a person's values, priorities, and perceptions throughout life.[4]

Each of us enters the work force with a unique perspective shaped by these dimensions and our own past experiences. Building effective human relationships

---

**TOTAL PERSON INSIGHT**

*VERNON E. JORDAN, JR.*

Attorney and Civil Rights Leader

*"So long as black and white Americans see each other as stereotypes and not as people with the same dreams, ambitions and values, this nation will be frozen in suspicion and hate."*

is possible only when we learn to accept and value the differences in others. Without this acceptance, both primary and secondary dimensions of diversity can become roadblocks to further cooperation and understanding.

## *Prejudiced Attitudes—An Introduction*

**Prejudice** is a premature judgment or opinion that is formed without examination of the facts. Throughout life we often prejudge people in light of their primary and secondary dimensions. Attitudes in favor of or against people that are based solely on these traits are prejudices. Rather than treat others as unique individuals, prejudiced people tend to think in terms of **stereotypes**—generalizations made about all members of a particular group. They uncritically accept widely held beliefs about what various racial groups, socioeconomic classes, men, women, people living in a particular geographic region, and so forth are "really like." When we bring stereotypes to the workplace, we are likely to misinterpret or devalue some primary and secondary differences even after we have been exposed to them.

Stereotyping exists, in part, because it provides an easy and convenient way of dealing with people. Accepting a stereotype, you don't have to make the effort to understand who a person really is or might become.[5] Stereotypes bring some predictability to our lives and reduce the uncertainty of dealing with other people. Stereotypes are often based on one or several real experiences a person has had in dealing with others, and they are resistant to change because people more readily believe information that confirms their previous experience than evidence that challenges it. For example, people without a tendency to gain weight sometimes view an overweight person as someone who lacks the self-discipline and motivation to lose weight.

Stereotypes are more likely to change upon actual acquaintance with members of a particular group. For example, even twenty years ago, gender stereotypes were very common. Women were often viewed as indecisive, passive, and too emotional to succeed in leadership positions. Research conducted by the 1990s characterized women as intelligent, logical, dependable, and skilled at relationships.[6] As the work force became increasingly female, and women began holding a greater proportion of management and executive positions, stereotypes were contradicted by facts.

In some cases, the distorted stereotypes we hold on to are shaped by news and entertainment media. For example, many people believe that the African American community is characterized by a pattern of heavy drug and alcohol use, abuse, and dependence. If you watch a lot of television and rely on the mass media for news, this stereotype will be reinforced. In reality, this stereotype is contradicted by the fact that African Americans are less likely to use alcohol and illegal drugs than are whites.[7]

## HUMAN RELATIONS *in* ACTION

### Tools for Tolerance: Personal

- Attend a play, listen to music, or go to a dance performance by artists whose race or ethnicity is different from your own.

- Visit a local senior citizens center and collect oral histories. Donate large-print reading materials and books on tape. Offer to help with a craft project.

- Learn sign language.

- Take a conversation course in another language that is spoken in your community.

- Sign the Declaration of Tolerance (see Figure 7.5 on page 174).

- Speak up when you hear slurs. Let people know that biased speech is always unacceptable.

## How Prejudicial Attitudes Are Formed and Retained

Three major factors contribute to the development of prejudice: childhood experiences, ethnocentrism, and economic conditions.

**Childhood Experiences**   Today's views toward others are filtered through the experiences and feelings of childhood. Children learn attitudes and beliefs from family, friends, and other authority figures, and they learn how to view and treat different racial, ethnic, religious, and other groups. The *emotions* of prejudice are formed in childhood. Later in life you may want to change your prejudice, but it is much easier to change your intellectual beliefs than your deep feelings.[8]

**Ethnocentrism**   The tendency to regard our own culture or nation as better or more "correct" than others is called **ethnocentrism.** The word is derived from *ethnic,* meaning a group united by similar customs, characteristics, race, or other common factors, and *center.* When ethnocentrism is present, the standards and values of our own culture are being used as a yardstick to measure the worth of other cultures.

   **Ethnic identity**, that part of our personal identity that reflects the racial, religious, and cultural group we belong to, tends to perpetuate ethnocentrism. As children, we are conditioned to respond to various situations as we see others in our culture respond to them. Some cultures value emotional control and avoid open conflicts and discussions of such personal topics as money or values. Other cultures encourage a bolder, more open expression of feelings and values.

In the book *Valuing Diversity,* the authors compare ethnocentrism in an organization to icebergs floating in an ocean. We can see the tips of icebergs above the water level, just as we can see our diverse coworkers' skin color, gender, mannerisms, and job-related talents and hear the words they use and their accents. These are basically "surface" aspects of a person that others can easily learn through observation. However, just as the enormous breadth of an iceberg's base lies beneath the water's surface, so does the childhood conditioning of people from different cultures. As icebergs increase in number and drift too close together, they are likely to clash at their base even though there is no visible contact at the water's surface.[9] As organizations increase the diversity of their work force, the potential for clashes resulting from deep-seated cultural conditioning and prejudiced attitudes also increases.

Racial profiling is the practice by which police officers stop motorists of certain racial or ethnic groups because the officers believe that these groups are more likely than others to commit certain types of crimes. The American Civil Liberties Union is trying to educate the public about this unfair practice and is working to have it declared illegal and stopped across the country.

**Economic Conditions**  When the economy goes through a recession or depression, and housing, jobs, and other necessities become scarce, people's prejudices against other groups often increase. Prejudice based on economic factors has its roots in people's basic survival needs, and as a result, it is very hard to eliminate. The recent backlash against immigrants can be traced, in part, to a fear that the new arrivals will take jobs that would otherwise be available to American workers. For example, when Mexico's President Vicente Fox asked America to enact more liberal immigration laws, organized anti-immigrant groups erected highway billboards that warned, "Deport all illegal aliens. The job you save may be your own."[10] Some fear that new immigrant arrivals will work for rock-bottom wages and thus depress the earning power of low-income Americans.

Rising income and wealth inequality in America is viewed by many as a serious barrier to racial harmony. Ronald Walters, University of Maryland political scientist, says, "You can only have meaningful racial reconciliation when people of roughly equal socioeconomic status can reach across the divide of race."[11] The gap in well-being between whites and nonwhites did not budge throughout the booming 1990s and remains huge. The racial divide in wealth (value of all assets) and income shows no sign of narrowing.[12]

---

## THINKING / LEARNING STARTERS

1. Have you ever been the object of prejudice? What were the circumstances? How did this behavior affect your self-esteem?

2. Do you carry any prejudices that are obvious carryovers from your childhood? Explain.

3. Are you doing anything to overcome these prejudices? What would the benefits be if you could overcome them?

---

## The Many Forms of Discrimination

**Discrimination** is behavior based on prejudiced attitudes. If, as an employer, you believe that overweight people tend to be lazy, that is an attitude. If you refuse to hire someone simply because that person is overweight, you are engaging in discriminatory behavior.

**Prejudice is a premature judgment or opinion that is formed without examination of the facts. Discrimination is behavior based on prejudiced attitudes.**

Individuals or groups that are discriminated against are denied equal treatment and opportunities afforded to the dominant group. They may be denied employment, promotion, training, or other job-related privileges on the basis of race, lifestyle, gender, or other characteristics that have little or nothing to do with their qualifications for a job.

## ■ *Gender*

Discrimination based on gender has been, and continues to be, the focus of much attention. The traditional roles women have held in society have undergone tremendous changes in the past few decades. More and more women are entering the work force not only to supplement family income but also to pursue careers in previously all-male professions. Men have also been examining the roles assigned them by society and are discovering new options for themselves. Most companies have recognized that discrimination based on gender is a reality and are taking steps to deal with the problem.

## ■ *Age*

Discrimination based on age can apply to workers in the 40-to-70 age range and to the younger workers from 18 to 25.

Youth can be a disadvantage when potential employers show a reluctance to hire young people because of their lack of practical experience in the workplace. Such employers fail to appreciate that everyone begins his or her career with no experience and needs an opportunity to prove himself or herself. Older workers between the ages of 40 and 70 are protected against discrimination by the Age Discrimination in Employment Act. The law states that if you are fired, demoted, denied a raise given to others, or otherwise mistreated primarily because of your age, you have legal recourse.

Age discrimination is on the rise, according to recent research studies. One in four Americans 40 years old and older suspects that he or she has been subjected to age-related employment discrimination.[13] As companies search for ways to cut costs, they often find creative ways (see Table 7.1) to get rid of older workers and replace them with younger workers who earn less. These same companies often refuse to hire older workers.

Many corporate leaders have a stereotypical notion that older workers are no longer capable of effective work performance. In reality, age often equates with wisdom and experience. Recent studies indicate that workers 55 and over are productive, cost-effective employees who can be trained in new technologies as easily as younger people. In addition, they often have lower turnover and absenteeism.[14] Progressive companies view age as an important element of their diversity program.

## ■ *Race*

Few areas are more sensitive and engender more passion than issues surrounding race. Throughout history we have seen attempts to place people in racial categories and judge them as racial symbols rather than as unique individuals. Until

## TABLE 7.1

**Age-Related Discriminatory Practices**

Many organizations have fostered cultures of age bias. This bias is expressed in a variety of age-related discriminatory practices:

■ Cutting off older workers from job-related training and career development opportunities.

■ Excluding older workers from important activities.

■ Favoring younger job applicants over older, better qualified candidates.

■ Forcing older workers out of the work force with negative performance evaluations.

■ Pressuring older workers to accept financial incentives and retire early.

*Source:* Sheldon Steinhauser, "Age Bias: Is Your Corporate Culture in Need of an Overhaul?" *HR Magazine,* July 1998.

the early decades of the twentieth century, the Irish Catholic "race" was stereotyped as lazy and violent. In the 1930s Jews in the United States were considered a separate "race" by many Christian Americans. Italians were once considered "nonwhite."[15]

**The Race Paradox**   Critics of racial categories view them as social inventions that intensify and reinforce racist beliefs and actions. They believe that one way to break down racial barriers and promote a race-free consciousness is to get rid of racial categories. A growing number of geneticists and social scientists reject the view that "racial" differences have an objective or scientific foundation.[16] Recently the American Anthropological Association (AAA) took the official position that "race" has no scientific justification in human biology. The AAA position is that "There is as much genetic variability between two people from the same 'racial group' as there is between two people from any two different 'racial' groups."[17] Put another way, individual differences are much greater than group differences, regardless of how the group is defined.[18]

A growing number of Americans have mixed-race identity and want to decide which part of their ancestry is relevant. Golf champion Tiger Woods (his father is African American and his mother is from Thailand) is proud of his multiracial background. He joins a growing number of Americans who believe that identities can evolve; that people needn't be locked into the identities bestowed on them at birth.[19]

The Heritage Multi-Racial Alliance, whose motto is "One world for us; no color lines," has sponsored multiracial diversity campaigns. A major goal of the Alliance was use of a multiracial category on the 2000 U.S. census form. Their efforts paid off. Respondents had the opportunity to check more than one box for race, allowing for sixty-three racial options.[20] The traditional nonwhite race categories (black, Hispanic, Asian, and Native American) will continue to be used in a variety of reporting systems. For example, agencies responsible for enforcement of nondiscriminatory housing laws, employment laws, and so forth will break down the many census report categories in ways that allow them to enforce the current laws.

Those who oppose getting rid of racial categories hold that in order to ensure that individuals of all races and national origins are treated fairly, we must categorize people according to these characteristics. They say the current system is needed to create minority voting districts and to administer an array of federal laws and programs designed to ensure that minorities get equal housing, education, health care, and employment opportunities.[21] Groups that are working to build race pride, such as the American Indian Movement, also oppose efforts to get rid of racial categories.

Many people still have an irrational suspicion of a particular ethnic or racial group. However, because of affirmative action programs and diversity training programs (discussed later in this chapter), and the threat of legal action, blatant racism has evolved into a new, subtler form of discrimination that is difficult to recognize and hard to combat.

## Disability

Wilfredo "Freddy" Laboy is described by his coworkers at Gap Inc. as the "wild man in a wheelchair." Freddy practically dances across the store, popping wheelies and spinning himself around to the beat of the ever-present pop music. The fast-talking, goateed, 36-year-old, who lost both legs when he fell off a freight train at age 9, never hesitates to hop off his chair to retrieve an item that has fallen on the floor. Freddy loves working at The Gap, and The Gap loves Freddy.[22]

Freddy Laboy is one of the country's 15 million disabled persons of working age. Despite the Americans with Disabilities Act (ADA) passed over a decade ago, only 25 percent of the disabled people who are of working age are currently employed. The ADA sets forth requirements for businesses with fifteen or more employees. It bans discrimination against workers with disabilities and requires employers to make "reasonable accommodations" so that they can work. It covers a wide range of disabilities, including mental impairments, AIDS, alcoholism, visual impairments, and physical impairments that require use of a wheelchair.

With this legal protection in place, why are so many disabled people still unemployed? The physical barriers are falling, but many psychological ones persist. Some employers are still unwilling to hire the person with a stutter, the person who uses a wheelchair, or the person who is blind. The good news is that several companies are setting a good example with major programs to accommodate both employees and customers with disabilities (see Table 7.2).

**TABLE 7.2**

**Enabling Those with Disabilities**

| Company | Type of Assistance |
|---------|--------------------|
| Crestar Bank | Provides voice-activated technology for disabled customer-service representatives. Makes special services available to customers with disabilities. |
| Honeywell | Participates in Able to Work program, a consortium of 22 companies that find ways to employ disabled persons. Uses its high-tech innovations to assist employees with disabilities. |
| Johnson & Johnson | Has established a comprehensive disability management program that tailors work assignments to employees returning to work after an injury. |
| Caterpillar | Serves as a model of high-tech accessibility for the disabled; sponsors Special Olympics. |

*Sources:* John Williams, "The List—Enabling Those with Disabilities," *Business Week*, March 6, 2000, p. 8; and "The New Work Force," *Business Week*, March 20, 2000, pp. 64–74.

## HUMAN RELATIONS *in* ACTION

### Meeting Someone with a Disability

Here are a few suggestions for making a good impression. If the person . . .

**. . . is in a wheelchair.** Sit down, if possible. Try to chat eye to eye. Don't touch the wheelchair. It is considered within the boundaries of an individual's personal space.

**. . . has a speech impediment.** Be patient, actively listen, and resist the urge to finish his or her sentences.

**. . . is accompanied by a guide dog.** Never pet or play with a guide dog; you will distract the animal from its job.

**. . . has a hearing loss.** People who are deaf depend on facial expressions and gestures for communication cues. Speak clearly and slowly. Speak directly to the person, not to an interpreter or assistant if one is present.

### ■ *Sexual Orientation*

Discrimination based on a person's sexual orientation is motivated by *homophobia,* an aversion to homosexuals. Not long ago, gays and lesbians went to great lengths to keep their sexuality a secret. But today many gays and lesbians are "coming out of the closet" to demand their rights as members of society. Indeed, many young

people entering the work force who are used to the relative tolerance of college campuses refuse to hide their orientation once they are in the workplace.

Gay rights activists are working hard to create awareness that discrimination based on sexual orientation is no less serious than discrimination based on age,

Gay rights activist Mary Cheney (left) confers with her sister and father, Vice President Dick Cheney. Mary, who is gay, was corporate-relations manager for Coors Brewing Co., which included serving as liaison to the gay and lesbian community in Golden, Colorado. Because the Coors family had donated to antigay causes, she worked to dispel negative notions about Coors. As a result of her efforts, Coors committed $110,000 to GLAAD, the Gay & Lesbian Alliance Against Defamation. Her visibility as the vice president's daughter is offering new opportunities to share her message throughout the country.

gender, race, or disability. Activists are also working to rid the workplace of anti-gay behaviors such as offensive jokes, derogatory names, or remarks about gays. An atmosphere in which gays and lesbians are comfortable about being themselves is often more productive than an atmosphere in which they waste their time and energy maintaining alternate, and false, personalities.

Brian McNaught, a consultant who conducts a workshop called "Homophobia in the Workplace," points out that it is not productive to ask gays and lesbians to completely ignore their private lives when they come to work. Heterosexuals bring their personal lives to work all the time. Being unable to participate in casual conversations about weekend events or after-work activities can leave gays and lesbians feeling isolated.[23]

Some companies have established lesbian and gay employee associations that provide a point of contact for previously invisible employees. Many companies have added sexual orientation to their nondiscrimination policies, and nationwide over 200 major public and private employers have extended medical benefits to same-sex partners. Some major companies such as American Express and J.P. Morgan & Company are targeting recruiting efforts at gay and lesbian college students.[24]

Many states have passed laws that help protect gays and lesbians from harm (see Figure 7.3). In the absence of such laws, however, every organization must provide workers with an environment that is safe and free of threats and intimidation. Progressive companies are taking the additional step of discovering ways in which they can provide an open, productive work atmosphere. They do not want to lose their intelligent, highly motivated lesbian and gay employees to companies that might provide a more open environment.

**FIGURE 7.3**

States Whose Hate-Crime Laws Include Sexual Orientation

*Sources:* From *USA Today*, May 18, 2000. Copyright © 2000, *USA Today*; and "U.S. Hate Crimes: Definitions and Facts," ReligiousTolerance. org., Copyright ©1999 to 2001 incl. by Ontario Consultants on Religious Tolerance. See http://www. religioustolerance.org/ hom_hat3.htm.

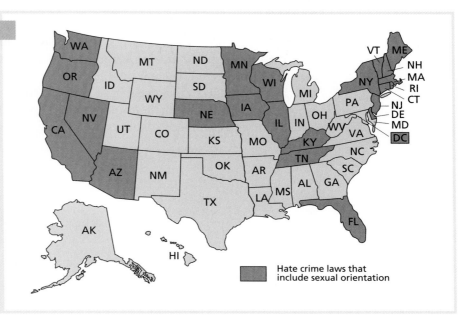

### ■ *Subtle Forms of Discrimination*

Discrimination based on gender, age, race, or disability is prohibited under Title VII of the 1964 Civil Rights Act. This prohibition applies to discrimination in all aspects of employment, including recruitment, hiring, promotion, discharge, classification, training, compensation, and other terms, privileges, and conditions of employment.[25] A person who feels she or he has been the victim of these types of discrimination can take legal action by filing a complaint with the state office of the Equal Employment Opportunity Commission.

But the laws do not specifically protect workers from subtler discrimination. For example, although some state laws protect gay men and lesbians from discrimination or illegal discharge from their jobs, an atmosphere that allows cruel comments and jokes about their lifestyles can nevertheless occur, adversely affecting their job performance. This lower job performance can be used as a valid reason for dismissing the lesbian or gay person. This subtler form of discrimination can, of course, be directed against any group and may be based on any of the secondary dimensions of diversity (religious beliefs, personal appearance, marital status). Those who are from another region of the country, speak with an accent, have too much education or too little, or possess some other personal characteristic that marks them as "different" may find themselves victims of subtle discrimination. Many people are inclined to equate a difference with a deficiency.

### ■ *What Can You Do?*

What can you do if you discover you are the target of discrimination? If you wish to stay in the organization, you will need to determine whether the "difference" is something you can change—your weight, the way you dress, your manner of speaking. If the difference is something you cannot or choose not to change, you may need to address the situation directly. Your assertiveness may help change other people's attitudes and in turn alter their discriminatory behaviors. Another powerful method of eliminating subtle discrimination is to compensate for it by excelling in your work. Become an expert on the job, and work to increase your skills and your value to the organization. As your colleagues gain respect for your talents, they will change their attitudes toward you. But if your future appears blocked, investigate other workplaces, where management may be more open to diversity.

---

| THINKING / LEARNING STARTERS

1. Describe your own primary and secondary dimensions of diversity.

2. Do you hold any prejudices that might create problems for you in your career? In your personal life?

## The Issue of Valuing Diversity

As we look back through the previous decades, we see a pattern of workers continually struggling to be treated alike. The new millennium, however, has brought a strong shift away from treating everyone the same and toward **valuing diversity.** In a work setting, valuing diversity means that an organization intends to make full use of the ideas, talents, experiences, and perspectives of all employees at all levels of the organization.

Many organizations have traditionally valued assimilation over diversity, placing emphasis on changing people to conform to traditional norms and performance expectations. Most old-economy organizations were shaped primarily by the values and experiences of western European, white, heterosexual, able-bodied men. Achieving high productivity has frequently been a matter of trying to fit all workers into the same mold and rewarding those who fit best. The dominant group set and controlled the agenda of the traditional organization and expected other groups to follow, conform, or disappear.

As the U.S. work force changes from being mainly Caucasian and male-dominated to representing almost equal numbers of men and women, along with a variety of racial and ethnic groups, organizations must break away from this traditional management approach. To remain competitive in the age of information, organizations are being forced to recognize and hire the best talent available in the labor pool, regardless of skin color, gender, and cultural background. Once on board, these talented individuals will choose to stay only in an atmosphere where they are appreciated and valued.

### ■ The Economics of Valuing Diversity

Valuing diversity is not only a legal, social, and moral issue; it is also an economic issue because an organization's most valuable resource is its people. The price tag for *not* helping employees learn to respect and value each other is enormous in terms of lost time, wasted energy, delayed production, and increased conflict among employees.

> **Valuing diversity is not only a legal, social, and moral issue; it is also an economic issue because an organization's most valuable resource is its people.**

- Highly skilled and talented employees may leave an organization that does not value diversity.

- Substantial dollars will be spent on recruiting and retraining because of high employee turnover.

- A comment, gesture, or joke delivered without malice but received as an insult will create tension between coworkers.

- Time will be wasted because of miscommunication and misunderstanding between diverse employees.[26]

Recognizing the value of diversity and managing it as an asset can help eliminate these negative effects and exert a positive influence on productivity and cooperation within the work force. Companies that pursue diversity and make it part of their culture usually outperform companies that are less committed to diversity.

*THINKING / LEARNING STARTERS*

1. Describe how closely the student body of your school or your coworkers reflect the cultural makeup of your community.

2. Is there a disproportionate number of students of a certain race, sex, or age bracket in your college? What accounts for this situation? What effects does it have on the environment of your school?

## Enhancing Diversity

By now you should be aware of the negative effects of prejudice and discrimination as well as the positive effects of valuing diversity. Many employers are no longer asking whether to diversify the work force but rather how best to enhance diversity. After all, a person's differences don't create human relations problems. Other people's responses to those differences do.

### ■ What Individuals Can Do

People tend to hang on to their prejudices and stereotypes. If certain white people believe people of color are inferior, they are likely to notice any incident in which a person of color makes a mistake. But when a person of color exhibits competence and sound decision-making abilities, these same white people may not notice, or they may attribute the positive results to other circumstances. You cannot totally eliminate prejudices that have been deeply held and developed over a long time. But you can learn to do the following:

1. *Monitor and analytically evaluate these prejudices in light of your increased personal involvement with others who are different from you.* As noted previously, it is not easy to free yourself from confining stereotypes. You need to not only change your intellectual beliefs but also change the emotions of prejudice formed throughout life. If you feel you are prejudiced against a particular group, develop a plan to curb prejudiced behaviors. Many people harbor prejudiced thoughts but have learned to avoid acting on them.

2. *Learn to look critically and honestly at the particular myths and preconceived ideas you were conditioned to believe about others.* Psychologists and sociologists have found that contact among people of different races, cultures, and lifestyles can break down prejudice when people join together for a common task. The more contact there is among culturally diverse individuals, the more likely it will be that stereotypes based on myths and inaccurate generalizations will not survive.

**Learn to look critically and honestly at the particular myths and preconceived ideas you were conditioned to believe about others.**

3. *Develop a sensitivity to differences.* Do not allow gender-based, racist, or anti-gay jokes or comments in your presence. If English is not a person's first lan-

guage, be aware that this person might interpret your messages differently from what you intended. When in doubt as to the appropriate behavior, ask questions. "I would like to open the door for you because you are in a wheelchair, but I'm not sure whether that would offend you. What would you like me to do?"

4. ***Develop your own diversity awareness program.*** The starting point might be creation of a "diversity profile" of your friends, coworkers, and acquaintances. How much diversity do these individuals have in terms of race? Ethnicity? Religion? Assess the cultural diversity reflected in the music you listen to and the books you read. Visit an ethnic restaurant and try to learn about more than the food. Attend services at a variety of churches, synagogues and temples, and mosques to learn about different faiths.[27]

### ■ *What Organizations Can Do*

A well-planned and well-executed diversity program can promote understanding and defuse tensions between employees who differ in age, race, gender, religious beliefs, and other characteristics. Programs that are poorly developed and poorly executed often backfire, especially in organizations where bias and distrust have festered for years.[28] Most of the programs that fail are those that are not comprehensive and do not have the full support of top management. A comprehensive diversity program has three pillars:[29] organizational commitment, employment practices, and training and development (see Figure 7.4).

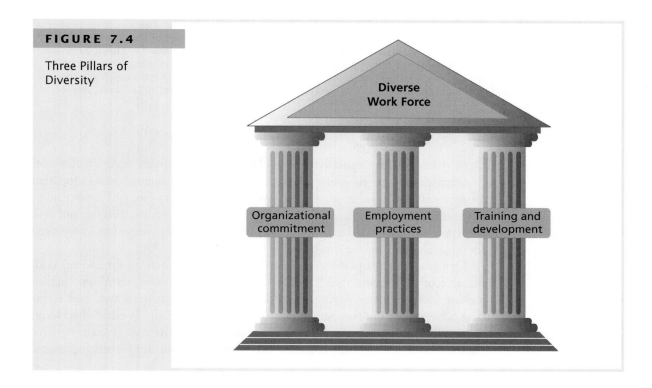

**FIGURE 7.4**

Three Pillars of Diversity

Diverse Work Force

Organizational commitment

Employment practices

Training and development

**TABLE 7.3**

**The High Cost of Discrimination and Harassment**

| Company | Award | Complaint |
|---------|-------|-----------|
| Coca-Cola Company | $192.5 million | Race discrimination class action lawsuit involving approximately 2,000 current and former employees. |
| Merrill Lynch | $5.6 million | Sexual discrimination lawsuit initiated by eight women employees. |
| Smith Barney | $40 million | Sexual harassment and discrimination lawsuit by thousands of women employees. |
| Kmart Corporation | $7.5 million | Age discrimination lawsuit involving 80 former store managers. |
| Texaco | $175 million | Racial discrimination lawsuit filed by African American employees. |
| Denny's | $54.4 million | Two class action lawsuits brought by black customers who were refused seating and service. |
| Adams Mark Hotels | $8 million | Racial discrimination suit by the Justice Department (Florida) and black guests at a college reunion. |
| American General Corporation | $215 million | Civil lawsuit alleging that African Americans were charged higher premiums. |
| First Union Corporation | $58.5 million | Age discrimination suit by former employees. |

*Sources:* Betsy McKay, "Coke Settles Bias Suit for $192.5 Million," *Wall Street Journal*, November 17, 2000, p. A3; Patrick McGeehan, "Merrill Lynch Settles Sex-Bias Lawsuit, Creating a System to Resolve Complaints," *Wall Street Journal*, May 6, 1998, p. B7; "Settlement of $7.5 Million Reached in Age-Bias Case," *Wall Street Journal*, September 23, 1997, p. B15; Kenneth Labich, "No More Crude at Texaco," *Fortune*, September 6, 1999, p. 205; Theodore Kinni, "Book Reviews," *Training*, August 2000, pp. 74–76 (includes a review of *The Denny's Story*, published by John Wiley & Sons); "Race-Discrimination Suits Cost Hotel Chain $8 Million," *Wall Street Journal*, March 22, 2000, p. B9; Greg Jaffe and Rochelle Sharpe, "First Union to Pay $58.5 Million to Settle Age-Discrimination Suit by Ex-Workers," *Wall Street Journal*, October 23, 1997, p. B4; Scot J. Paltrow, "Insurer to Settle Race Suit," *Wall Street Journal*, June 22, 2000, p. C1; Tom Lowry, "Judge Approves Smith Barney Bias Settlement," *USA Today*, July 27, 1998, p. 5B.

**Organizational Commitment**   Do diversity programs make a difference? Companies that see diversity programs as an *event*—a one-day workshop that promotes the advantages of a diverse work force—are very likely to answer no to this question. In fact, some of these quick-fix programs create greater, not less, divisiveness among workers. Companies that see diversity programs as a *process* are more likely to answer this question in the affirmative.

Denny's Inc., a large restaurant chain that had a reputation for racism, is an example of a company that has taken a comprehensive, long-term approach to making amends. After paying more than $54 million to settle two civil rights class action suits, the company vowed to change its culture. It established long-term hiring and purchasing goals, developed nondiscriminatory training programs, created a program to increase the number of minority-owned franchises,

Denny's has established a number of diversity initiatives in recent years. The company vowed to change its culture after paying more than $54 million to settle two civil rights class action suits.

and made it clear that evidence of bigotry toward customers or employees would result in immediate termination.[30] Subsequently, Denny's parent company, Advantica, has been in the top ten of *Fortune* magazine's list of "50 Best Companies for Asians, Blacks, and Hispanics" for two consecutive years.[31]

The quest for diversity is difficult, and some companies struggle for years without achieving success in this area. Publicly, Coca-Cola Company has been a strong backer of civil rights, but it is not a model for diversity in corporate America. Former black employees recently sued the company, alleging vast discrepancies in pay, promotions, and performance evaluations. Reporting on the lawsuit, *Business Week* said, "The cola giant needs a cultural overhaul. Just as Texaco needed to scrub its 'oil rig' culture clean of racism, Coke needs to scrap the insular environment that ex-employees say is dominated by good ol' boys. . . ."[32]

### Employment Practices

To achieve work force diversity, organizations need to seek out a broad variety of workers, including people of different ethnicity, family situations, and sexual orientation. Diversity should not be limited to race and gender. The starting point is active recruitment of people who are underrepresented in the work force. One approach is to recruit in places where minorities attend school or work.

**FIGURE 7.5**

Declaration of
Tolerance

*Source:* Excerpted, with
permission, from *Teaching Tolerance.* Copyright
© 2000, Southern Poverty
Law Center, Montgomery,
AL. *101 Tools for
Tolerance* is available
free from the SPLC. For
more information, visit
www.splcenter.org or
send a fax to (334)
264-7310.

*DECLARATION OF TOLERANCE*

*Tolerance is a personal decision that comes from a belief
that every person is a treasure. I believe that America's
diversity is its strength. I also recognize that ignorance,
insensitivity, and bigotry can turn that diversity
into a source of prejudice and discrimination.*

*To help keep diversity a well-spring of strength and make
this country a better place for all, I pledge to have respect
for people whose abilities, beliefs, cultures, race, sexual
identity or other characteristics are different from my own.*

*To fulfill this pledge, I will . . .*
- *examine my own biases and work to overcome them,*
- *set a positive example for my family and friends,*
- *work for tolerance in my own community, and*
- *speak out against hate and injustice.*

_____

*Signature*

Please sign and mail a copy to:
National Campaign for Tolerance,
400 Washington Avenue
Montgomery, AL 36104.

**To achieve work force diversity, organizations need to seek out a broad variety of workers, including people of different ethnicity, family situations, and sexual orientation. Diversity should not be limited to race and gender.**

Some companies form partnerships with schools and colleges that have great diversity in the student body. Merrill Lynch & Co., Inc., for example, helps high schools in multiracial New Jersey prepare students for careers in the financial services area by teaching them to use personal computers and industry-specific software programs. Other companies sponsor professors' research, provide employees as guest lecturers, award scholarships, and hire students for summer jobs. These activities give company recruiters an opportunity to learn more about the specific details of the college's academic programs as well as the qualifications of individual graduates.[33]

**Training and Development**   To develop a culture that values and enhances diversity, organizations need training programs that give managers and employees the tools they need to work more effectively with one another regardless of their diverse backgrounds. These programs should also reduce an organization's liability for discrimination.[34]

Dallas-based Texas Instruments is often cited as a company that has distinguished itself through effective diversity training initiatives. It has been named to

"GENTLEMEN, THERE'S BEEN SOME CRITICISM FROM SOME QUARTERS ABOUT THE SUPPOSED LACK OF DIVERSITY IN THE TOP RANKS OF THIS COMPANY."

the honor roll of *Hispanic Magazine*'s "100 Best Companies for Hispanics" and *Black Professional* magazine's "200 Great Places to Work." The starting point is a one-day seminar to learn to value diversity and uncover unconscious behavioral patterns that could impede the progress of women and minority employees. Senior managers attend a two-day session. Follow-up courses focus on ways to foster inclusiveness at Texas Instruments and respect for the individual.[35]

Many other companies have adopted the approach used at Texas Instruments. Done well, diversity training programs can promote harmony and reduce conflict. We cannot stop people from bringing prejudices to work, but we can explain that they must learn to act as though they have none.[36]

## Affirmative Action: Yesterday and Today

Does affirmative action right the wrongs of the past or create new ones? This issue is being debated by some of America's best thinkers, and we are hearing strong arguments for and against this controversial program. **Affirmative action** can be defined as a program that encourages the hiring and promotion of members of groups that have been discriminated against in the past. Affirmative action, in all of its various forms, amounts to a major effort to make up for past wrongs.[37]

## HUMAN RELATIONS *in* ACTION

### Tools for Tolerance: Community

- Frequent minority-owned businesses and get to know the proprietors.
- Start a language bank of volunteer interpreters for all foreign languages used in your community.
- Host a "multicultural extravaganza" such as a food fair or an art, fashion, and talent show.
- Conduct a "diaper equity" survey of local establishments. Commend managers who provide

changing tables in men's as well as women's restrooms.
- Bring people of diverse faiths together for retreats, workshops, or potluck dinners. Be welcoming to agnostics and atheists, too.
- Participate in a blood drive or clean up a local stream. Identify issues that reach across racial, ethnic, and other divisions and forge alliances for tackling them.

The Civil Rights Act of 1964, subsequent amendments, and related laws provide employment protection for women, minorities, and other categories of disadvantaged individuals. Affirmative action programs have attacked employment discrimination with four methods:[38]

1. Active recruitment of women and minorities

2. Elimination of prejudicial questions on employment application forms

3. Establishment of specific goals and timetables for minority hiring

4. Validation of employment testing procedures

Affirmative action was originally designed to level the playing field of employment by outlawing discrimination in hiring. Many years ago "Whites only" was a common hiring standard, and you could find a "Help Wanted, Female" section in your daily newspaper.[39] There is no doubt that antidiscrimination legislation was needed. Affirmative action allowed a tremendous influx of diverse individuals through the front door of thousands of schools and organizations. Many were able to work their way into advanced, top-level positions. At the same time, however, affirmative action reinforced the historical view that the members of protected groups are not qualified for various positions and therefore need assistance just to get a job.

### ■ *Rethinking Affirmative Action*

Many people say it is time to rethink affirmative action or even eliminate it. Recent political and legal interpretations of affirmative action have stimulated a nationwide debate over the merits of any program that grants preferential treatment to specific groups. Terry Eastland, author of *Ending Affirmative Action—The*

*Case for Color Blind Justice,* has outlined some of the most common arguments voiced by those who want to end preferential policies:[40]

- *Preferences are discriminatory.* They tend to discriminate against those who are not members of the "right" race or gender.

- *Preferences do not counter discrimination.* Efforts by a company or a government to police presumed discrimination tend to move the focus away from real instances of discrimination that should be at the heart of law enforcement efforts.

- *Preferences do not make sense, given changing demographics.* The population eligible for affirmative action continues to grow several times faster than the nonpreferred population.

Secretary of State Colin Powell, a distinguished African American military leader and statesman, takes a more moderate position on affirmative action. He says, "If affirmative action means programs that provide equal opportunity, then I am all for it. If it leads to preferential treatment or helps those who no longer need help, I am opposed."[41] Barbara Bergmann, professor at American University and author of *In Defense of Affirmative Action,* presents the view that affirmative action is the only practical way to rectify discrimination in hiring. She states that many companies and government agencies will not embrace fairness in hiring and promotion as long as guidelines are voluntary.[42] Arthur A. Fletcher, considered by many the father of affirmative action, believes that a great deal of progress has been made but that achieving diversity in the workplace will take many more years. He says that hiring women and minorities can be done without compromising work performance. His views have been supported by recent research findings.[43]

The debate about affirmative action will continue for many years. The concept and the means for implementing it have been challenged in court repeatedly in recent years. We can anticipate a move to focus preferences on class or socioeconomic factors rather than race or gender. And we can anticipate that voluntary efforts to establish a diverse work force are likely to continue because they can influence profits. As one author noted, "Appreciating diversity isn't just a nice idea, it's a business imperative."[44] Companies that ignore diversity will struggle to survive in the global market place during the 21st century.

## Summary

Work force diversity has become an important issue for organizations that want to remain competitive in a global economy. These organizations are beginning to move away from focusing on prejudice and discrimination and toward valuing diversity. Two dimensions, or sets of characteristics, are the basis of every individual's diversity. Primary dimensions include gender, age, race, physical and mental abilities, and sexual orientation. Secondary dimensions include health habits, religious beliefs, ethnic customs, communication style, relationship status, income, general appearance, and education and training.

Prejudice and discrimination are major barriers to effective human relations. Prejudice is an attitude based partly on observation of others' differences and partly on ignorance, fear, and cultural conditioning. Prejudiced people tend to see others as stereotypes rather than as unique individuals. Prejudicial attitudes are formed through the effects of childhood experiences, ethnocentrism, and economic factors. Discrimination is behavior based on prejudicial attitudes. Groups protected by law from discrimination in the workplace include women, people of color, older and younger workers, and those who have disabilities. Subtler forms of discrimination include discrimination arising from personal appearance, marital status, and so on. These subtle forms of discrimination are often difficult to prove but may be offset through assertiveness, a change in the behavior that causes the discrimination, or a move to a more tolerant organization.

The issue of valuing diversity is an economic one for most organizations. The changing demographics of American society mean that the work force will soon be made up of a minority of white men and a majority of women, people of color, and immigrants. Companies cannot afford to ignore this change in the pool of human resources.

Individuals can enhance diversity by letting go of their stereotypes and learning to critically and honestly evaluate their prejudiced attitudes as they work and socialize with people who are different. They will need to develop a sensitivity to differences and develop their personal diversity awareness programs. Organizations must develop a culture that respects and enhances diversity. Their diversity training programs should become an internal process rather than an event. They need to seek out, employ, and develop people from diverse backgrounds.

Affirmative action guidelines have helped bring fairness in hiring and promotion to many organizations. Today, however, some people believe these guidelines are discriminatory because they allow preferential treatment for the people they were designed to protect. These preferences may no longer make sense, critics say, given the changing demographics of today's work force.

## Career Corner

**Q:** I receive phone calls at work from customers located all over the world. Most of them speak English, but because of their accents, I often have difficulty understanding what they are trying to say to me. How can I handle these calls more effectively?

**A:** The fact that your customers can speak two languages indicates that they are probably educated and intelligent, so treat them with respect. Statements like "I can't understand you," or "What did you say?" are rude and should be avoided. Instead, take personal responsibility for improving the communications and gently say, "I am having a little difficulty understanding you, but if you will be patient with me I am sure I will be able to help." Ask them to slow down so that you can hear all the information correctly. Listen for key words and repeat them back to the caller. Identify coworkers who are fluent in a particular language, and ask them to help when calls come in from customers who share the same ethnic identity. Remember, people with foreign accents are not necessarily hard of hearing, so don't shout.

## Key Terms

diversity
primary dimensions
secondary dimensions
prejudice
stereotypes

ethnocentrism
ethnic identity
discrimination
valuing diversity
affirmative action

## Review Questions

1. Distinguish between the primary and secondary dimensions of diversity, and give examples of each.
2. Why should organizations be concerned about valuing diversity?
3. How do the changing demographics of American culture affect the human resources pool of the future? Be specific.
4. Define *prejudice* and *discrimination*. How do these two terms differ in meaning?
5. What are some of the ways in which people acquire prejudices?
6. In what ways might valuing diversity impact an organization economically?
7. How can subtle forms of discrimination hurt the victim's chances to succeed in his or her career?
8. What role does affirmative action play in today's organizations? What are some of the positive and negative outcomes of affirmative action?
9. How can organizations enhance work force diversity?
10. What flaws in diversity training programs can cause a negative backlash among participants?

## Application Exercises

1. Select a professional journal, the want ads from a local or national paper, or any magazine publication. Examine the ads, articles, and pictures for evidence that the publishers and advertisers are attempting to attract and respect readers from diverse races and cultures. For example, which racial or ethnic groups are pictured in expensive cars, offices, or homes? If your chosen career is traditionally dominated by one gender, do articles in your professional journals include references to both sexes?
2. For one week, keep a diary that records every instance in which you see actions or hear comments that reflect outmoded, negative stereotypes. For instance, watch a movie, and observe whether the villains are all of a particular race or ethnic group. As you read textbooks from other courses you are

taking, notice whether the pictures and examples reflect any stereotypes. Listen to your friends' conversations, and notice any time they make unfair judgments about others based on stereotypes. Finally, reflect on your own attitudes and perceptions. Do you engage in stereotyping?

Share your experiences with class members, and discuss what steps you can take to help rid the environment of negative stereotyping.

3. John Hope Franklin, professor of history at Duke University, was selected to lead former President Clinton's advisory board on race. In an interview conducted shortly after he accepted the assignment, he noted that there are constant reminders of the deep racial divide that exists in America and that cannot easily be bridged unless people from different ethnic or racial groups begin to establish a dialogue.

Meet with someone who is a member of a racial or ethnic group different from your own, and attempt to build a relationship by discussing the things that are important to each of you. As you get to know this person, become aware of his or her beliefs and attitudes. Try not to be diverted by accent, grammar, or personal appearance; rather, really listen to the person's thoughts and ideas. Search for things you and your new acquaintance have in common, and do not dwell on your differences.

## Internet Exercise

Religious beliefs represent an important secondary dimension of diversity. Unfortunately, some people do not have very much tolerance for religious beliefs and practices that differ from their own. A 19-year-old woman living in Denver showed up for work at Domino's Pizza wearing a hijab, the traditional Muslim head scarf. The manager told her to remove the scarf or leave. She had recently converted to Islam and was not sure if the manager was being rude or intolerant of her religion. Later, company officials discovered that the manager's order was a violation of Title VII of the Civil Rights Act of 1964. The employee was then told she could wear a scarf as long as it was red and blue, the company colors.[45] Using the search engine of your choice, search for the keywords "Anti-Defamation League"; then click on either Law or Latest News to discover any new developments in regard to discrimination based on religious beliefs and customs. Also, www.diversityhotwire.com may offer additional information that will give you a greater understanding of this volatile issue.

## Self-Assessment Exercise

For each of the following statements, circle the number from 1 to 5 that best represents your response: (1) strongly disagree (never do this); (2) disagree (rarely do this); (3) moderately agree (sometimes do this); (4) agree (frequently do this); (5) strongly agree (almost always do this).

A. I refuse to perpetuate negative stereotypes, and I accept each person as a unique individual worthy of my respect.  1  2  3  4  5

B. I make every effort to identify my own prejudiced attitudes and avoid stereotypical attitudes toward people of color, older people, persons with disabilities, and others who are different from me.  1  2  3  4  5

C. I work hard to combat prejudice because it has a negative impact on my self-esteem and the self-esteem of the victim.  1  2  3  4  5

D. When I witness discriminatory behavior, I speak up and/or take action to defend the victim.  1  2  3  4  5

E. I understand the economics of valuing diversity and support my employer's efforts to hire and retain minority employees.  1  2  3  4  5

Select an appropriate attitude or a skill you would like to improve. Write your goal in the space provided, and describe the steps you will take to achieve this goal.

GOAL: _____

_____

_____

_____

**Case Problem**    *Denny's Racial Bias = $54.4 Million*

Denny's, the $1.7 billion restaurant chain, has been fighting racial discrimination charges since the early 1990s. Court documents record a host of charges, including refusing to serve nonwhites, forcing African American customers to prepay for their meals, temporary closings of restaurants with mostly African American customers, unfair hiring and treatment of nonwhite employees, and blocking nonwhite employees from franchise opportunities and management positions.

One lawsuit was filed when six African American Secret Service officers, who had allegedly been snubbed by service personnel at a Denny's in Annapolis, Maryland, claimed Denny's "service lapse" had been "racially motivated." Another lawsuit, filed in San Jose, California, alleged that thirty-two black customers were ordered to prepay for meals or pay a cover charge though white customers had no such requirement. Denny's parent company agreed to pay

$54.4 million to settle two class action suits. In addition, the landmark deal committed the organization to NAACP hiring and purchasing goals.

Since then, Denny's has made major progress. Eight of the twelve all-white top executives have left the company, almost half of its franchisees are people of color, and roughly 20 percent of its vendors are minority suppliers. Immediately following the settlement, management sent a clear warning throughout the organization: "If you discriminate, you're history." The same day that another discrimination suit was filed by a group of Asian American students in Syracuse, New York, all management, staff, and security personnel at the allegedly offending Denny's location were fired. (Denny's has since been exonerated of the Syracuse charges.) Denny's parent company, Advantica, now spends several million dollars annually on compliance with the courts' rulings and employee training, having discovered that a company cannot simply mandate firing racist employees or those who refuse to comply with the rules. Advantica's ongoing diversity training program is designed to help employees at all levels understand the difficulties and ambiguities inherent in racial conflicts. *Fortune* magazine now lists Advantica as one of the top ten best employers for minorities in the United States, and it has become a model for other organizations struggling with this sensitive issue.[46]

### Questions

1. Beyond the $54.4 million fines, what other losses might Denny's experience as a result of the charges of discriminatory behaviors?
2. Do you believe that top management officials in the Denny's organization were responsible for creating a climate that encouraged restaurant managers to engage in racially biased activities? Why?
3. How would you respond if your manager asked you to blatantly discriminate against a minority?

# 8

# Resolving Conflict and Achieving Emotional Balance

## CHAPTER PREVIEW

After studying this chapter you will be able to

- List and describe some of the major causes of conflict between people in the work setting.

- Explain the three ways to approach conflict resolution.

- Understand the role that assertiveness and cooperation play in conflict resolution.

- Identify the five steps of the conflict resolution process.

- Describe how emotions influence our thinking and behavior.

- Understand the factors that help us achieve emotional balance.

- List and describe the major factors that influence our emotional development.

- Learn how to deal with your anger and the anger of others.

- Describe strategies for achieving emotional control.

As director of team development at Damark, Mark Johansson thinks a more appropriate job title would be manager of relationships. He helps executives, middle managers, and employees sort out their individual conflicts with specific coworkers. "People conflicts at work are inevitable, but when people are angry at each other for hours or days, decisions don't get made and work doesn't get done." It is like "helping people take pebbles out of their shoes. A pebble won't disable you, but it hurts and slows your gait. Once you remove it, there's a lot of relief."[1] Unfortunately, Johansson's position at Damark is unique. Most organizations rely on the employees themselves to resolve day-to-day conflicts. The fast pace of today's work environment offers too little time for management personnel to stop and resolve the conflicts that may wound your ego or hurt your feelings. Conflict resolution has become a necessary human relations skill for workers and managers alike.

A key element of conflict resolution is emotional balance. This is achieved, in part, by learning to deal with your anger and the anger of others. The factors that contribute to emotional balance will be discussed later in this chapter.

## A New View of Conflict

Most standard dictionaries define **conflict** as a clash between incompatible people, ideas, or interests. These conflicts are almost always perceived as negative experiences in our society. But when we view conflict as a negative experience, we may be hurting our chances of dealing with it effectively. Many books and articles imply that we must do everything in our power to eliminate the conflicts in our lives. In reality, conflicts can serve as opportunities for personal growth if we develop and use positive, constructive conflict resolution skills.[2]

Much of our growth and social progress comes from the opportunities we have to discover creative solutions to conflicts that surface in our lives. Dudley Weeks, professor of conflict resolution at American University, says conflict can provide additional ways of thinking about the *source* of conflict and open up possibilities for improving a relationship.[3] When people work together to resolve conflicts, their solutions are often far more creative than they would be if only one person addressed the problem. Creatively managed conflict can shake people

---

**TOTAL PERSON INSIGHT**

*CHERYL SHAVERS*

Senior Manager, Intel Corporation

*"Companies pay a high price for conflict. Productivity drops, work relationships suffer and energy is wasted, as workers become increasingly angry, stressed and defensive."*

out of their mental ruts and give them a new point of view. The heart of effective human relations lies not in trying to eliminate conflict (an impossible task) but in making constructive use of the energy released by conflict.

## ◼ *The Cost of Conflict*

The amount of time and money invested in conflict resolution is surprisingly high. It is estimated that management personnel spend about 20 percent of their time resolving disputes among staff members.[4] Most managers have learned that when they address the source of a conflict rather than suppress it, lines of communication open and people begin talking *to* each other rather than *about* each other. This open communication helps workers feel that their opinion is valued and that they are a part of the team.

In some cases, the revenue loss due to unresolved conflict can be extremely high. General Motors gave up $2 billion in lost production from two strikes that crippled its output across North America for more than seven weeks.[5] American Airlines said the cost of its latest labor conflict—a pilot sickout over wage issues that scrubbed hundreds of flights—was $150 million.[6] In addition to dealing with this loss of revenue, GM and American had to find ways to rebuild employees' and customers' trust and loyalty after the conflicts were ended.

 HUMAN RELATIONS *in* ACTION

### Look Beyond the Résumé

A management recruiter with a placement firm received a résumé showing that the job candidate had broad knowledge about the position that was open. The applicant had even won two prestigious awards from previous employers for work showing thoughtfulness, diligence, and daring. He looked perfect for the job—on paper. During a private two-hour interview with the recruiter, however, the candidate failed to make eye contact and said nothing positive about anyone he had worked with or for in the past. He made comments such as "I like to work things out on my own" and "I don't like to be second-guessed by superiors."

His references spoke highly of his intelligence but said he was a loner who not only disliked collaborating with colleagues but resented direction and feedback of any kind from anyone. One former boss described him as "arrogant and stubborn." Since the organization that hired the recruiter expected considerable teamwork among its staff members, the applicant was not hired.

One of the recruiter's colleagues, however, did sponsor the candidate for another position. She convinced that client's management personnel that they could train him to work effectively with others, yet the candidate quit 6 months later. Though he may look good on paper, it is obvious that he is difficult to get along with and is likely to fail in a work setting where collaboration is important.

## *Finding the Root of the Conflict*

### ■ *The Root of a Conflict*

If left unattended, weeds can take over a garden and choke all the healthy plants. When inexperienced gardeners cut weeds off at the surface instead of digging down to find the roots, the weeds tend to come back twice as strong. Conflicts among people at work often follow the same pattern. Those attempting to keep peace in the workplace try to fix the immediate problem by asking those involved in the conflict to "get over it" or shake hands and move on with the business at hand. Yet unless the root of the conflict is addressed, the conflict is likely to recur with a vengeance. As a result, just like the garden choked by weeds, productivity within the organization suffers. This segment of the chapter discusses the most common causes of conflicts in the workplace.

**Ineffective Communication**   A major source of personal conflict is the misunderstanding that results from ineffective communication. In Chapter 2 we discussed the various filters that messages must pass through before effective communication can occur. In the work setting, where many different people work closely together, communication breakdowns are inevitable.

> **Unless the root of the conflict is addressed, the conflict is likely to come back with a vengeance. As a result, just like the garden choked by weeds, productivity within the organization suffers.**

Often it is necessary to determine if the conflict is due to a misunderstanding or a true disagreement. If the cause is a *misunderstanding*, you may need to explain your position again or provide more details or examples to help the other person understand. If a *disagreement* exists, one or both parties have to be persuaded to change their position on the issue. Those involved in the conflict can attempt to explain their position over and over again, but until someone changes, the root problem will persist.[7] This issue is discussed in greater detail later in this chapter.

**Value Clashes**   In Chapter 4 you read that differences in values can cause conflicts between generations, among men and women, and among people with different value priorities. Consider the conflicts that might arise between "loyalists," who join their organization for life and make decisions for their own good as well as the good of the company, and "job-hoppers," who accept a job in order to position themselves for the next opportunity that might further their personal career advancement. The opportunities for value clashes are almost limitless in today's diverse organizations.

**Culture Clashes**   For generations, culture clashes have occurred between workers not only from other countries but also from different parts of the United States. Today's diverse work force reflects a kaleidoscope of cultures, each with its own unique qualities. The individual bearers of these different cultural traditions could easily come into conflict with one another. The issues may be as simple as

When Eileen Gittins, CEO of Personify, purchased Anubis Solutions, she anticipated that it would take time for employees of both companies to adjust to each other's styles. Gittins and her new partners Adeeb Shana and Amit Desai selected several workers to serve as "cultural ambassadors" who helped employees from both companies get acquainted.

one person's desire to dress in ethnic fashion and a supervisor's insistence on strict adherence to the company dress code, or as complex as work ethics. When a colleague's culturally based customs conflict with yours, perhaps the Golden Rule— Do unto others as you would have them do unto you—should be your guiding light. Respect the other person's right to follow his or her customs (as long as they do not endanger the workplace); expect others to respect your customs as well.

**Work Policies and Practices**    Interpersonal conflicts can develop when an organization has arbitrary or confusing rules, regulations, and performance standards. Many organizations are experimenting with nontraditional workweek rules and regulations. For example, management at Boeing wants the freedom to assign workers to schedules that could cover any of the seven days of the week. At Verizon Communications Inc., about 90,000 employees walked off their jobs to demonstrate their frustration with 10–15 hours of forced overtime a week. Workers at Boeing and Verizon resent the new rules, which leave little time for personal or family life. In fact, policies involving employees with children and those who are child-free are becoming a hot issue in some organizations. Many firms cover day-care expenses and allow flexible work schedules to accommodate parents who need to be home when their children arrive from school. These same companies often ask child-free workers to pick up the slack when other employees need family time.[8]

**Adversarial Management**    Under adversarial management, supervisors may view their employees and even other managers with suspicion and distrust and treat them as "the enemy." Employees usually lack respect for adversarial managers, resenting their authoritarian style and resisting their suggestions for change. This atmosphere makes cooperation and teamwork difficult. Supervisors who display genuine concern for both people and production and are sensitive to employee needs have far fewer conflicts than do adversarial managers. Because of this, most organizations are encouraging a leadership style that encourages openness and mutual respect.

**Noncompliance**    Conflict also surfaces when some workers refuse to comply with the rules and neglect their fair share of the workload. Coworkers get angry if they have to put forth extra effort to get the work done because others are taking two-hour lunch breaks, sleeping on the job, making personal phone calls during office hours, and wasting time. Now that so many organizations are organizing their work forces into teams, noncompliance has the potential for becoming a major source of conflict. The good news is that noncompliance is probably one of the easiest types of conflict to resolve. All employees—not just the supervisors—need to develop effective assertiveness skills so that they feel comfortable confronting the errant workers and asking for compliance.

### ■ *Responding Assertively*

Many times, coworkers, supervisors, and managers say or do something that irritates you. They get on your nerves. They may be model employees who do their job and meet their deadlines, so management fails to notice the frustration they create. Your challenge is to deal professionally with these personal irritations before they overwhelm you and negatively affect *your* job performance. Disruptive or uncooperative coworkers can be disabling to you and very time-consuming. Many professionals advise going directly to the offending person and calmly discussing his or her irritating behavior, rather than complaining to others.[9] Figure 8.1,

## HUMAN RELATIONS *in* ACTION

### Fire the Client?

Lisa Zwick knew her client, the CEO of an Internet start-up company, was a problem. He was irritable and extremely hard to work with. When he called her California home at 5:00 A.M. one Monday morning from his New York City hotel room and asked her to order a limousine for him, she refused and took the issue to her boss. With his support, Lisa fired the client, telling him, "This isn't working out for several reasons; but most of all, you're a jerk!" Many firms are concluding that firing cantan-

kerous clients can be a good business decision. One company fired a client who was bringing in $1 million a year, or 20 percent of the company's revenue, for making nasty, digging comments about employees. The owner of the company believed that if the irritating client was going to drive her employees crazy, the relationship wasn't worth it. Her respected employees replaced the lost business and have since doubled revenue to $10 million.

**The Tanks:**

Pushy and ruthless, loud and forceful, they assume that the end justifies the means.

**Strategy:** When under attack, hold your position, make direct eye contact, focus on breathing slowly and deeply. When they finish, say, "When you're ready to speak to me with respect, I'll be ready to discuss this matter."

**The Snipers:**

They identify your weaknesses and use them against you through sabotage behind your back or putdowns in front of the crowd.

**Strategy:** Stop in midsentence and focus your full attention on them. Ask them to clarify a grievance. If it is valid, take action; if invalid, express your appreciation and calmly offer new information.

**The Know-It-Alls:**

They will tell you what they know—for hours at a time—but they won't take a second to listen to your "clearly inferior" ideas.

**Strategy:** Acknowledge their expertise and be prepared with your facts. Use plural pronouns (*we, us*). Present your information as probing questions rather than statements so that you appear less threatening and willing to learn.

**The Think-They-Know-It-Alls:**

They don't know much, but they don't let that get in the way. They exaggerate, brag, mislead, and distract.

**Strategy:** Acknowledge their input, but question their facts with "I" statements, such as "From what I've read and experienced. . . ."

**The Grenades:**

When they blow their tops, they are unable to stop. When the smokes clear and the dust settles, the cycle begins again.

**Strategy:** When their explosion begins, assertively repeat the individual's name to get his/her attention. Calmly address their first few sentences, usually the real problem. Suggest taking time out to cool down, then listen to their problem.

**The Yes Persons:**

They are quick to agree but slow to deliver, leaving a trail of unkept commitments and broken promises.

**Strategy:** When they say yes, ask them to summarize their commitment and write it down. Arrange a deadline and describe the consequences that will result if they do not follow through.

**The Maybe Persons:**

When faced with a crucial decision, they keep putting it off until it's too late and the decision makes itself.

**Strategy:** List advantages and disadvantages of the decision or option. Help them feel comfortable and safe, and stay in touch until the decision is implemented.

**The Whiners:**

They wallow in their woe, whine incessantly, and carry the weight of the world on their shoulders.

**Strategy:** Listen and write down their main points. Interrupt and get specifics; identify and focus on possible solutions. If they remain in "It's hopeless" mode, walk away saying,"Let me know when you want to talk about a solution."

"Dealing with People You Can't Stand," offers specific strategies you might use. Keep in mind that some people are unaware of the impact of their behavior and if you draw their attention to it, will change it.

Whereas these strategies may be comfortable for some people, such a direct approach may be very uncomfortable for many others. This is the time to reinforce your assertiveness skills. Assertiveness is based on rights. **Assertive behavior** involves standing up for your rights and expressing your thoughts and feelings in a direct, appropriate way that does not violate the rights of others. It is a matter of getting the other person to understand your viewpoint.[10] People who exhibit assertive behavior skills are able to handle their conflicts with greater ease and assurance while maintaining good interpersonal relations. Use assertive behaviors when you sense someone is taking advantage of you, ignoring your needs, or disregarding your point of view.

Some people do not understand the distinction between being aggressive and being assertive. **Aggressive behavior** involves expressing your thoughts and feelings and defending your rights in a way that violates the rights of others. Aggressive people may interrupt, talk fast, ignore others, and use sarcasm or other forms of verbal abuse to maintain control. They do not view conflict resolution as a strategy for improving relationships. Aggressive behavior, of course, may bring out the worst in those on the receiving end. The receivers are likely to behave defensively, which just escalates the conflict.

People who attempt to avoid conflict by simply ignoring things that bother them are exhibiting **nonassertive behavior.** Nonassertive people often give in to the demands of others, and their passive approach makes them less likely to make their needs known. If you fail to take a firm position when such action is appropriate, colleagues may take advantage of you, and management may question your ability to lead.[11] Table 8.1 may give you a clearer understanding of how assertive, aggressive, and nonassertive individuals respond when confronted with conflict situations.

### How to Become More Assertive

If you are aggressive, nonassertive, or less assertive than you would like to be in certain situations, do not be discouraged. With practice, you can acquire the sense of well-being that comes with knowing that you can communicate your wants, dislikes, and feelings in a clear, direct manner without threatening or attacking others. Entire books are written describing assertiveness skills, so it is impossible to explain the various techniques within the context of this one chapter. Nevertheless, we can offer you practical guidelines that may help you develop assertiveness skills.

**In the beginning, take small steps.**　Being assertive may be difficult at first, so start with something that is easy. You might decline the invitation to keep the minutes at the weekly staff meeting if you feel others should assume this duty from time to time. If you are tired of eating lunch at Joe's Diner (the choice

**TABLE 8.1**

**Behaviors Exhibited by Assertive, Aggressive, and Nonassertive Persons**

| | *Assertive Person* | *Aggressive Person* | *Nonassertive Person* |
|---|---|---|---|
| *In conflict situations* | Communicates directly | Dominates | Avoids the conflict |
| *In decision-making situations* | Chooses for self | Chooses for self and others | Allows others to choose |
| *In situations expressing feelings* | Open, direct, honest, while allowing others to express their feelings | Expresses feelings in a threatening manner; puts down, inhibits others | Holds true feelings inside |
| *In group meeting situations* | Direct, clear, "I" statements: "I believe that . . ." | Clear but demeaning "you" statements: "You should have known better . . ." | Indirect, unclear statements: "Would you mind if . . ." |

of a coworker), suggest a restaurant that you would prefer. If someone insists on keeping the temperature at a cool 68 degrees and you are tired of being cold all the time, approach the person and voice your opinion. Asking that your desires be considered is not necessarily a bad thing.[12]

**Use communication skills that enhance assertiveness.** A confident tone of voice, eye contact, firm gestures, and good posture create nonverbal messages that say, "I'm serious about this request." Using "I" messages can be especially helpful in cases where you want to assert yourself in a nonthreatening manner. If you approach the person who wants the thermostat set at 68 degrees and say, "You need to be more considerate of others," the person is likely to become defensive. However, if you say, "I feel uncomfortable when the temperature is so cool," you will start the conversation on a more positive note.

**Be soft on people and hard on the problem.** The goal of conflict resolution is to solve the problem but avoid doing harm to the relationship. Of course, relationships tend to become entangled with the problem, so there is a tendency to treat the people and the problem as one. Your coworker Terry is turning in projects late every week, and you are feeling a great deal of frustration each time it happens. You must communicate to Terry that each missed deadline creates serious problems for you. Practice using tact, diplomacy, and patience as you keep the discussion focused on the problem, not on Terry's personality traits.

---

### THINKING / LEARNING STARTERS

1. Identify some of the causes of conflict in an organization in which you worked as an employee or volunteer. What types of conflict seemed to cause the most trouble among people?

2. Have you ever experienced a conflict with a coworker? Explain. How did you handle the situation? Could you have handled the situation in a more assertive manner? Explain.

---

## Learn to Negotiate Effectively

In baseball, if two runners try to occupy the same base at the same time, there is conflict. It is an exciting situation, but if a positive solution is not found quickly, both they and their team will be losers. We must accept the fact that any time two or more people are brought together, the stage is set for potential conflict. When conflict does occur, the results may be positive or negative, depending on how those involved choose to approach it. One of the most effective ways of handling conflicts with another person, department, or organization is to learn how to negotiate.

### Think Win/Win

There are basically three ways to approach negotiations: win/lose, lose/lose, and win/win. When you use the **win/lose approach**, you are attempting to reach your goals at the expense of the other party's. For example, a manager can say, "Do as I say or find a job somewhere else!" The manager wins; the employee loses. Although this approach may end the conflict on a short-term basis, it doesn't usually address the underlying cause of the problem. It may simply sow the seeds of another conflict because the "losers" may seek revenge. (This strategy may be effective in those rare instances when it is more important to get the job done than it is to maintain good human relations among the work force.)

When the **lose/lose approach** is used to settle a dispute, each side must give in to the other. If the sacrifices are too great, both parties may feel that too much has been given. This strategy can be applied when there is little time to find a solution through effective negotiation techniques, or when negotiations are at a standstill and no progress is being made. Union-management disputes, for example, often fall into the lose/lose trap when neither side is willing to yield. In these cases an arbitrator, a neutral third party, may be called in to impose solutions on the disputing parties.

In general, the win/lose and lose/lose approaches to negotiating create a "we versus they" attitude among the people involved in the conflict, rather than a "we versus the problem" approach. "We versus they" (or "my way versus your way")

In several departments at America Online, workers communicate nonverbally with each other with foam balls and blocks in various colors and shapes. When a colleague needs privacy, a yellow ball might be perched on his or her cubicle wall. If an officemate can be heard being loud and obnoxious on the phone, a red block might be vaulted into his or her cubicle. What might the blue ball mean?

means that participants focus on whose solution is superior, instead of working together to find a solution that is acceptable to all. Each person tends to see the issue from his or her viewpoint only and does not approach the negotiations in terms of reaching the goal.

The basic purpose of the **win/win approach** to negotiating is to fix the problem—not the blame! Don't think hurt; think help. Negotiating a win/win solution to a conflict is not a debate where you are attempting to prove the other side wrong; instead, you are engaging in a dialogue where each side attempts to get the other side to understand its concerns and both sides then work toward a mutually satisfying solution. Your negotiating skills are usually much better when you shift your emphasis from the tactical approach of how to counter your opponent's every comment to the more strategic one of how to solve the problem collaboratively with them.[13]

Perhaps the most vital skill in effective negotiations is listening. Don't demand; listen. When you concentrate on learning common interests, not differences, the nature of the negotiations changes from a battle to win to a discussion of how to meet the objectives of everyone involved in the dispute.

> **Negotiating a win/win solution to a conflict is not a debate where you are attempting to prove the other side wrong; instead, you are engaging in a dialogue where each side attempts to get the other side to understand its concerns and both sides then work toward a mutually satisfying solution.**

## ■ Beware of Defensive Behaviors

Effective negotiations are often slowed or sidetracked completely by defensive behaviors that surface when people are in conflict with each other. When one person in a conflict situation becomes defensive, others may mirror this behavior. In a short time, progress is slowed because people stop listening and begin thinking about how they can defend themselves against the other person's comments.

We often become defensive when we feel our needs are being ignored. That is why improving your assertiveness skills is so important. Our needs form one of the essential foundations of our relationships, and when they are ignored or treated as unimportant, the relationship cannot realize its full potential.[14] If you feel you are trapped on the losing end of a win/lose negotiation and can hear yourself or the other person becoming defensive, do everything in your power to refocus the discussion toward resolving the conflict.

## ■ Negotiating Styles Vary

Depending on personality, assertiveness skills, and past experiences in dealing with conflict in the workplace, individuals naturally develop their own negotiating styles. But negotiating is a skill, and people can learn how and when to adapt their style to deal effectively with conflict situations.

Robert Maddux suggests that there are five different behavioral styles that can be strategically implemented during a conflict situation. These styles are based on the combination of two factors: assertiveness and cooperation (see Figure 8.2). He takes the position that different styles may be appropriate in different situations.

**Avoidance Style (Uncooperative/Nonassertive)**   This style is appropriate when the conflict is too minor or too great to resolve. Any attempt to resolve the conflict might result in damaging a relationship or simply wasting time and energy. Avoidance might take the form of diplomatically sidestepping an issue or postponing your response until a more appropriate time.

**Accommodating Style (Cooperative/Nonassertive)**   This style is appropriate when resolving the conflict is not worth risking damage to the relationship or general disharmony. Individuals who use this approach relinquish their

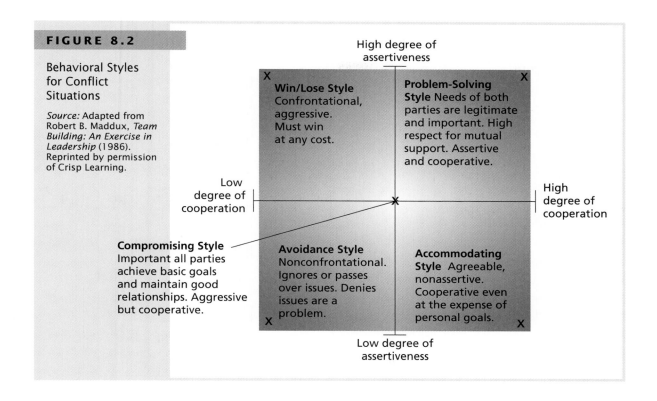

**FIGURE 8.2**

Behavioral Styles
for Conflict
Situations

*Source:* Adapted from
Robert B. Maddux, *Team
Building: An Exercise in
Leadership* (1986).
Reprinted by permission
of Crisp Learning.

own concerns to satisfy the concerns of someone else. Accommodating might take the form of selfless generosity or blind obedience to another's point of view.

**Win/Lose Style (Uncooperative/Aggressive)**    This style may be appropriate when the conflict involves "survival of the fittest," when you must prove your superior position, or when your opinion is the most ethically or professionally correct. This power-oriented position allows you to use whatever means seem appropriate when it is time to stand up for your rights.

**Compromising Style (Moderately Aggressive/Moderately Cooperative)**    This style is appropriate when no one person or idea is perfect, when there is more than one good way to do something, or when you must give to get what you want. Compromise attempts to find mutually acceptable solutions to the conflict that partially satisfy both sides. Never use this style when unethical activities are the cause of the conflict.

**Problem-Solving Style (Assertive/Cooperative)**    This style is appropriate when all parties openly discuss the issues and a mutually beneficial solution can be found without anyone making a major concession. Problem solvers attempt to uncover underlying issues that may be at the root of the problem and then focus the discussion toward achieving the most desirable outcome. They seek to replace conflict with collaboration.

*On Manners by Jerry Marcus*

*"Let me finish! You always say 'You win' before I've won."*

## Conflict Resolution Process

In the past, the responsibility for conflict resolution was often given to supervisors, department heads, team leaders, shop stewards, mediators, and other individuals with established authority and responsibility. Today, the picture is changing as more companies are organizing workers into teams. The trend toward increased worker participation in decision making and problem solving (employee empowerment) is also having an impact on conflict resolution practices. Many progressive organizations want employees to resolve their own conflicts whenever possible. This means that every employee needs to possess conflict resolution skills. The **conflict resolution process** consists of five steps that can be used in both work and family situations.

### THINKING / LEARNING STARTERS

1. Imagine and describe the human relations atmosphere in an organization where win/lose strategies are consistently applied.

2. Briefly describe the most recent conflict you had with another person. How might you have changed your conflict resolution style to better handle the situation?

To apply the five steps requires understanding and acceptance of everything we have discussed up to this point in the chapter: application of assertiveness skills, understanding how to deal with various types of difficult people, and support for the win/win approach to conflict resolution.

### ■ Step One: Decide Whether You Have a Misunderstanding or a True Disagreement

David Stiebel, author of *When Talking Makes Things Worse!*, says a misunderstanding is a failure to accurately understand the other person's point. A disagreement, in contrast, is a failure to agree that would persist despite the most accurate understanding. In a true disagreement, people want more than your explanation and further details; they want to change your mind.[15] When we fail to realize the distinction between these two possibilities, a great deal of time and energy may be wasted. Consider the following conflict situation.

> **A misunderstanding is a failure to accurately understand the other person's point. A disagreement, in contrast, is a failure to agree that would persist despite the most accurate understanding.**

As Sarah entered the driveway of her home, she could hardly wait to share the news with her husband Paul. Late that afternoon she had met with her boss and learned she was the number-one candidate for a newly created supervisory position. Sarah entered the house and immediately told Paul about the promotion opportunity. In a matter of seconds, it became apparent that he was not happy about the promotion. He said, "We don't need the extra money, and you do not need the headaches that come with a supervisory position." Expecting a positive response, Sarah was very disappointed. In the heat of anger, Sarah and Paul both said things they would later regret.

If Sarah and Paul had asked each other a few questions, this conflict might have been avoided. Prior to arriving home, Sarah had already weighed the pros and cons of the new position and decided it was not a good career move; however, she wanted her husband's input before making the final decision. This conflict was not a true disagreement, in which one person tries to change the other person's mind; it was a misunderstanding that was the result of incomplete information. If Sarah and Paul had fully understood each other's position, it would have become clear that a true disagreement did not exist.

### ■ Step Two: Define the Problem and Collect the Facts

The saying "A problem well defined is a problem half solved" is not far from the truth. It is surprising how difficult this step can be. Everyone involved needs to focus on the real cause of the conflict, not on what has happened as a result of it. At this stage, it is helpful to have everyone write a one- or two-sentence definition of the problem. When everyone is allowed to define the problem, the real cause of the conflict will often surface.

As you begin collecting information about the conflict, it may be necessary to separate facts from opinions or perceptions. Ask questions that focus on who is

The not-for-profit American Arbitration Association offers a variety of arbitration and mediation services. AAA clients often seek help in drafting arbitration clauses and arbitration advocacy training.

involved in the conflict, what happened, when, where, and why. What policies and procedures were involved?

Conflict resolution in the age of information offers us new challenges. As we are faced with information overload, we may be tempted to use the information we already have rather than search for the new information needed to guide a decision.[16]

### ■ *Step Three: Clarify Perceptions*

Your perception is your interpretation of the facts surrounding the situations you encounter. Perceptions can have a tremendous influence on your behavior. In a conflict situation, it is therefore very important that you clarify all parties' perceptions of the problem. You can do this by attempting to see the situation as others see it. Take the case of Laura, a sales representative who was repeatedly passed over for a promotion even though her sales numbers were among the best in the department.

Over a period of time Laura became convinced that she was the victim of gender discrimination. She filed charges with the Equal Employment Opportunity Commission (EEOC), and a hearing was scheduled. When Laura's boss was given a chance to explain his actions, he described Laura as someone who was very dedicated to her family. He said, "It's my view that she would be unhappy in a sales management position because she would have to work longer hours and travel more." He did not see his actions as being discriminatory. Laura explained that she valued the time she spent with her husband and children but achieving a management position was an important career goal. Laura's and her boss's perceptions of the same situation were totally different.

### ■ *Step Four: Generate Options for Mutual Gain*

Once the basic problem has been defined, the facts surrounding it have been brought out, and everyone is operating with the same perceptions, everyone involved in the conflict should focus on generating options that will fix the problem. Some people, however, do not consider generating options to be part of the conflict resolution process. Rather than broadening the options for mutual gain, some individuals want to quickly build support for a single solution. The authors of the best-selling book *Getting to Yes* say, "In a dispute, people usually believe that they know the right answer—their view should prevail. They become trapped in their own point of view."[17] This is where brainstorming comes in. **Brainstorming** is a process that encourages all those involved in the conflict to generate a wide variety of ideas and possibilities that will lead to the desired results. No one should be allowed to evaluate, judge, or rule out any proposed solution until all options are on the table.

### ■ *Step Five: Implement Options with Integrity*

The final step in the conflict resolution process involves finalizing an agreement that offers win/win benefits to those in conflict. Sometimes, as the conflict resolution process comes to a conclusion, one or more parties in the conflict may be tempted to win an advantage that weakens the relationship. This might involve hiding information or using pressure tactics that violate the win/win spirit and weaken the relationship. Even the best conflict solutions can fail unless all conflict partners serve as "caretakers" of the agreement and the relationship.[18]

Establish timetables for implementing the solutions, and provide a plan to evaluate their effectiveness. On a regular basis, make it a point to discuss with others how things are going to be sure that old conflict patterns do not resurface. Conflict resolution agreements must be realistic and effective enough to survive as the challenges of the future confront them.[19]

## Achieving Emotional Balance

An **emotion** can be thought of as a feeling, such as jealousy, fear, love, joy, and sorrow, that influences our thinking and behavior. It is not an exaggeration to say that much of the human behavior we observe every day springs from feelings. An emotional experience often alters thought processes by directing attention toward some things and away from others.

Throughout each day our feelings are activated by a variety of events (see Figure 8.3). You might feel a sense of joy after learning that a coworker has just given birth to a new baby. You might feel overpowering grief after learning that your supervisor was killed in an auto accident. Angry feelings may surface when you discover that someone borrowed a tool without your permission. Once your feelings have been activated, your mind interprets the event. In some cases, the feelings trigger irrational thinking: "No one who works here can be trusted!" In other cases, you may engage in a rational thinking process: "Perhaps the person who borrowed the tool needed it to help a customer with an emergency repair." The important point to remember is that we can choose how we behave.

### Achieving Emotional Balance—A Daily Challenge

The need to discover ways to achieve emotional balance has never been greater. To be successful in these complex times, we need to be able to think and feel simultaneously. People make choices dictated primarily by either their heads (reason) or their hearts (feelings). The thinking function helps us see issues logically; the feeling function helps us be caring and human.[20] Many organizations are

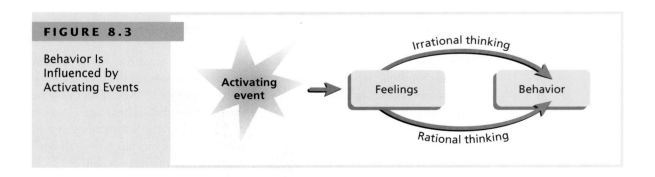

**FIGURE 8.3**

Behavior Is Influenced by Activating Events

spawning fear, confusion, anger, and sadness because the leaders lack emotional balance.

The basic emotions that drive us—such as fear, love, greed, joy, and anger—have scarcely changed over the years. However, we are now seeing enormous differences in the expression of emotions. Today, people are much more likely to engage in aggressive driving, misbehave during commercial airline flights, or become abusive when they are unhappy with service. In the workplace many people experience emotional pain because of disagreeable bosses.

## ■ *Emotional Intelligence*

Daniel Goleman, author of two popular books on emotional intelligence, challenges the traditional view of the relationship between IQ and success. He says there are widespread exceptions to the rule that IQ predicts success: "At best, IQ contributes about 20 percent to the factors that determine life success, which leaves 80 percent to other forces."[21] The focus of Goleman's research are the human characteristics that make up what he describes as *emotional competence.* The emotional competence framework is made up of two dimensions:[22]

**Personal Competence**    This term refers to the competencies that determine how we manage ourselves. Recognizing one's emotions and their effects, keeping disruptive emotions and impulses in check, and maintaining standards of honesty and integrity represent a few of the competencies in this category.

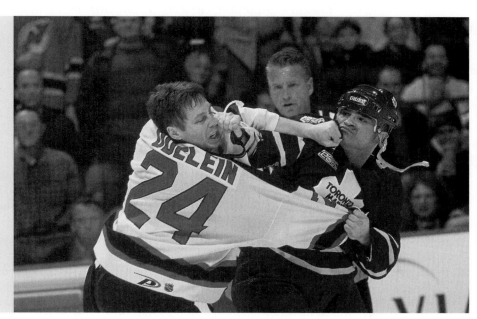

Emotional balance is sometimes missing when athletes compete. Hockey players in particular are known for losing their cool on the ice, as shown in this example between the Toronto Maple Leafs' Tie Domi and the New Jersey Devils' Lyle Odelein.

**Social Competence**    This refers to the competencies that determine how we handle relationships. Sensing others' feelings and perspectives, listening openly and sending convincing messages, and negotiating and resolving disagreements represent some of the competencies in this category.

Although IQ tends to be stable throughout life, emotional competence is learnable and tends to increase throughout our life span. The emotional competencies that really matter for work can be learned.

## ■ *Emotional Expression*

We carry inside us a large array of emotions that have been with us since birth and will be with us until death. However, we sometimes suffer from a lack of emotional balance because we learn to inhibit the expression of certain emotions and to overemphasize the expression of others. Some families, for example, discourage the expression of love and affection. Some people are taught from an early age to avoid expressing anger. Others learn that a public display of grief (crying, for example) is a sign of weakness. If as a child you were strongly encouraged to avoid the expression of anger, fear, love, or some other emotion, you may repress or block these feelings as an adult.[23]

Emotional imbalance also develops if we become fixated on a single emotion. The high incidence of violent crime in America has motivated some people to become almost totally infused with the emotion of fear. One writer noted that people who are preoccupied with fear may be intensifying the problem: "We have a habit of keeping ourselves overwhelmed, through the news media, with bad and scary things that have happened all over the world each day; and then the chronic pattern of worrying about which of these bad things might happen to us in the future."[24] To focus on one emotion to the exclusion of others creates a serious imbalance within us.

  *HUMAN RELATIONS in ACTION*

### Savvy Thinking on Super Bowl Sunday

It was Super Bowl Sunday and the departing flight from New York to Detroit was delayed two hours. Tension among the passengers—mostly businessmen—was increasing. When the plane finally arrived in Detroit, a glitch with the boarding ramp required the plane to stop about a hundred feet from the gate. Frantic passengers, concerned about being late, leaped to their feet. At that point the flight attendant needed to get everyone to sit down so that the plane could finish taxiing to the gate. She could have gone to the intercom and announced in a stern voice, "Federal regulations require that you be seated before we can move to the gate." Instead, she warbled in a singsong tone reminiscent of a playful warning to an adorable child who has done something naughty, "You're staaan-ding!" The passengers laughed and sat back down until the plane reached the gate.

## ■ *The Emotional Factor at Work*

Emotions play a critical role in the success of every organization, yet many people in key decision-making positions—leaders with outstanding technical skills—fail to understand the important role emotions play in a work setting. In part, the problem can be traced to leadership training that emphasizes that "doing business" is a purely rational or logical process. Some leaders learn to value only those things that can be arranged, analyzed, and defined. One consultant put the problem into proper perspective when he said, "We are still trying to do business as if it requires only a meeting of the minds instead of a meeting of the hearts."[25]

In some cases, emotional blindness can be very costly. Helen Barrett, a 57-year-old social work manager and former employee of Yale–New Haven Hospital, was awarded $105,000 by a jury that decided she was fired in a manner that caused emotional distress. Barrett was forced to leave her personal belongings in a plastic bag and was escorted out the door by security guards in full view of coworkers. A supervisor told her she would be arrested for trespassing if she returned. This threat was made even though there had been no indications of disloyalty or criminal wrongdoing.[26]

---

**TOTAL PERSON INSIGHT**

*JAMES C. GEORGES*

Chief Executive Officer,
The Par Group

*"All of our technology is underutilized and will remain so until we put the emotion of doing business onto parity with the logical and rational aspects of performance improvement."*

---

**Relationship Strategy** Emotional undercurrents are present in almost every area of every organization. Most banks, hospitals, retail firms, hotels, and restaurants realize that they need a relationship strategy—a plan for establishing, building, and maintaining quality relationships with customers. This type of plan is essential for success in today's marketplace, which is characterized by vigorous competition, very similar products, and customer loyalty dependent on quality relationships and quality products.[27] Front-line employees, those persons responsible for delivering quality service and building relationships, engage in "emotional labor," and those who have frequent contact with the public often find the work very stressful.[28] *Emotional labor,* which taxes the mind, is often more difficult to handle than physical labor, which strains the body.

> **Emotional labor, which taxes the mind, is often more difficult to handle than physical labor, which strains the body.**

Relationships are no less important in the international arena. James Georges, a consultant with considerable international experience, believes our preoccupation with purely rational processes is a barrier to success in the global marketplace. "Our preoccupation with logic, knowledge, data, facts, rational systems

*THINKING / LEARNING STARTERS*

1. Recall a situation at work or at school where the leadership displayed emotional blindness. What are some of the reasons the important role of emotions was not taken into consideration?

2. Do you agree that emotional undercurrents are present in almost every area of the typical organization? Can you think of any exceptions?

and procedures gets in the way of developing the 'heart skills' we need in order to do business successfully in a highly competitive, global market."[29]

## Factors That Influence Our Emotions

The starting point in achieving greater emotional balance is to determine the source of emotional difficulties. Why do we sometimes display indifference when the expression of compassion would be more appropriate? Why is it so easy to put down a friend or coworker and so hard to recognize that person's accomplishments? Why do we sometimes worry about events that will never happen? To answer these and other questions, it is necessary to study the factors that influence our emotional development.

### ■ Temperament

**Temperament** refers to a person's individual style and frequency of expressing needs and emotions; it is biological and genetically based. It reflects a contribution by nature to the beginning of an individual's personality.[30] Researchers have found that certain temperamental characteristics are apparent in children at birth and remain somewhat stable over time. For example, the traits associated with extroversion and introversion can be observed when a baby is born. Of course, many events take place between infancy and adulthood to alter or shape a person's temperament. Personality at every age reflects the interplay of temperament and of environmental influences, such as parenting.[31]

### ■ Subconscious Influences

The **subconscious mind** is a vast storehouse of forgotten memories, desires, ideas, and frustrations, according to William Menninger, founder of the famed Menninger Foundation.[32] He noted that the subconscious mind can have a great influence on behavior. It contains memories of past experiences as well as memories of feelings associated with past experiences. The subconscious is active, continuously influencing conscious decision-making processes.

Although people cannot remember many of the important events of the early years of their lives, these incidents do influence their behavior as adults. Joan Borysenko offers this example:

> Inside me there is a seven-year-old who is still hurting from her humiliation at summer camp. Her anguish is reawakened every time I find myself in the presence of an authority figure who acts in a controlling manner. At those moments, my intellect is prone to desert me, and I am liable to break down and cry with the same desolation and helplessness I felt when I was seven.[33]

This example reminds us that childhood wounds can cause us to experience emotions out of proportion to a current situation. Also, we often relive the experience in a context very different from the one we experienced as a child. A worker who is strongly reprimanded by an angry supervisor may experience the same feelings that surfaced when he was scolded by his mother for breaking an expensive vase.

**Transactional Analysis**    A promising breakthrough in understanding the influence of the subconscious came many years ago with the development of the **Transactional Analysis** (TA) theory by Eric Berne. After years of study, Berne concluded that from the day of birth, the brain acts like a two-track stereo tape recorder. One track records events, and the other records the feelings associated with those events.

To illustrate how feelings associated with early childhood experiences can surface later in life, picture in your mind's eye a 3-year-old walking around his mother's sewing room. He picks up a pair of sharp scissors and begins walking toward the staircase. The mother spots the child and cries, "Tommy, drop those scissors! Do you want to kill yourself?" Tommy's tape recorder records both the event (walking with scissors) and the emotions (fear and guilt). Ten years later, Tommy is taking an art class and his teacher says, "Tommy, bring me a pair of scissors." As he begins to walk across the room, his mind is flooded by the feelings of fear and guilt attached to that earlier childhood event.

## ■ *Cultural Conditioning*

A professor at Dartmouth College said, "Culture is what we see and hear so often that we call it reality. Out of culture comes behavior."[34] Culture helps shape just about every aspect of our behavior and our mental processes. Culture is frequently associated with a particular country; but actually, most countries are multicultural. African Americans, Hispanic Americans, Asian Americans, and American Indians represent a few of the subcultures within the United States.[35]

The rate of interpersonal violence in the United States is the highest among all industrialized countries. Americans of all ages encounter fictionalized violence in movies, TV programs, and video games. They witness real violence at many sporting events and in their homes. The authors of *No Safe Haven,* a major report on violence against women by an American Psychological Association task

Incidents of flight attendants being verbally abused or assaulted have increased in recent years. This ad, sponsored by the SKYRAGE Foundation, is trying to make the skies a calmer place.

force, notes that as many as 4 million women experience a severe or life-threatening assault from a male partner in an average twelve-month period.[36] Many people—both men and women—are victims of verbal aggression, which may take the form of insults or swearing. Verbal aggression can affect people in ways similar to physical aggression, and it is also sometimes the first step toward physical aggression.[37]

 ## Coping with Your Anger and the Anger of Others

In the presence of disagreement or conflict we often experience primary feelings such as frustration, hurt, embarrassment, guilt, or insecurity. These feelings are often followed by the secondary feeling of anger. If someone strongly criticizes your work in front of coworkers, you may experience shame, alarm, or insecurity, which are primary feelings. Later, in the privacy of your office or home, you may begin to feel a strong sense of anger. You may say to yourself, "She didn't have to criticize my work in front of everybody!"

**Anger** may be defined as the thoughts, feelings, physical reactions, and actions that result from unacceptable behavior by others.[38] The negative emotion of anger often triggers hostility. Learning to deal effectively with anger is a key to a healthy relationship and to your physical and mental health. The authors of *Anger Kills* say that about 20 percent of the general population has levels of hostility high enough to be dangerous to health, another 20 percent has very low levels, and the rest of the population falls somewhere in between.[39]

## HUMAN RELATIONS *in* ACTION

### Stick Swinging, Choking, and Trash Talk

Marty McSorley, a member of the Boston Bruins hockey team, was suspended for knocking out Donald Brashear, a player for the Vancouver Canucks. Near the end of a tension-filled game, McSorley skated up—out of Brashear's view—and swung his stick with both hands against Brashear's head. Later McSorley said, "I have to come to terms with what I did. There's no excuse. It was so stupid, I can't believe I did it."

In some cases, the coach is the victim of violence. Latrell Sprewell was suspended from the Golden State Warriors basketball team for choking his coach, P. J. Carlesimo. Sprewell had been the target of several of Carlesimo's tirades that involved screaming and profanity.

Trash talk, the practice of boasting and insulting one's foe, sometimes results in physical violence. Commercials from athletic companies such as Nike often glorify trash talking, implying that bad manners are essential to good basketball. Critics of professional sports say there are too few good role models and too many negative messages.

## ■ *Managing Your Anger*

**Learning to deal with your anger, and the anger of other people, is one of the most sophisticated and mature skills people are ever required to learn.**

Learning to deal with your anger, and the anger of other people, is one of the most sophisticated and mature skills people are ever required to learn. Intense anger takes control of people and distorts their perceptions, which is why angry people often make poor decisions.[40]

Dr. Art Ulene, author of *Really Fit Really Fast,* says the first step in anger management is to monitor your anger. How often do you get angry each day? What are the causes of irritation in your life? How upsetting is each episode of anger? How well do you manage each episode? Ulene suggests using a diary or journal to record this information. This self-monitoring activity will help you determine the impact of anger in your life. Record not only the source of the irritation, but the feelings that surfaced when you became angry. Also record the behaviors you displayed when angry. Ulene says that people who monitor their behavior carefully see positive results: "Without even trying, their behavior begins to change in ways that are usually desirable."[41]

What makes you angry? The anger journal will help you identify your most common anger triggers. You may find that irritations and annoyances such as traffic delays, interruptions, or loud noise are very irritating. You may discover that your anger is frequently connected to disappointment in someone or something. Tiger Woods, who has dominated the sport of golf in recent years, has sometimes struggled to control his temper in major tournaments. After a missed putt, or hitting a poor tee shot, he sometimes becomes very upset with himself. Another outstanding golfer, Jose Maria Olazabal, can also become very angry with himself. The two-time winner of the Masters once returned to his hotel room after a bad round of golf and punched the wall with great force. The result was a broken bone in his right hand.[42]

## ■ *Effective Ways to Express Your Anger*

Buddha said, "You will not be punished for your anger, you will be punished by your anger." Intense anger that is suppressed will linger and become a disruptive force in your life unless you can find a positive way to get rid of it. Expressing feelings of anger can be therapeutic, but many people are unsure about the best way to self-disclose this emotion. To express anger in ways that will improve the chances that the other person will receive and respond to your message, consider these suggestions:

1. *Avoid reacting in a manner that could be seen as emotionally unstable.* If others see you as reacting irrationally, you will lose your ability to influence them.[43] Failure to maintain your emotional control can damage your image.

2. *Do not make accusations or attempt to fix blame.* It would be acceptable to begin the conversation by saying, "I felt humiliated at the staff meeting this morning." It would not be appropriate to say, "Your comments at the morning staff meeting were mean spirited and made me feel humiliated." The latter statement invites a defensive response.[44]

3. *Express your feelings in a timely manner.* The intensity of anger can actually increase with time. Also, important information needed by you or the person who provoked your anger may be forgotten or distorted with the passing of time.

4. *Be specific as you describe the factors that triggered your anger, and be clear about the resolution you are seeking.* The direct approach, in most cases, works best.

In some cases the person who triggers your anger may be someone you cannot confront without placing your job in jeopardy. For example, one of your best customers may constantly complain about the service he receives. You know he receives outstanding service, and you feel anger building inside you each time he complains. But any display of anger may result in loss of his business. In this situation you rely on your rational thinking power and say to yourself, "This part of my work is very distasteful, but I can stay calm each time he complains."

**TOTAL PERSON INSIGHT**

KIMES GUSTIN

Author, *Anger, Rage, and Resentment*

*"We all want to live sufficiently free from anger so that it isn't a problem, so that it doesn't prevent us from living successfully and harmoniously with other people and at peace within ourselves. This requires not just a philosophy, or a way of looking at things, it requires some skill-building."*

Research conducted by the Yale School of Management found that nearly one out of four working men and women were "chronically" angry at work. The most common reason for their anger was believing that their employers had violated basic promises and had not fulfilled the "expected psychological contract with their workers." This problem, according to the authors of the study, remains mostly "underground" because workers tend not to express their anger openly.[45]

## ■ *How to Handle Other People's Anger*

Dealing with other people's anger may be the most difficult human relations challenge we face. Most of us are not well prepared to deal with our own anger or the anger of others. The following skills can be learned and applied to any situation where anger threatens to damage a relationship.

1. *Recognize and accept the other person's anger.* The simple recognition of the intense feelings of someone who is angry does a lot to defuse the situation.[46] In a calm voice you might say, "I can see that you are very angry," or "It's obvious that you are angry."

2. *Encourage the angry person to vent his or her feelings.* By asking questions and listening carefully to the response, you can encourage the person to discuss the cause of the anger openly. Try using an open-ended question to encourage self-disclosure: "What have I done to upset you?" or "Can you tell me why you are so angry?"

Tiger Woods, an outstanding golf professional, sometimes struggles to control his temper. He often becomes visibly angry after a poor t-shot or a missed putt.

---

*THINKING / LEARNING STARTERS*

1. Think about the last time someone expressed his or her anger to you. Were you able to respond in an appropriate way? Was the relationship between you and the angry person damaged?

2. Try to recall a situation where you either suppressed your feelings or overexpressed your feelings. How did your behavior affect the other person?

---

3. ***Do not respond to an angry person with your own anger.*** To express your own anger or become defensive will only create another barrier to emotional healing. When you respond to the angry person, keep your voice tone soft. Keep in mind the old biblical injunction, "A soft answer turns away wrath."[47]

4. ***Give the angry person feedback.*** After venting feelings and discussing specific details, the angry person will expect a response. Briefly paraphrase what seems to be the major concern of the angry person, and express a desire to find ways to solve the problem. If you are at fault, accept the blame for your actions and express a sincere apology.

## Strategies for Achieving Emotional Control

We live our lives in two distinct worlds—one of fact and certainty and one of emotions and ambiguity. The world of certainty is that part of our lives that deals with objects and our rational side; the world of ambiguity deals with people and our feeling, or emotional, side—our human world. Too often we try to handle our human world in the same way that we handle our factual world.[48] Most of us are better prepared to deal with the rational side of our life because most of our previous education (formal and informal) emphasized this area. In this, the final part of the chapter, we share with you some practical suggestions for achieving greater control of the emotions that affect your life.

### ■ *Identifying Your Emotional Patterns*

We could often predict or anticipate our response to various emotions if we would take the time to study our emotional patterns—to take a running inventory of circumstances that touch off jealousy, fear, anger, or some other emotion. Tamra Reed, a graphic designer employed by a large newspaper, felt anger and frustration every time a coworker delivered material late. New to her position, Tamra was hesitant to discuss her feelings with the offending person, but she did record them in a journal. She recorded not only her conscious feelings, such as anxiety, but also other feelings in her body—a knot in her stomach and muscle tension when material arrived late. Tamra soon began to identify some patterns. The late arrival of the material meant she had less time to work on the final design, so her completed work often fell short of the high-quality standards she set for herself.

The journal entries helped Tamra become aware of ways to cope with her problem. She discovered that she had lost touch with the power of her own resources. Each time she accepted late material, she gave her power to the offending person. This was followed by feelings of anger toward herself and toward the person who turned in the material late. She finally resolved to stop accepting late material and made her intentions known to those who were missing deadlines.

If you don't feel comfortable with journal writing, consider setting aside some quiet time to reflect on your emotional patterns. A period of quiet reflection will help you focus your thoughts and impressions. Becoming a skilled observer of your own emotions is one of the best ways to achieve greater emotional control.

In addition to journal writing and quiet reflection, there is one more way to discover emotional patterns. At the end of the day, construct a chart of your emotional landscape. Make a chart (see Table 8.2) of the range of emotions you experienced and expressed during the day.[49] Your first entry might be "I woke up at 6:00 A.M. and immediately felt _____." The final entry might be "I left

**TABLE 8.2**

**Charting Your Emotional Landscape**

| Time | Circumstance | Emotion |
|------|-------------|---------|
| 6:00 A.M. | Alarm goes off. Mind is flooded by thoughts of all the things that must be done during the day. | Anxiety |
| 7:10 A.M. | Depart for work. Heavy traffic interferes with plan to arrive at work early. | Anger and helplessness |
| 8:00 A.M. | Thirty-minute staff meeting scheduled by the boss lasts fifty minutes. No agenda is provided. Entire meeting seems a waste of time. | Anger and frustration |
| 9:35 A.M. | Finally start work on creative project. | Contentment |
| 10:15 A.M. | Progress on project interrupted when coworker enters office, sits down, and starts sharing gossip about another coworker. | Anger and resentment |
| 11:20 A.M. | Progress is made on creative project. | Contentment |
| 1:45 P.M. | Creative project is complete and ready for review. | Joy and contentment |
| 2:50 P.M. | Give project to boss for review. She says she will not be able to provide any feedback until morning. This delay will cause scheduling problems. | Frustration |
| 4:00 P.M. | Attend health insurance update seminar sponsored by human resources department. No major changes are discussed. | Boredom |
| 5:40 P.M. | Give up on a search for a missing document, turn off computer, and walk to parking lot. | Relief and fatigue |

the office at 5:30 P.M. with a feeling of _____." What emotions surfaced throughout your workday? Resentment? Creative joy? Anxiety? Boredom? Contentment? Anger? Satisfaction? Reflect on the completed chart and try to determine which patterns need to be changed. For example, you might discover that your behavior is too often influenced by irrational thinking. Repeat this process over a period of several days in order to identify your unique emotional patterns.

## ■ *Fine-Tuning Your Emotional Style*

**Getting rid of emotional imbalances can help you live a fuller, more satisfying life.**

Once you have completed the process of self-examination and have identified some emotional patterns you want to change, it is time to consider ways to fine-tune your emotional style. Getting rid of emotional imbalances can help you live a fuller, more satisfying life. Here are four things you can begin doing today.

■ *Take responsibility for your emotions.* How you view your emotional difficulties will have a major influence on how you deal with them. If your anger is triggered by thoughts such as "I can never make my boss happy" or "Things always go wrong in my life," you may never find an effective way to deal with this emotion. By shifting the blame to other people and events, you cannot achieve emotional control.

■ *Put your problems into proper perspective.* Why do some people seem to be at peace with themselves most of the time while others seem to be in a perpetual state of anxiety? People who suffer from an emotional imbalance often are unable or unwilling to look at problems realistically and practically, and they view each disappointment as a major catastrophe. To avoid needless misery, anxiety, and emotional upsets, use an "emotional thermometer" with a scale of 0 to 100. Zero means that everything is going well, and 100 denotes something life-threatening or truly catastrophic. Whenever you feel upset, ask yourself to come up with a logical number on the emotional thermometer. If a problem surfaces that is merely troublesome but not terrible, and you give it 60 points, you are no doubt overreacting. This mental exercise will help you avoid mislabeling a problem and feeling upset as a result.[50]

### TOTAL PERSON INSIGHT

GERARD EGAN

Author, *You and Me*

*"It's unfortunate that we're never really taught how to show emotion in ways that help our relationships. Instead, we're usually told what we should* not *do. However, too little emotion can make our lives seem empty and boring, while too much emotion, poorly expressed, fills our interpersonal lives with conflict and grief. Within reason, some kind of balance* in the expression of emotion *seems to be called for."*

■ *Take steps to move beyond anger and resentment.* Some people are upset about things that happened many years ago. Some even nurse grudges against people who have been dead for years. The sad thing is that the anger remains long after we can achieve any positive learning from it.[51] Studies of divorce, for example, indicate that anger and bitterness can linger a long time. Distress seems to peak one year after the divorce, and many people report that it takes at least two years to move past the anger.[52] When anger dominates one's life, whatever the reason, therapy or counseling may provide relief. Membership in a support group is often helpful.

■ *Give your feelings some exercise.* Several prominent authors in the field of human relations have emphasized the importance of giving our feelings some exercise. Leo Buscaglia, author of *Loving Each Other,* says, "Exercise feelings. Feelings have meaning only as they are expressed in action."[53] Sam Keen, author of *Fire in the Belly,* said, "Make a habit of identifying your feelings and expressing them in some appropriate way."[54] If you have offended someone, how about sending that person a letter of regret? If someone you work with has given extra effort, why not praise that person's work? If you have been nursing a grudge for some time, how about practicing forgiveness?

Every day of our personal and work life we face some difficult decisions. One option is to take only actions that feel good at the moment. In some cases, this means ignoring the feelings of customers, patients, coworkers, and supervisors. Another option is to behave in a manner that is acceptable to the people around you. If you choose this option, you will have to make some sacrifices. You may have to be warm and generous when the feelings inside you say, "Be cold and selfish." You may have to avoid an argument when your feelings are insisting, "I'm right and the other person is wrong!" To achieve emotional control often requires restructuring our ways of feeling, thinking, and behaving.

## Summary

Conflicts among people happen every day and can arise because of poor communications, values and culture clashes, confusing work policies and practices, adversarial management, or noncompliance. Conflicts also surface when we must deal with disruptive or uncooperative coworkers. While unresolved conflicts can have a negative effect on an organization's productivity, a difference of opinion sometimes has a positive effect by forcing team members toward creative and innovative solutions to the problem.

There are several approaches for dealing with conflict: win/lose, lose/lose, and win/win. Using the win/win strategy can not only resolve a conflict but also preserve effective human relations. Regardless of the strategy implemented, your ability to display assertiveness and cooperative behaviors are key factors in the effective resolution of conflicts with others. There are five steps in the conflict resolution process.

We carry inside us a vast array of emotions that come into play when we encounter a conflict situation. An emotion can be thought of as a feeling that influences our thinking and behavior. We sometimes experience emotional imbalance because we learn to inhibit the expression of certain emotions and overemphasize the expression of others.

Our emotional development is influenced by temperament (the biological shaper of personality), our subconscious mind, and cultural conditioning. Throughout the long process of emotional development we learn different ways to express our anger. Appropriate expressions of anger contribute to improved interpersonal relations, help us reduce anxiety, and give us an outlet for unhealthy stress. We must also learn how to handle other people's anger. It takes a great deal of effort to learn how to deal with our own anger and the anger of others.

Emotional control is an important dimension of emotional style. The starting point in developing emotional control is to identify your current emotional patterns. One way to do this is to record your anger experiences in a diary or journal. Once you have completed the process of self-examination, you should consider appropriate ways to fine-tune your emotional style.

## Career Corner

Q: I am in my mid-40s, have spent twenty-two years working my way up to be supervisor of my department in a major department store, and love my job. The new 31-year-old store manager has started to exclude me from memos and weekly management meetings, saying, "There's no reason for you to attend." Many of my coworkers are much younger than I, dress in jeans instead of professional suits, and seem to lack the traditional work ethic. Those of us over 40 are finding it difficult to keep our mouths shut. Any suggestions?

A: It is obvious your conflict stems from a values clash that sometimes develops between older and younger workers. There also seems to be a breakdown in communication. Your younger coworkers and the store manager may be consciously or unconsciously building an "us versus them" scenario in relation to the more experienced members of the team. You need to establish more effective communication with your store manager. Openly discuss your concerns, and assertively seek an explanation for the changes that have taken place. When you allow others to ignore your needs and disregard your point of view, you display passive behaviors that will get you nowhere.

## Key Terms

| | |
|---|---|
| conflict | conflict resolution process |
| assertive behavior | brainstorming |
| aggressive behavior | emotion |
| nonassertive behavior | temperament |
| win/lose approach | subconscious mind |
| lose/lose approach | Transactional Analysis |
| win/win approach | anger |

## Review Questions

1. What are some of the major causes of conflicts between people in organizations?
2. Discuss the positive aspects of conflict in an organization.
3. What results might you expect when you implement the win/lose approach? The lose/lose approach? The win/win approach?
4. How does assertive behavior differ from aggressive behavior?
5. How does a misunderstanding differ from a true disagreement?
6. What is the relationship between feelings and emotion? What role do feelings play in our life?
7. What is meant by the term *emotional balance*? What factors create an emotional imbalance?
8. What four steps can improve the chances that another person will receive and respond to your feelings of anger?
9. List four skills that can be used effectively to handle anger in other people.
10. List and briefly describe four ways to fine-tune your emotional style.

## Application Exercises

1. Recall the last time you were angry at another person or were the victim of a situation that made you angry. For example, a housemate or roommate refuses to pay her share of the grocery bill, or your manager accuses you of wrongdoing without knowing all the facts. Then answer the following questions:
   a. Did you express your anger verbally, physically, or emotionally?
   b. Did you suppress any of your anger? Explain.
   c. What results did you experience from the way you handled this situation? Describe both positive and negative results.
   d. If the same situation arose again, would you do anything differently? Explain.
2. To develop your assertiveness skills, find a partner who will join you for a practice session. The partner should assume the role of a friend, family member, or coworker who is doing something that causes you a great deal of frustration. (The problem can be real or imaginary.) Communicate your dislikes and feelings in a clear, direct manner without threatening or attacking. Then ask your partner to critique your assertiveness skills. Participate in several of these practice sessions until you feel confident that you have improved your assertiveness skills.
3. To learn more about how emotions influence your thinking and behavior, complete each of the following sentences. Once you have completed them all, reflect on your written responses. Can you identify any changes you would like to make in your emotional style?
   a. "When someone makes me angry, I usually . . ."
   b. "The most common worry in my life is . . ."
   c. "When I feel compassion for someone, my response is to . . ."
   d. "My response to feelings of grief is . . ."
   e. "When I am jealous of someone, my response is to . . ."

## *Internet Exercise*

Many people have an anger management problem. Although anger is a natural human emotion, the mismanagement of anger can result in serious human relations problems. Help with anger management is as close as your computer. The American Psychological Association has a Web page on "Controlling Anger— Before It Controls You." The address is *www.apa.org/pubinfo/html.* Visit this site and prepare a written summary of the information presented. If you wish to study anger management in greater detail, visit *www.angermgmt.com* or *www. angermgt.com.*

## *Self-Assessment Excercise*

For each of the following statements, circle the number from 1 to 5 that best represents your response: (1) strongly disagree (never do this); (2) disagree (rarely do this); (3) moderately agree (sometimes do this); (4) agree (frequently do this); (5) strongly agree (almost always do this).

A. When I experience conflict with others I strive to determine how much assertive behavior and how much cooperative behavior to display.   1   2   3   4   5

B. In my attempts to resolve conflict I strive for a solution that all parties can accept.   1   2   3   4   5

C. I am able to solve problems and make decisions in a logical manner without allowing my emotions to interfere.   1   2   3   4   5

D. My relationships with people at home, school, and work do not suffer because of my expressions of anger or impatience.   1   2   3   4   5

E. I have developed effective ways to cope with my own anger and the anger of others.   1   2   3   4   5

F. I am familiar with, and can apply, several strategies for achieving emotional control.   1   2   3   4   5

Select an appropriate attitude or skill you would like to improve. Write your goal in the space provided, and describe the steps you will take to achieve this goal.

GOAL: _____

_____

_____

_____

**Case Problem** | *Helping Employees Who Behave Badly*

Organizations that want to survive in today's highly competitive global economy must learn how to deal with employees who behave badly. This includes the boss who frequently becomes angry and yells at employees. It also includes employees who treat customers with indifference and disrespect. Team members who cause friction and engage in infighting also need help. Many employees who behave badly are persons with valuable technical skills, so termination may not be an option. To salvage the career of an employee who possesses strong technical skills but lacks effective people skills is a challenge. Here is how some companies are meeting this challenge.

- At Chemical Bank, based in New York City, some candidates for management positions have been encouraged to complete the Dale Carnegie human relations course. One enrollee was a 32-year-old employee who had a degree in accounting. He had good technical skills, but Chemical wanted him to develop his people skills.

- David Prosser, chief executive officer of RTW Inc., a worker's compensation management firm in Minneapolis, received complaints about one of his managers. This person would become angry and yell at other employees. Most of the targets of his wrath were lower-level employees who wouldn't dare fight back. Other managers met with him to discuss his behavior, but he denied he had done anything wrong. Prosser viewed the manager as a valued employee, so he sent him to Executive to Leader Institute, a local coaching firm. After several months of personal coaching, the manager learned to control his anger.

More serious cases include employees who have substance addictions or serious personality disorders such as depression. A potentially violent employee can present the greatest challenge because discharging an employee with a mental disability may be viewed as illegal by the courts. Antibias laws such as the Americans with Disabilities Act can make it difficult for employers to fire mentally unstable workers. Legal pitfalls exist because it is often difficult to distinguish between conduct that is the result of a mental disability and conduct that is the result of generally unacceptable behavior. Companies must also determine the best way to deal with domestic violence that spills over to the job. For example, many women who are victims of domestic abuse are threatened or abused while at work.[55]

### Questions

1. At Chemical Bank some employees are encouraged to complete the Dale Carnegie human relations course. What are the advantages and disadvantages of this approach?

2. A manager at RTW Inc. was given help in the form of personal coaching. What are the advantages and disadvantages of this approach?

3. What would be your response if a fellow worker suddenly became moody and caused friction in your department? Would you attempt to offer assistance, or would you wait for someone else to deal with the problem?

# 9 A Life Plan for Effective Human Relations

CHAPTER PREVIEW

After studying this chapter you will be able to:

- Define success by standards that are compatible with your needs and values.

- Learn how to cope with the forces that influence work/life balance.

- Discuss the meaning of *right livelihood*.

- Describe four nonfinancial resources that can enrich your life.

- Provide guidelines for developing a healthy lifestyle.

- Develop a plan for making needed changes in your life.

Joe Sizemore used to hunt and fish as well as collect Star Trek memorabilia, but he doesn't do these things anymore. He abandoned these leisure-time activities after he started working long hours at the Corning plant in Blacksburg, Virginia. It is not uncommon for him to work 60 hours or more a week. He eagerly volunteers for overtime in order to increase his earnings. Sizemore is not the most prominent overtime worker at the plant—that distinction belongs to Michael Tucker, who usually works between 67 and 70 hours a week.

Sizemore's wife works full-time at another industrial plant, so he doesn't get to spend much time with her and their two daughters. The Sizemores have adopted many trappings of middle-class life: a nice home on a hilltop, two cars, vacation trips, and a time-share at a Virginia ski resort.[1]

David and Lisa Keyko recently decided to adopt a more traditional lifestyle. He is a lawyer and she is now a housewife. Prior to this change they were the classic high-powered career couple. He was a commercial litigator, and she was a director at a design firm. At that time they split most of the household chores, left their children with a babysitter, and came home exhausted most nights. Mr. Keyko is now the sole breadwinner, and most weekdays he's at the office until 9:00 P.M.[2]

The Sizemores and the Keykos are in many ways typical new economy families. They are struggling to achieve some degree of balance between work and their personal lives. Many observers of the American scene say you can have a good job or a life, but not both. The Corning plant prefers paying overtime to hiring more workers, so Joe Sizemore will very likely continue working long hours. Lawyers are expected to work long hours, so David Keyko may not be able to spend much time with his family.

Before you start feeling sorry for Joe Sizemore and David Keyko, remember that they do have choices. Joe can stop volunteering for so much overtime, and David can find ways to spend less time at the office. They have burdened themselves with demanding work schedules, but to what end? Are the rewards worth the loss of time and vitality from life outside work?

## Achieving Balance in a Chaotic World

We are being told to envision a future filled with sharp detours and many redefinitions of our work lives. Tom Peters, noted author and consultant, talks about the disappearing career ladder:

> A typical career path today isn't linear or even always upward. It's more like a maze, full of hidden turns, zigs, and zags that go in all sorts of directions—even backward sometimes, when that makes sense. The satisfaction that you derive from the job is what should matter most, not the directions [in which] you appear to be going.[3]

The dream of finding job security and knowing that we have "arrived" seems sadly obsolete. As we change jobs eight or more times during our working lives, we will need to reshape our work identity.[4]

In this chapter we help you construct a life plan that will enhance your relationships with people in your personal life and in your work life. This plan will also help you better manage the relationship you have with yourself. We discuss the meaning of success and suggest ways to cope with major disappointments that will surface in your work life. You will learn how to avoid being trapped by a lifestyle that offers financial rewards but little else. This chapter also helps you define your relationship with money and describes four nonfinancial resources that give meaning to life. Finally, you will learn how to develop the mental and physical fitness needed to keep up in today's frantic, fast-paced world.

## Toward a New Definition of Success

Most of us have been conditioned to define success in narrow terms. Too frequently we judge our own success, and the success of others, by what is accomplished at work. Successful people are described as those who have a "good job" or have "reached the top" in their field. We sometimes describe the person who has held the same job for many years as successful. We do not stop to consider that such a person may find work boring and completely devoid of personal rewards.

From early childhood on we are taught to equate success with pay increases and promotions. Amy Saltzman, author of *Downshifting,* notes that many people

**From early childhood on we are taught to equate success with pay increases and promotions.**

tend to set goals and measure success along a vertical career path that is often described as the "career ladder" or the "fast track." Saltzman says, "One is not successful, according to this school of thought, unless one is consistently moving up the ladder in some clearly quantifiable way."[5] Too often the person who is striving to achieve an immediate career goal (one more rung on the career ladder, for example) is forced to give up everything else that gives purpose and meaning to life. This may mean spending less time with family members and friends, spending less time keeping physically fit, abandoning vacation plans, and spending weekends at work.

Of course, the fast track is no longer an option for many employees. Today there are fewer rungs on the corporate ladder. One major goal of downsizing is to reduce the number of layers of management. The flattening of organizations is likely to continue.[6]

---

**TOTAL PERSON INSIGHT**

*AMY SALTZMAN*

Author, *Downshifting: Reinventing Success on a Slower Track*

*"When it comes to defining a successful life in American Society, today's career professionals seem stuck between two ultimately dissatisfying extremes: dropping out completely and creating their own vision of a better world, or working within the system and speeding up their pace on the success treadmill."*

Cynthia Cunningham (left) and Shelley Murray worked 60-hour workweeks to achieve success as BankBoston branch managers. They wanted more time with their children, but the long hours created a major barrier to motherhood. Then they decided to package themselves and share one job. Later, a senior BankBoston executive accepted their proposal.

## ■ *The Need for New Models of Success*

In recent years, a growing number of people are angry, disillusioned, and frustrated because they had to abruptly change their career plans. They gave their best efforts to an employer for ten, fifteen, or twenty years, and then the company eliminated their jobs. For years the firm said, "Take care of business and we'll take care of you," but then the situation changed. Under pressure from new global competition, hostile takeovers, and the need to restructure, companies started getting rid of experienced workers. The unwritten and unspoken contract between the company and the employee was broken. Many of the people who lost their jobs during the past decade were once told that if they had ambition and worked tirelessly to achieve their career goals, success would be their reward. But the "reward" for many people has been loss of a job, loss of self-esteem, and increased anxiety about the future.

We should certainly feel sympathy for persons who have lost their jobs and watched their dreams dissolve. But there is another group of people who also merit our concern. These are the persons who put in long hours, climbed the ladder of success, and still have a job but have discovered that something important is missing from their lives. These people have a good job, a regular paycheck, and in some cases an impressive title, but they do not *feel* successful. How should we feel about the person who invested ten, fifteen, or twenty years in a job, gave up all or most of his or her leisure time, gave up quality time with friends and family, climbed the career ladder, and then discovered that life was empty and unfulfilling?

**One-Dimensional Model**   The traditional success model defined success almost exclusively in terms of work life. The model emphasized working long hours, reaching work-related goals, and meeting standards often set by others. Lynn Lannon, president of the Lannon Group, a San Francisco–based consulting firm, says the old model results in "judging one's success by the standards of others, never feeling quite good enough and often feeling dissatisfied."[7]

The old model of success required us to be "one-dimensional" people for whom work is the single dimension. In the life of such a person, everything that has meaning seems to be connected to the job. When a person defines himself or herself by a job and then loses that job, what does that person have left? Of course, the loss of a job encourages some people to search for meaning beyond their work. People who are able to broaden their perspectives, develop interests beyond their jobs, and put balance in their lives not only usually achieve more self-fulfillment but also are more valuable as employees.[8]

## Loss of Leisure Time

Throughout history Americans have burdened themselves with a very demanding work ethic. A study released by the United Nations International Labor Organization indicated that Americans spend more time on the job than employees in any other industrialized nation. What's more, downsizing efforts have left fewer people to do the same amount of work, so many people are working harder. Most of these workers yearn for more leisure time.

U.S. workers not only work long hours, they spend less time on vacation than do workers in most other industrialized countries. A typical American worker receives only ten days of paid vacation after one year of service. By comparison, a worker in Sweden, Denmark, or Germany would receive thirty days off after one year of service.

Some of America's best-managed companies are beginning to realize the negative consequences of long hours on the job and loss of leisure time. The director of human resource strategy and planning for Merck and Company says, "You can't build an effective company on a foundation of broken homes and strained personal relationships." A senior executive at Price Waterhouse says, "We want the people who work for our firm to have lives outside Price Waterhouse—people with real lives are well rounded, and well-rounded people are creative thinkers."[9]

## Developing Your Own Life Plan

The goal of this chapter is to help you develop a life plan for effective relationships with yourself and others. The information presented thus far has, we hope, stimulated your thinking about the need for a life plan. We have noted that personal life can seldom be separated from work life. The two are very much intertwined. We have also suggested that it is important for you to develop your own definition of success. Too frequently people allow others (parents, teachers, counselors, a spouse) to define success for them. Judging your success by the standards established by someone else may lead to a life of frustration.

Many people today are discovering that true success is a combination of achievements. Becoming too focused on one narrow goal may not provide the self-satisfaction you are seeking. One author makes this observation: "Everyone wants to be successful. But each person must have a personal definition of what success will feel like, and understand that true success rarely means having just

## HUMAN RELATIONS *in* ACTION

### Volvo's Swedish Paradise

When Ford Motor Company purchased the Sweden's Volvo AB's car division factory in Gothenburg, Swedish employees worried about losing access to the company gym, Olympic-size swimming pool, badminton and tennis courts, outdoor track, tanning beds, and the physical therapy hot-water pool. Their worries were justified, as Ford executives contemplated the cost effectiveness of the perks. Workers paid $1.50 a day to get into the facilities, but it cost $605,500 a year to support the center. For Ford, the Volvo facility raised the question of "perk parity" for its U.S. employees, who usually have free-of-charge fitness centers and weight-reduction programs, but none of the other goodies normally found only at the most exclusive health clubs. Jacques Nasser, Ford CEO, planned to make Volvo a high-volume car in the United States, which meant a three-shift, round-the-clock production schedule. Swedish employees currently worked only two shifts. The night shift worked less than 30 hours, but earned as much as the 40-hour day shift because of the Swedish government–mandated allocation for late-shift employees. A Swedish economist stated that Sweden's high income taxes were offset by these perks as well as by profit-sharing programs, fine art, and trendy equipment for offices. However, Swedish workers' eyes lighted up when they heard about the high wages earned by Ford employees.

one goal."[10] A narrow definition of success may actually prove to be counterproductive if it means giving up everything else that adds meaning to life.

Because work is such an important part of life, we now move to a discussion of items that will help you in your career planning. We discuss the concept of "right livelihood."

## Toward Right Livelihood

Kirk Korley gave up a lucrative career as a computer scientist to start Doggie Spa & Day Care in Chapel Hill, North Carolina. He started this business because he had a vision of what pet care could be. At age 49 Susan Marshall earned an MBA at the Mandel Center for Nonprofit Organizations at Case Western Reserve University. Three months before receiving the degree, she accepted the position of executive director of the Cleveland Zoological Society, a nonprofit organization that operates the Cleveland Zoo. And Nora Fascenelli accepted a cub reporter position at the Yuma Daily Sun newspaper after spending 20 years as a lawyer.[11]

What do these three people have in common? Each person is searching for "right livelihood." The concept of right livelihood is described in the core teachings of Buddhism. In recent years, the concept has been described by Michael Phillips in his book *The Seven Laws of Money* and by Marsha Sinetar in her book *Do What You Love . . . The Money Will Follow.* **Right livelihood** is work consciously chosen, done with full awareness and care, and leading to enlightenment. Barbara Sher, contributor to *New Age* magazine, says right livelihood

Keith Seeley, a data processing manager for SunTrust Banks in Tifton, Georgia, is in search of right livelihood. He is taking farrier courses to learn the horse-shoeing trade and hopes to start his own business in the near future. He is shown with his mare, Dandy.

means that you wake up in the morning and spend all day working at something you really want to do.[12] Ronald Sheade, once a vice president at a Fortune 1,000 company, now teaches eighth-grade science in a suburb of Chicago. He doesn't make big money anymore, but he loves teaching and now gets to spend more time with his family.[13] There are three characteristics to right livelihood.

### Right Livelihood Is Based on Conscious Choice

Marsha Sinetar says, "When the powerful quality of conscious choice is present in our work, we can be enormously productive."[14] She points out that many people have learned to act on what others say, value, and expect and thus find conscious choice very difficult:

> It takes courage to act on what we value and to willingly accept the consequences of our choices. Being able to choose means not allowing fear to inhibit or control us, even though our choices may require us to act against our fears or against the wishes of those we love and admire.[15]

To make the best choices, you must first figure out what you like to do, as well as what you are good at doing. What you like doing most is often not obvious. It may take some real effort to discover what really motivates you. Students often get help from career counselors or explore a career option during a summer internship. If you are employed, consider joining a temporary project team. A team assignment may give you the opportunity to work closely with experts in such diverse areas as finance, marketing, or manufacturing.[16]

### ■ *Right Livelihood Places Money in a Secondary Position*

People who embrace this concept accept that money and security are not the primary rewards in life. Michael Phillips explains that "right livelihood has within itself its own rewards; it deepens the person who practices it."[17] For example, people who work in the social services usually do not earn large amounts of money, but many receive a great deal of personal satisfaction from their work. Nora Fascenelli may not make much money as a reporter, but the work may provide enormous personal satisfaction.

Many people who once viewed success in terms of wealth, material possessions, and status are realizing that something is missing from their lives. They do not *feel* successful. They once felt pressured to "have it all" but now feel disappointed that their achievements have not brought them real happiness.

### ■ *Right Livelihood Recognizes That Work Is a Vehicle for Personal Growth*

Most of us spend from forty to sixty hours each week at work. Ideally, we should not have to squelch our real abilities, ignore our personal goals, and forget our need for stimulation and personal growth during the time we spend at work.[18] Most employees know intuitively that work should fulfill their need for self-expression and personal growth, but this message has not been embraced by many leaders. Too few organizations truly empower workers and give them a sense of purpose. When employees feel that the company's success is their own success, they will be more enthusiastic about their work.

> **Most employees know intuitively that work should fulfill their need for self-expression and personal growth, but this message has not been embraced by many leaders.**

The search for right livelihood should begin with a thoughtful review of your values. The values clarification process (see Table 4.1) should be completed *before* you interview for a job. Mark Buzek, a graduate of Ohio State University, decided not to take a job that would require frequent relocation and excessive travel. Although he is not married, he has strong ties with his parents, two sisters, and a brother in Ohio. Staying close to family members is an important value in his life. Sarah Schroeder, another college graduate, says she cut off interviews with several employers who expect continuous sixty-hour-plus workweeks.[19]

When a job fails to fulfill your expectations, consider changing jobs or changing careers. If the job isn't right for you, your body and your mind will begin sending you messages. When you begin feeling that something is lacking, try to answer these basic questions: What is making me feel this way? What, exactly, about my current position is unpleasant? Choosing a satisfying career and lifestyle requires understanding what contributes to your job satisfaction. Self-

---

### THINKING / LEARNING STARTERS

1. Do you agree that many people define success in terms that are too narrow? Reflect on your personal knowledge of friends and family members before answering this question.

2. In your opinion, does the concept of right livelihood seem realistic? Is right livelihood an option for everyone, or only a select few? Explain.

---

exploration and continual evaluation of your needs, goals, and job satisfaction are important. Don't wait for a crisis (layoff) to clear your vision.[20]

### ■ *Defining Your Relationship with Money*

Money is a compelling force in the lives of many people. It often influences selection of a career and the amount of time and energy invested in that career. Joe Sizemore, introduced at the beginning of this chapter, says that his longest workday was 18 hours and his longest workweek, 82.[21] Why do we work such long hours and give up so much leisure time? One major reason is that we are so caught up in the cycle of consumption, we have lost our free will. We work so that we may spend.

According to Juliet Schor, author of *The Overspent American*, Americans spend a great deal of time and money keeping up with the Joneses. Schor argues that people compete for status within "reference groups," persons they work with at the office or factory, members of their professions, and friends or relatives. When we strive to keep up, but fall short, we often feel anxious and poorer. She also believes that consumers have become slaves to advertising and status symbolism. The desire to own a Lexus, a Rolex, or a second home can be very powerful.[22]

The way we choose to earn, save, and spend our money determines, in large measure, the quality of our lives. For example, if you think that having *more* money is going to produce happiness or peace of mind, will you ever earn enough? Many people accept the "myth of scarcity." They have a mind-set or belief that "I don't have enough _____." Money becomes the lightning rod for the scarcity notion.[23] With this mind-set, any extra money earned is quickly spent on the things you think you do not have enough of. Once you turn your "wants" into "needs," then the need to work more overtime, hold down a second job, or continue a dual-earner arrangement intensifies.[24] When you live in a competitive culture—a culture of *more*—it's hard to set limits.

Many people do not have a mature relationship with money. They spend everything they earn and more (thanks to the convenience of credit cards) and then experience bouts of money anxiety and money worry. These unpleasant emotions often weaken interpersonal relationships. Money issues continue to be the number one cause of divorce in the United States. About 70 percent of divorcing couples attribute the breakdown of their marriage to arguments about money. Two-income families are often more careless when it comes to spending. Linda Kelley, author of *Two Incomes and Still Broke?*, says it's not how much you make that counts; it's how much you keep.[25]

**Mature Money Management** Competence in managing your personal finances is no less important than competence in managing your career. It is difficult to take career risks (leaving a job you dislike) unless you are able to build a financial cushion. Early retirement may not be an option unless you prepare for it. Here are some tips on how to manage your personal finances:

- *Determine where your income is going.* With a simple record-keeping system, you can determine how much you spend each month on food, housing, clothing, transportation, and other things. Search for spending patterns you may want to change.

- *Spend less than you earn.* To do this, you may need to get rid of some credit cards, eat fewer meals at restaurants, use public transportation instead of driving your car, or make some other lifestyle change. The personal savings rate recently reached a new low point. Try to make savings a habit.

- *Maintain a cash cushion.* If you lost your job today, how long could you live on your current cash reserves? Financial consultants suggest that cash reserves should be equal to the amount you earn during a two-month period.

- *Develop a personal financial plan.* With a financial plan, you are more likely to achieve your financial goals. Without a plan, you are likely to follow a haphazard approach to management of your finances.

## HUMAN RELATIONS *in* ACTION

### Who Wants to Be a Millionaire?

Chances are, you won't have an opportunity to win top prize on the *Who Wants to Be a Millionaire* TV show. One alternative is to build a large fund with a regular savings plan. A mixture of the following three things can produce amazing results:
- A small amount of money
- An average rate of return
- A period of time for your investment to grow

Steve Moore of the Cato Institute and Tom Kelly of the Savers and Investors Foundation provide a simple illustration of the stunning results that can be achieved. If your parents placed $1,000 in a mutual fund in 1950, and the money was allowed to grow at the stock market's average rate of return, they would now have $217,630. This is a reminder that fortunes can be made even by low-wage earners who save regularly during their working years.

*JULIE CONNELLY*

Contributing Editor, *Fortune*

*"Keep in mind that there is no harder work than thinking— really thinking—about who you are and what you want out of life. Figuring out where your goals and your skills match up is a painful, time-consuming process."*

Com-Corp Industries, a manufacturing plant based in Cleveland, Ohio, sees personal money management skills as one key to reducing conflict in the workplace. Employees who cannot live within their means are often under great stress and are more likely to experience interpersonal problems at work and at home. The company provides employees with classes on such subjects as developing a household budget and wise use of credit.[26]

## Nonfinancial Resources

If you become totally focused on your financial resources, if you are caught up in the work-and-spend cycle, then chances are you have ignored your **nonfinancial resources.** And it is often the nonfinancial resources that make the biggest contribution to a happy and fulfilling life. A strong argument can be made that the real wealth in life comes in the form of good health, peace of mind, time spent with family and friends, learning (which develops the mind), and healthy spirituality. Paul Hwoschinsky, author of *True Wealth,* makes this observation about nonfinancial resources: "If you are clear about who you are, and clear about what you want to do, and bring your financial and non-financial resources together, it's extraordinary what can happen. I encourage people to really honor their total resources, and magical things happen. New options occur."[27]

If you focus most or all of your attention on work, and you suffer a major work-related disappointment, then the result is likely to be feelings of depression and despair. Thoughts such as "Now I have lost everything" can surface when you fail to get a promotion, find out that you were not selected to be a member of a special project team, or learn that your job has been eliminated. If you fully understand the power of your nonfinancial resources, then work-related disappointments are easier to cope with. The starting point is to realize that *most* of your resources are nonfinancial. During periods of great uncertainty, it is especially important that you think about your nonfinancial assets and consider ways to enhance them. We briefly discuss four nonfinancial resources that can enrich your life: physical and mental health, education and training (intellectual growth), leisure time (time for family, socializing, recreation), and healthy spirituality (see Figure 9.1).

**Physical and Mental Health**    Is the statement "Health means wealth" just a worn-out cliché, or is this slogan a message of inspiration for people who

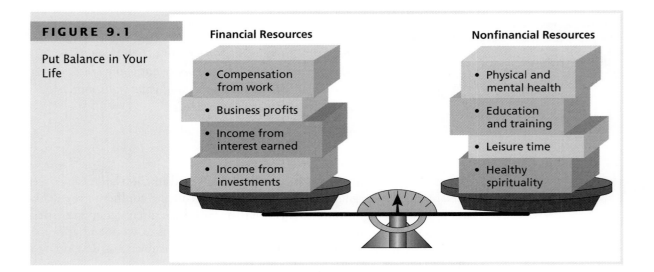

**FIGURE 9.1**

Put Balance in Your Life

Financial Resources

- Compensation from work
- Business profits
- Income from interest earned
- Income from investments

Nonfinancial Resources

- Physical and mental health
- Education and training
- Leisure time
- Healthy spirituality

want to get more out of life? If good health is such an important nonfinancial asset, then why are so many people flirting with self-destruction by eating the wrong foods, drinking too much, exercising too little, and generally choosing unhealthy lifestyles? The answer to the second question may be lack of awareness of the benefits of physical fitness. Susan Smith Jones, a fitness instructor at UCLA and author of *Choose to Be Healthy,* offers these benefits of good health:

- There is an interrelationship between health and outlook on life. For example, when the physical body is fit, toned, and strong, this condition has a positive effect on the mind. We are more likely to experience higher levels of self-esteem, feel a greater sense of self-confidence, and have a more positive outlook on life.

- Poor health tends to interfere with everything else in life: family harmony, work schedules, and relationships.

- Regular exercise and a healthy diet produce greater mental clarity, a higher energy level, and a more youthful appearance.[28]

Jones states that good health is something you must *choose* to have. She says, "Regardless of the lifestyle you've lived until now, you can, at any moment, choose differently."[29] If your breakfast is currently five cups of coffee and a danish, you can choose to change your diet. If you are spending thirty hours a week sitting in front of a TV set, you can choose to spend that time in a different way. Your current level of health is the result of many choices you made in the past. Later in this chapter we discuss ways to form new habits that will help you achieve vibrant health.

**Education and Training (Intellectual Growth)**   The new economy thrives on a well-educated and well-trained work force. It rewards workers who take personal responsibility for their learning. The National Study of the Changing Workforce reports that 90 percent of American workers say their jobs require them to "keep learning new things." They also associate learning opportunities with higher job satisfaction and less stress at home.[30]

Throughout life we must continue to acquire new knowledge and skills. The time when you could achieve career success with just hard work and loyalty has passed. Today, employees are likely to be judged and rewarded on the basis of performance. Michael Hammer, co-author of *Re-Engineering the Corporation*, says, "You have to get results, and you have to continually update, train and develop yourself so that you're ready for tomorrow's jobs."[31] The expression "never stop learning" has never had more relevance than it does today. Here are some tips on how to acquire the skills and abilities you need:

- *Think of yourself as a unique product.* To maintain value in the marketplace, you must keep up-to-date. What skills and capabilities do you need to maintain or increase your value?[32]

- *Be selective in what you learn.* Learning often requires large amounts of time and energy, so consider carefully what unit of knowledge or skill will generate the most improvement.[33]

- *Take advantage of various learning pathways.* It helps to think of your job as a learning resource. Take full advantage of instructional programs offered by your employer. Volunteer for team assignments that will provide new learning opportunities. Peter Senge, author of *The Fifth Discipline*, says the fundamental learning unit in any organization is a team.[34] And look outside the company at community college classes or programs offered by Toastmasters, Dale Carnegie, or other organizations.

In his best-selling book *The Art of Happiness*, the Dalai Lama says the role of learning and education in achieving happiness is widely overlooked. He notes that numerous surveys have conclusively found that higher levels of education have a positive correlation with better health and a longer life, and even protect us from feelings of depression.[35]

**Leisure Time**    Leisure time can provide an opportunity to relax, get rid of work-related stress, get some exercise, spend time with family and friends, or simply read a good book. Many people think they want more leisure time, but when it is available, they do not know what to do. Some people even feel guilty when they are not working. In her book *Downshifting,* Amy Saltzman talks about the problems Americans have with leisure time:

> The fact is, leisure today has something of a negative connotation. Having too much leisure implies we are wasting time and not working hard enough to get ahead. With so little time and so much of it devoted to professional pursuits, spending a Saturday afternoon on the front porch reading a book, talking to the neighbors or writing a letter to a friend is out of the question.[36]

If you are working for someone who is on the fast track, someone who may have given up all or most of his or her leisure time, you may be pressured to work at the same pace. If your boss is constantly trying to meet impossible deadlines and deal with last-minute rushes, you may feel the need to give up time for recreation or family. If this happens, try to identify the consequences of being overworked. Look at the situation from all points of view. If you refuse to work longer hours, what will be the consequences for your relationship with the boss, your relationship with other employees, your future with the organization?[37] You have choices, but they may be difficult ones. If it looks as though the pressure to work longer hours will never end, you may want to begin searching for another job.

Is it worth taking some risks to protect the leisure time you now have? Should you increase the amount of leisure time available in your life? Consider the following benefits of leisure time:

- As we noted previously in this text, maintaining social connections with friends and family can be good for your health. A growing number of studies show that if you have strong and fulfilling relationships, you may live longer, decrease your chances of becoming sick, and cope more successfully when illness strikes.[38] Time spent with friends and family can be a powerful source of mental and physical renewal. An excellent way to increase your social connections and improve your own health is to become a volunteer. Research indicates that volunteers experience pleasurable physical sensations such as feelings of warmth, well-being, and calmness, and increased energy levels.[39]

- One of the best ways to feel satisfied about your work is to get away from it when you begin to feel worn out. People who take time off from work often return with new ideas, a stronger focus, and increased energy. When you discover that end-of-the-week exhaustion is still hanging around Monday morning, it's time to take some vacation or personal days.[40]

- Find some quiet time for yourself each day. You might use it to meditate, take the dog for a walk, or just sit quietly. Use this time to nourish yourself and bring balance to your life.

If you want more leisure time, then you must establish your priorities and set your goals. This may mean saying no to endless requests to work overtime or rejecting a promotion. Sometimes you must pull back from the endless demands of work and "get a life."

**Healthy Spirituality**   A discussion of nonfinancial resources would not be complete without an introduction to healthy spirituality. To become a "whole" or "total" person requires movement beyond the concrete, material aspects of life to the spiritual side of the human experience. Healthy spirituality can bring a higher degree of harmony and wholeness to our lives and move us beyond self-centeredness.

Julius Walls, CEO of Greyston Bakery, has discovered that healthy spirituality can coexist with successful business practices. The Yonkers, New York, based bakery is staffed by poor African-Americans and Hispanics who ar233e given an opportunity to achieve self-sufficiency in the context of a caring workplace.

**Spirituality** can be defined as an inner attitude that emphasizes energy, creative choice, and a powerful force for living. It involves opening our hearts and cultivating our capacity to experience reverence and gratitude. It frees us to become positive, caring human beings.[41]

Spirituality encompasses faith, which can be described as what your heart tells you is true when your mind cannot prove it. For some people, faith exists within the framework of a formal religion; for others it rests on a series of personal beliefs such as "Give others the same consideration, regard, kindness, and gentleness that you would like them to accord you."[42]

**An understanding of the many aspects of spirituality can give us an expanded vision of what it means to be human.**

An understanding of the many aspects of spirituality can give us an expanded vision of what it means to be human. Although spirituality is often associated with religion, it should be viewed in broader terms. Robert Coles, of Harvard Medical School, likes a definition of spirituality given to him by an 11-year-old girl:

I think you're spiritual if you can escape from yourself a little and think of what's good for everyone, not just you, and if you can reach out and be a good person—I mean live like a good person. You're not spiritual if you just talk spiritual and there's no action. You're a fake if that's what you do.[43]

*ROBERT WUTHNOW*

Author, *After Heaven—
Spirituality in America Since
the 1950s*

*"Faced with growing uncertainties and with ample
opportunities for choice, people will need to spend more time
than ever before reflecting on the deep values that make life
worth living and the sources of those values, including
spirituality."*

The words of this young girl remind us that one dimension of spirituality involves showing concern and compassion for others. It means turning away from
rigid individualism and investing some time and energy in helping others. It
means in some cases rolling up our sleeves and getting involved. We can enhance
our spirituality through volunteer work, taking the time to listen to a coworker
who is trying to resolve a serious personal problem, or simply writing a personal
note of appreciation to someone at work who has given us assistance.

In many ways, large and small, work can be made more spiritual. The philosophy of Worthington Industries is expressed in a single sentence: "We treat our
customers, employees, investors and suppliers as we would like to be treated."[44]
Hudson Food Inc. hired a chaplain to provide needed support and counseling to
troubled employees.[45] Lotus Development Corporation formed a "soul" committee to examine the company's management practices and values. The company wants to find ways to make the work environment as humane as possible.[46]
Edward Bednar teaches Zen Buddhist meditation techniques to employees working in the Wall Street area. He is attempting to help them live a more contempla-
tive life.[47] At the Hazelwood, Missouri, Ford Motor plant a nondenominational
prayer group meets regularly.[48]

Spirituality is present in people who have a zest for life and are enthusiastic
about experiencing its richness. Visiting an art gallery, listening to a concert, or
walking near the ocean can stimulate healthy spirituality. Table 9.1 describes
some ways to begin your journey to healthy spirituality.

Healthy spirituality can often serve as a stabilizing force in our lives. The various twelve-step programs (Alcoholics Anonymous is one example) emphasize the
need for a spiritual connection. "Working the steps" means, among other things,
turning life over to a higher power. This spiritual connection seems to give hope to
persons who feel a sense of loneliness and isolation.

For many people, a commitment to a specific religion is an important dimension of spirituality. Active membership in a religious group provides an opportunity to clarify spiritual values and achieve spiritual direction. If you do not attend
the services of some religious group at a church, synagogue, temple, mosque,
whatever—investigate a place of worship that seems compatible with your general orientation and attend a few times. If this experience tends to nurture your
spiritual life, try to incorporate the core beliefs into your life. For many people,

**TABLE 9.1**

**Ways to Achieve Healthy Spirituality**

As interest in healthy spirituality grows, people are searching for ways to become more spiritual. The following spiritual practices draw our focus away from ourselves and the anxieties in our lives.

■ **Meditation**   Oprah Winfrey described the powerful influence of meditation this way: "There is no greater source of strength and power for me in my life now than going still, being quiet and recognizing what real power is."

■ **Prayer**   Dr. Larry Dossey, physician and author of numerous books on the role of spirituality in medicine, says prayer can be a powerful force in our lives. Prayer groups have been established at many organizations.

■ **Spiritual Reading**   In addition to sacred readings, consider *Healing and the Mind* by Bill Moyers, *The Soul of a Business* by Tom Chappell, and *The Hungry Spirit* by Charles Handy.

■ **Time with Nature**   Spiritual contemplation during a walk in the woods or a visit to a quiet lake can help us balance mind, body, and spirit.

*Sources:* David Elkins and Amanda Druckman, "Four Great Ways to Begin Your Spiritual Journey," *Psychology Today*, September/October 1999, p. 46; Larry Dossey, M.D., "Can We Change the World?" *The Inner Edge*, June/July 2000, pp. 22–23.

membership in a religious community provides social connections—an extended family that they can depend on for social support.[49]

As more companies accept the whole person in the workplace, healthy spirituality will grow in importance. Hyler Bracey, consultant and author of *Managing from the Heart*, said, "We used to check our feelings, health, sexuality, spirituality and family problems at the door of the workplace. We've matured enough to get beyond that. The unspeakable is now acceptable."[50]

**TOTAL PERSON INSIGHT**

*AUTHOR UNKNOWN*

*"Don't get crispy fried in business. The insidious suction of achievement could leave you with no soul."*

## Developing a Healthy Lifestyle

Earlier in this chapter we noted that a healthy lifestyle can provide a higher energy level, a greater sense of self-confidence, and generally a more positive outlook on life. People who maintain good health usually have more endurance, spend less time feeling tired or ill, and miss less work than persons who are not

Alcoholic beverages can cause serious health risks when used in excess. If you drink alcohol, do so in moderation.

healthy. Good health is receiving greater attention today because many Americans are investing more time and energy in their work. They are being asked to work longer hours and do more in less time. Good health can help combat stress and tension at work and at home.

There is another important reason to adopt a healthy lifestyle. Throughout the past decade, the cost of health care has steadily increased, and several million Americans do not have health insurance. The old saying "I can't afford to get sick" is on the minds of many workers today.

The first step toward adopting a healthy lifestyle is to become well informed—to read, study, and learn what can be done to maintain your current level of health or improve your health. In this section we offer guidelines that form the framework for a good diet and a good exercise program. The second step is to determine what changes you need to make in your lifestyle and then make those changes.

## Guidelines for a Healthy Diet

Eating the right foods can improve your health, boost your energy level, and in some cases extend your life. The link between health and diet is quite clear. We will review several important dietary guidelines.[51]

**Maintain a Diet That Is Balanced and Varied**　　The best guide to a balanced diet is the Food Guide Pyramid (see Figure 9.2). The pyramid can be used to create a diet weighted toward vegetarian foods. Eating a variety of foods is important because you need more than forty different nutrients for good health: vitamins and minerals, amino acids (from proteins), essential fatty acids

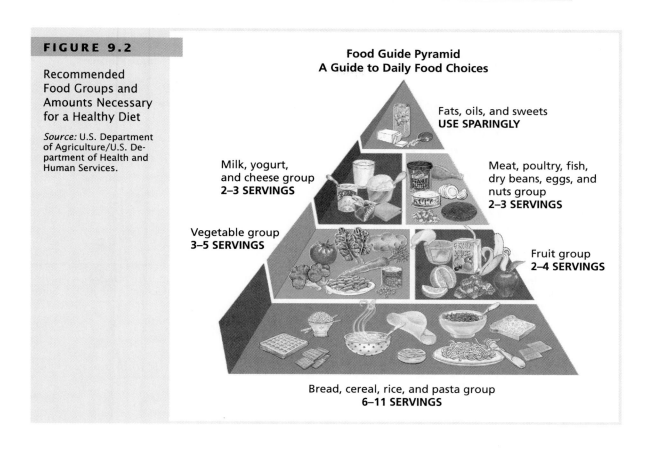

**FIGURE 9.2**

Recommended Food Groups and Amounts Necessary for a Healthy Diet

*Source:* U.S. Department of Agriculture/U.S. Department of Health and Human Services.

(from fats and oils), and sources of energy (calories from carbohydrates, fats, and proteins). Variety counts most in the fruit and vegetable categories because these foods are so rich in nutrients, and nutrients vary from species to species.[52] The number of servings you need each day depends on your total calorie intake. Keep in mind that servings are small—just one slice of bread or piece of fruit; half a cup of cooked rice, pasta, or vegetables; three ounces of cooked lean meat, poultry, or fish.

**Cut Down on Fatty Foods**    The foods that are popular with many Americans are relatively high in fat, especially saturated fat, which contributes to high blood cholesterol levels. Many restaurant foods are high in fat because it gives menu items the flavor people often seek when eating out (see Table 9.2). Heart disease and certain kinds of cancer are byproducts of a high-fat diet. Although diet is the most important factor in lowering cholesterol, exercise can help.

**Eat Foods with Adequate Starch and Fiber**    Foods high in starch, such as breads made with whole grains, dry beans and peas, and potatoes, contain many essential nutrients. Many starches also add dietary fiber to your diet. A growing number of scientists believe that high-fiber diets can help reduce the

**TABLE 9.2**

**Food Choices High in Fat, Sodium, and Calories—Followed by Healthy Alternate Choices**

|  | Fat (grams) | Sodium (milligrams) | Calories |
|---|---|---|---|
| McDonald's Big Breakfast | 51 | 1580 | 760 |
| Burger King Biscuit (with sausage, egg, and cheese) | 43 | 1650 | 620 |
| Denny's Grand Slam | 50 | 2240 | 800 |
| Dunkin' Donuts Bagel (plain) | 1 | 710 | 340 |
| Eggo Nutri-Grain Whole Wheat Waffles | 3 | 430 | 140 |
| Scrambled Egg Substitute (2 eggs' worth) | 6 | 190 | 130 |

*Source:* Excerpt from "The Breakfast Breakdown." Copyright 1999, CSPI. Reprinted/adapted from *Nutrition Action Healthletter,* published by the Center for Science in the Public Interest (CSPI), 1875 Connecticut Avenue, NW, Suite 300, Washington, DC 20009-5728. $24.00 for 10 issues.

odds of getting cancer of the colon. Some cereals and most fruits and vegetables are good sources of fiber.

**Avoid Too Much Sodium**  A common byproduct of excess sodium is high blood pressure. In the United States, where sodium-rich diets are very common, about one in four adults has elevated blood pressure. In populations with low sodium intakes, high blood pressure is very uncommon.[53] The recommended daily intake of sodium is 1,100 to 2,400 milligrams.

**If You Drink Alcohol, Do So in Moderation**  Alcoholic beverages are high in calories and low in nutrients and cause serious health risks when used in excess. When alcohol is consumed in excess of one or two drinks per day, there tends to be a strong relationship between alcohol intake and high blood pressure. Excessive alcohol consumption has been linked to liver damage and certain types of cancer.[54]

With the help of these healthy diet guidelines, you can develop your own plan for achieving a healthful diet. Keep in mind that good nutrition is a balancing act. You want to select foods with enough vitamins, minerals, protein, and fiber but avoid too much fat and sodium. You want to consume enough calories to maintain the energy level required in your life but avoid weight gain.

### Improving Your Physical Fitness

With regard to exercise, people often choose one of two extreme positions. Some adopt the point of view that only high-intensity activities (marathon running, high-impact aerobics) increase physical fitness. These people believe in the "no-pain, no-gain" fitness approach. The other extreme position is to become a "couch potato" and avoid all forms of exercise. Both positions should be avoided.

**Physical fitness** can be defined as the ability to perform daily tasks vigorously and have enough energy left over to enjoy leisure activities. It is the ability to endure difficult and stressful experiences and still carry on. Physical fitness, which involves the performance of the lungs, heart, and muscles, can also have a positive influence on mental alertness and emotional stability. Research indicates that even a moderate level of physical activity can have a surprisingly broad array of health benefits on virtually every major organ system in the body.[55] For most people, a program that involves regular physical activity at least three times a week and includes sustained physical exertion for twenty to thirty minutes during each activity period is adequate.[56] This modest investment of time and energy will give you a longer and healthier life.

You do not need to become an obsessive fitness fanatic to achieve lifesaving benefits from exercise. Start slowly with an aerobic fitness activity you feel you will enjoy. Walking, swimming, running, low-impact aerobics, and jogging are aerobic exercise. When we engage in aerobic exercise, the body is required to improve its ability to handle oxygen.[57] These exercises strengthen the heart, burn up calories, increase stamina, and help release tension.

If you are younger than 35 and in good health, you probably do not need to see a doctor before beginning an exercise program. If you are older than 35 and have been inactive for several years, consult your doctor before engaging in vigorous exercise.[58]

 HUMAN RELATIONS *in* ACTION

### Dare to Change!

In the New Economy there are no rules about how young or how old you should be to relaunch your career. Melissa is the director of training and development for a large retail outlet, and she loves the job. She spent many years searching for a meaningful and fulfilling career. She was first a flight attendant, then a high school teacher, and then a manager of a retail store. Today Melissa feels content because she feels she is doing something worthwhile. Her advice to those who feel their current position is lacking something important? Dare to change!

 *Planning for Changes in Your Life*

Throughout this book we have emphasized the concept that you can control your own behavior. In fact, during these turbulent times changes in your behavior may be one of the few things under your control. If making changes in your life seems to be a logical course of action at this point, then it is time to do some planning.

The starting point is to clearly identify the personal growth goals that can make a difference in your life. What are some behaviors you can adopt (or alter) that will make an important positive change in your life? Once you have identified these behaviors, you can set goals and do what is necessary to achieve them.

## ■ *The Power of Habits*

Before we discuss specific goal-setting methods, let us take a look at the powerful influence of habits. Some habits, like taking a long walk three or four times a week, can have a positive influence on our well-being. Simply saying "Thank you" when someone does a favor or pays a compliment can be a habit. Other habits, such as smoking, never saying no to requests for your time, feeling jealousy, or constantly engaging in self-criticism, are negative forces in our lives. Stephen Covey, author of *The Seven Habits of Highly Effective People,* makes this observation: "Habits are powerful factors in our lives. Because they are consistent, often unconscious patterns, they constantly, daily, express our character and produce our effectiveness . . . or ineffectiveness."[59]

Breaking deeply embedded habits, such as impatience, procrastination, or criticism of others, can take a tremendous amount of effort. The influences supporting the habit, the actual root causes, are often repressed in the subconscious mind and forgotten.[60] How do you break a negative habit or form a positive habit? The process involves five steps.

**Motivation**   Once you are aware of the need to change, you must develop the willingness or desire to change. After making a major commitment to change, you must find ways to maintain your motivation. The key to staying motivated is to develop a mind-set powerful enough that you feel compelled to act on your desire to change. You must continuously remind yourself why you want to change a bad habit or form a new habit. Only when the activity (exercise, weight loss, etc.) becomes personally meaningful will you be motivated to do it regularly.

**Knowledge**   Once you clearly understand the benefits of breaking a habit or forming a new one, you must acquire the knowledge you need to change. Seek information, ask for advice, or learn from the experiences of others. This may involve finding a mentor, joining a group, or gathering sufficient material and teaching yourself. For example, suppose you decide you need to lose weight. Your first step might be to visit a bookstore or the Internet. Your next step might be to talk with others who share the same goal. You might consider joining a support group or talking to a counselor or an expert in nutrition. In the process of acquiring information, you are actually gaining a better understanding of the habit you want to learn or unlearn.

**Practice**   Information is only as useful as you make it. This means that to change your behavior you must *practice* what you have learned. If you are a shy person, does this mean you need to volunteer to make a speech in front of several hundred people? The answer is no. Although there is always the rare individual who makes a major change seemingly overnight, most people find that the best and surest way to develop a new behavior is to do so gradually. This is particularly true if you feel a lot of anxiety about changing. Take your time. Allow yourself to ease into your new behavior until you feel comfortable with it.

**Feedback**    Whenever you can, seek feedback as you attempt to change a habit. Dieters lose more weight if they attend counseling sessions and weigh-ins. People who want to improve their public speaking skills benefit from practice followed by feedback from a teacher or coach. Everyone has blind spots, particularly when trying something new. You will often need to rely on the feedback of others to tell you when you are off course or when you have really changed—sometimes you are too close to the process to tell.

**Reinforcement**    When you see yourself exhibiting the type of behavior you have been working to develop—or when someone mentions that you have changed—reward yourself! The rewards can be simple, inexpensive ones—treating yourself to a movie, a bouquet of flowers, a favorite meal, or a special event. This type of reinforcement is vital when you are trying to improve old behaviors or develop new ones. Do not postpone rewarding yourself until the goal is reached. Intermediate success is just as important as the final result.

## ■ The Goal-Setting Process

Many years ago J. C. Penney, founder of the large retail chain, made a strong statement regarding the value of having goals: "Give me a stock clerk with a goal, and I will give you a man who will make history. Give me a man without a goal, and I will give you a stock clerk."[61] Penney recognized that goals give direction to our lives. Setting and reaching personal goals contributes to emotional well-being. It gives us a sense of personal control and a greater feeling of confidence in ourselves.

Goals should be an integral part of your plan to break old habits or form new ones. You will need an assortment of goals that address the different needs of your life. After a period of serious reflection, you may be facing unlimited goal-setting possibilities. Where do you begin? We hope that reading the previous chapters in this book, completing the self-assessment exercises at the end of each chapter, and reviewing the material in this chapter will help you narrow the possibilities.

The goal-setting process requires that you be clear about what you want to accomplish. If your goal is too general or vague, progress toward reaching that goal will be difficult to observe. Goals such as "I want to be a success" or "I desire good health" are much too general. The more specific the goal, the easier it will be for you to reach.[62]

A very important step in the goal-setting process is to put the goal in writing. Although the power of written goals is widely recognized, many people do not put their goals in writing. A written goal, reviewed daily, is much more likely to be reached.

## The Choice Is Yours

Are you ready to develop a life plan for effective human relations? We hope the answer is yes. One of the positive aspects of personal planning is that you are making your own choices. You decide what kind of person you want to be and then set your own standards and goals. The results can mean not only career advancement and financial benefits but also the development of strong, satisfying relationships with others. These relationships may be the key to future opportunities, and you in turn may be able to help others reach their goals.

In the opening chapter of this text, we talked about the total person approach to human relations. By now, we hope you realize that you are someone special! You have a unique combination of talents, attitudes, values, goals, needs, and motivation—all in a state of development. You can decide to tap your potential to become a successful, productive human being, however *you* understand those terms. We hope this book helps you to develop your human relations skills and to become what you want to be. You can turn the theories, concepts, and guidelines presented here into a plan of action for your own life and career. We wish you the best!

## Summary

The traditional definitions of success that most of us know are too confining. They view success almost entirely in terms of measurable job achievements. These definitions leave out the intangible successes to be had in private and in professional life.

Many people today are discovering that true success is a combination of achievements. Achieving right livelihood is one important dimension of success. Right livelihood is work consciously chosen, done with full awareness and care, and leading to enlightenment. Right livelihood is based on conscious choice. Although right livelihood recognizes that work is a vehicle for self-expression, it is a concept that places money in a secondary position. People who choose right livelihood are more likely to have high self-esteem, are self-disciplined, and have established meaningful goals.

A person's nonfinancial resources make one of the biggest contributions to a happy and fulfilling life. Each of us has four nonfinancial resources that can enrich our lives: physical and mental health, education and training (intellectual growth), leisure time (time for family, socializing, recreation), and healthy spirituality. These nonfinancial resources can be acquired throughout our lives.

Many Americans are working to achieve healthy lifestyles. Healthy lifestyles can give us a higher energy level, a greater sense of self-confidence, and generally a more positive outlook. People who maintain good health usually have more endurance, spend less time feeling tired or ill, and miss less work than persons who are not physically fit.

Planning for changes in your life often requires breaking negative habits or forming positive habits. The process of breaking habits and forming new ones involves five steps: motivation, knowledge, practice, feedback, and reinforcement. Goal setting is also an integral part of a successful plan to make changes. Unspecified or vague goals, goals that are not put in writing, are harder to reach and contribute less than they could to a productive, enriching life.

## Career Corner

Q: Two years ago I accepted a job that was interesting and challenging. The work involved a great deal of human contact, and solving "people problems" was a rewarding experience. Recently the company purchased an automated customer-relationship management system, and now my major responsibility is working with the new technology. I miss the human contact. I have a great deal of job security, but my work is no longer satisfying. Is it time to move on?

A: Job satisfaction is a basic requirement for good mental health. If you find your duties repetitive, frustrating, or unmotivating, it's time to change jobs. Betsy Kyte Newman, author of *Getting Unstuck: Moving Ahead with Your Career,* notes that no one field or even one career will necessarily satisfy you for your entire life. Make a self-assessment and determine what type of work will be satisfying. Explore career options and the realities involved. Will you acquire new skills or some type of college degree? Will you need to relocate? Deciding when to move on is one of the hardest decisions you will make, so spend plenty of time thinking and planning.

## Key Terms

right livelihood
nonfinancial resources

spirituality
physical fitness

## Review Questions

1. What have been the traditional criteria used to measure success? What are some of the reasons we need a new model for success in our society?
2. Explain the reasons many Americans have experienced a decline in leisure time.
3. What does the term *right livelihood* mean? What are the common characteristics of right livelihood?
4. Critics say Americans live in a commercial culture that encourages spending. They say too many people have adopted a work-and-spend cycle. Do you agree? Explain.

5. List and describe the four nonfinancial resources.

6. Julie Connelly in the Total Person Insight says there is no harder work than thinking about who you are and what you want out of life. Do you agree or disagree with her point of view? Explain.

7. What are the major reasons we should adopt a healthy lifestyle?

8. List and describe the guidelines for a healthy diet.

9. Provide a brief description of physical fitness. Why is physical fitness so important in the life of a typical worker?

10. What are the five steps involved in breaking a negative habit or forming a positive habit?

## Application Exercises

1. In recent years, it has become popular for organizations to develop a mission statement that reflects their philosophy and objectives. The Gear for Sports Vision statement provides one example (see Chapter 4). Prepare a personal mission statement that reflects your goals and aspirations for a successful life. Your mission statement should cover the roles of financial and nonfinancial resources in your life.

2. Throughout this chapter you were encouraged to take control of your life and establish your own definition of success. This chapter has a strong "all development is self-development" theme. Can we really control our own destinies? Can we always make our own choices? Mike Hernacki, author of the book *The Ultimate Secret of Getting Absolutely Everything You Want,* says yes:

> To get what you want, you must recognize something that at first may be difficult, even painful to look at. You must recognize that *you alone* are the source of all the conditions and situations in your life. You must recognize that whatever your world looks like right now, you alone have caused it to look that way. The state of your health, your finances, your personal relationships, your professional life—all of it is *your* doing, yours and no one else's.[63]

Do you agree with this viewpoint? Take a position in favor of or in opposition to Hernacki's statement. Prepare a short one- or two-paragraph statement that expresses your views.

3. There are many ways to deepen and extend your spirituality. One way is to begin placing a higher value on silence, tranquillity, and reflection. If your life is extremely busy, you may not be taking time for thought or reflection. If you are accustomed to living in the presence of noise throughout the day, quiet times may make you feel uncomfortable at first. Over a period of one week, set aside a few minutes each day for your own choice of meditation, prayer, contemplation, or reflection. Try to find a quiet place for this activity. At the end of the week, assess the benefits of this activity, and consider the merits of making it part of your daily routine.[64]

## Internet Exercise

At some point in your life, full-time employment will become less appealing. You will begin thinking about part-time work that will give you time to pursue a personal interest, start a family, become an independent consultant, earn a degree, or simply enjoy more leisure time. Several Internet sites can help you acquire information:

| Name | URL | Services |
|------|-----|----------|
| Resources | *www.resourcesconnection.com* | Helps find work for legal, technical, and marketing professionals. |
| Aquent | *www.AquentPartners.com* | Helps find work for print, technical, and Web multimedia professionals. |
| Manpower | *www.Manpower.com* | Finds assignments in a wide variety of fields. |
| Adecro | *www.workflex.monster.com* | Lists several contract jobs and includes a ten-question quiz on whether "flex work" is right for you. |

Visit two of these Web sites and study the job opportunities. Prepare a written summary of your findings.

## Self-Assessment Exercise

For each of the following statements, circle the number from 1 to 5 that best represents your response: (1) strongly disagree (never do this); (2) disagree (rarely do this); (3) moderately agree (sometimes do this); (4) agree (frequently do this); (5) strongly agree (almost always do this).

A. I try to maintain balance in my life by avoiding addiction to work and by engaging in leisure-time activities.       1   2   3   4   5

B. I support the concept of right livelihood and seek work that will be consciously chosen and done with full awareness and care, and that will lead to enlightenment.       1   2   3   4   5

C. I envision my existence in a larger context and view healthy spirituality as a positive, enlightening force in my life.       1   2   3   4   5

D. I avoid rigid individualism (self-centered behavior) by investing time and energy in helping others.　　1　2　3　4　5

E. I seek advice and counsel from friends, coworkers, and professionals in order to cope with life's problems.　　1　2　3　4　5

F. I stay connected with family and friends and monitor the development of my nonfinancial resources carefully.　　1　2　3　4　5

G. I seek to develop a healthy lifestyle.　　1　2　3　4　5

H. I have established well-thought-out, realistic goals for my life, and these goals are tied to my values.　　1　2　3　4　5

Select an appropriate attitude or skill you would like to improve. Write your goal in the space provided, and describe the steps you will take to achieve the goal.

GOAL: _____

_____

_____

_____

## Case Problem　　*Friendships as a Source of Positive Energy*

Friendships formed on the job and off the job can be an important source of positive energy. Edward M. Hallowell, author of *Connect*, says, "To thrive, indeed just to survive, we need warm-hearted contact with other people." He believes that a human-contact deficiency weakens the body, the mind, and the spirit.

Research indicates that the ability to form friendships at work is an important characteristic of a productive workplace. Information age jobs tend to create a work environment where people draw close very fast and rely on one another for support. Diana Freeland, a former manager with a large energy company, says that enjoying friends at work went hand in hand with doing her best work. However, layoffs, reorganizations, and the movement of headquarters resulted in the loss of several good friends. In addition to various job upheavals, the struggle to balance career and family often leaves little room for time with friends.

The Dalai Lama, in his book *The Art of Happiness*, discusses the value of connecting with others through volunteer work. In addition to helping others, volunteer activities can bring us some significant health benefits. Research indicates that interacting in a warm and compassionate way increases life expectancy. He says showing compassion for others is "emotionally nourishing."

Making friends and staying connected with them takes effort and some degree of risk. Some people avoid developing new friendships because they fear being hurt or rejected, or they feel life is too busy to make room for a friendship. Yet when we hold back too often, it becomes a habit. We *need* those human moments—time spent with a friend—in order to thrive in life.[65]

## Questions

1. Many employees report that some of their closest friends are also their colleagues. Can you think of any problems that might surface if your closest friends were colleagues on the job?
2. Interacting with others in a warm and compassionate way seems to offer us improved health and vitality. What would explain these beneficial effects?

# NOTES

## Chapter 1

1. Kip Tindell, "Who Says a Trash Can Can't Make You Smile? Transcending Value at The Container Store," *Retailing Issues Letter*, January 2000, pp. 1–6; Daniel Roth, "My Job at The Container Store," *Fortune,* January 10, 2000, pp. 74–78; Robert Levering and Milton Moskowitz, "The 100 Best Companies to Work For," *Fortune,* January 8, 2001, p. 149.

2. Edward M. Hallowell, *Connect* (New York: Pantheon Books, 1999), pp. 1–14.

3. John Seely Brown and Paul Duguid, *The Social Life of Information* (Boston: Harvard Business School Press, 2000), pp. 2–13.

4. Seanna Browder, "Boeing's Revised Flight Plan," *Business Week,* December 21, 1998, p. 39; Carlos Tejada, "Work Week," *Wall Street Journal*, June 20, 2000, p. A1.

5. Joann S. Lublin, "Mergers Often Trigger Anxiety, Lower Morale," *Wall Street Journal*, January 16, 2001, pp. B1, B4.

6. Hal Lancaster, "Managing Your Career," *Wall Street Journal*, February 18, 1997, p. B1; David Wessel, "Temp Workers Have Lasting Effect," *Wall Street Journal*, February 1, 2001, p. A1.

7. Jeffrey Pfeffer, *The Human Equation* (Boston: Harvard Business School Press, 1998), pp. 293.

8. Chris Lee, "The Death of Civility," *Training*, July 1999, pp. 24–30.

9. Stephen L. Carter, *Civility* (New York: Basic Books, 1998), p. 11.

10. Bernard Avishai, "Companies Can't Make Up for Failing Schools," *Wall Street Journal*, July 28, 1996, p. A12.

11. Jeff Pettit, "Team Communication: It's in the Cards," *Training & Development*, January 1997, p. 12.

12. William C. Taylor, "Inspired by Work," *Fast Company*, November 1999, pp. 200–202; Katharine Mieszkowski, "Report from the Future," *Fast Company*, November 1999, pp. 66–68.

13. Gene Koretz, "A New Economy, but No New Deal," *Business Week*, July 10, 2000, p. 34; Lauren Storck, "The Rich Make Us Sick," *Psychology Today*, September/October 1999, p. 2; "Helping America's Working Poor," *Business Week*, July 17, 2000, p. 164.

14. Haidee Allerton, "Working Life," *Training & Development*, August 1995, p. 72.

15. Joseph Pereira, "Employers Confront Domestic Abuse," *Wall Street Journal*, March 2, 1995, p. B1.

16. Maggie Jackson, "Dads Speak Up About Work-Family," *Roanoke Times*, June 15, 1997, p. B1.

17. Kevin Dobbs, "Tires Plus—Taking the Training High Road," *Training*, April 2000, pp. 57–63.

18. Robert Kreitner, *Management*, 8th ed. (Boston: Houghton Mifflin, 2001), p. 282.

19. Allan A. Kennedy, interview by, in "The Culture Wars," *Inc.*, 20th Anniversary Issue, 1999, pp. 107–108.

20. David Stamps, "Going Nowhere: Culture Change at the Postal Service Fizzles," *Training*, July 1996, pp. 26–34.

21. William W. Arnold and Jeanne M. Plas, *The Human Touch* (New York: Wiley, 1993), pp. 1 and 2.

22. D. R. Hampton, C. E. Summer, and R. A. Webber, *Organizational Behavior and the Practice of Management* (Glenview, Ill.: Scott, Foresman, 1973), p. 215.

23. "Great Expectations," *Fast Company*, November 1999, p. 224.

24. Betsy Jacobson and Beverly Kaye, "Balancing Act," *Training & Development*, February 1993, p. 26.

25. Jacobson and Kaye, "Balancing Act," pp. 24–26.

26. Sue Shellenbarger, "For Harried Workers in the 21st Century, Six Trends to Watch," *Wall Street Journal*, December 29, 1999, p. B1.

27. Rochelle Sharpe, "Labor Letter," *Wall Street Journal*, September 13, 1994, p. 1.

28. Alan Farnham, "The Man Who Changed Work Forever," *Fortune*, July 21, 1997, p. 114.

29. George F. Will, "A Faster Mousetrap," *New York Times Book Review*, June 15, 1997, p. 8.

30. Bradley J. Rieger, "Lessons in Productivity and People," *Training & Development*, October 1995, pp. 56–58.

31. For a detailed examination of the Hawthorne criticisms and the legacy of the Hawthorne research, see David A. Whitsett and Lyle Yorks, *From Management Theory to Business Sense* (New York: American Management Association, 1983).

32. Jim Collins, "The Classics," *Inc.*, December 1996, p. 55.

33. Thomas J. Peters and Robert H. Waterman, Jr., *In Search of Excellence: Lessons from America's Best-Run Companies* (New York: Harper & Row, 1982), p. 14.

34. *Human Connections* (Englewood Cliffs, N.J.: Prentice-Hall, 1982), p. xii.

35. Stephen R. Covey, *The 7 Habits of Highly Effective People* (New York: Simon & Schuster, 1989), pp. 66–67.

36. Richard Koonce, "Emotional IQ, A New Secret of Success," *Training & Development*, February 1996, p. 19.

37. Denis Waitley, *Empires of the Mind* (New York: Morrow, 1995), p. 133.

38. Michael Crom, "Building Trust in the Workplace," *The Leader*, October 1998, p. 6; Ron Zemke, "Can You Manage Trust?" *Training*, February 2000, pp. 76–83.

39. Harold H. Bloomfield and Robert K. Cooper, *The Power of 5* (Emmaus, Pa.: Rodale Press, 1995), p. 61.

40. Thomas Petzinger, Jr., "The Front Lines," *Wall Street Journal*, May 21, 1999, p. B1; Lucy McCauley, "Relaunch!" *Fast Company*, July 2000, pp. 97–108; Liz Stevens, "In the Race, America Has the Most Rats," *The News and Observer*, November 21, 1999, p. E3.

## Chapter 2

1. Lin Grensing-Pophal, "Follow Me," *HR Magazine*, February 2000, p. 41.
2. Christopher Caggiano, "Low-Tech Smarts," *Inc.*, January 1999, p. 79.
3. Grensing-Pophal, "Follow Me," p. 41.
4. Don Clark, "Managing the Mountain," *Wall Street Journal*, June 21, 1999, p. R4.
5. John Stewart and Gary D'Angelo, *Together—Communicating Interpersonally* (New York: Random House, 1988), p. 5.
6. Carol Hymowitz, "Advice on Organizing from the (Clean) Desks of Some Busy Workers," *Wall Street Journal*, December 29, 1998, p. B1.
7. David Shenk, *Data Smog—Surviving the Information Glut* (San Francisco: Harper Edge, 1997), p. 54.
8. Sy Lazarus, *Loud and Clear* (New York: AMACOM, 1974), p. 3.
9. Ronald G. Shafer, "Government Bureaucrats to Learn a New Language: Simple English," *Wall Street Journal*, June 2, 1998, p. B1.
10. "Clean It Up—Or Else," *Business Week*, October 26, 1998, p. 8.
11. "Memos from Hell," *Fortune*, February 3, 1997, p. 120.
12. Matthew McKay, Martha Davis, and Patrick Fanning, *Messages: The Communication Skills Book* (Oakland, Calif.: New Harbinger, 1995), p. 108.
13. Ibid.
14. Deborah Tannen, *You Just Don't Understand* (New York: Ballantine Books, 1991), p. 42.
15. Judith C. Tingley, *Genderflex: Men and Women Speaking Each Other's Language at Work* (New York: AMACOM, 1994), p. 33.
16. Ginger Trumfio, "More Than Words," *Sales & Marketing Management*, April 1994, p. 55.
17. Phyllis Mindell, "The Body Language of Power," *Executive Female*, May/June 1996, p. 48.
18. Roger E. Axtell, ed., *Do's and Taboos Around the World*, compiled by Parker Pen Company, 3d ed. (New York: Wiley, 1993), p. 46.
19. Ibid, p. 47.
20. Ibid, p. 49.
21. William B. Gudykunst, Stella Ting-Toomey, Sandra Sudweeks, and Lea Stewart, *Building Bridges: Interpersonal Skills for a Changing World* (Boston: Houghton Mifflin, 1995), pp. 315–316.
22. C. Glenn Pearce, "How Effective Are We as Listeners?" *Training & Development*, April 1993, pp. 79–80.
23. Cheryl Shavers, "Stopping Your Chatty Boss Calls for Sensitivity, Insight," *San Jose Mercury News*, October 26, 1997, p. 3E.
24. John Chaffee, *Thinking Critically*, 5th ed. (Boston: Houghton Mifflin, 1996), pp. 40, 72.

25. Michael Toms, "Dialogue—the Art of Thinking Together—Sparks Spirit of 'Aliveness' in Organizations," *The Inner Edge*, August/September 1998, p. 8.
26. Ibid, p. 462.
27. Stephen R. Covey, *The 7 Habits of Highly Effective People* (New York: Simon & Schuster, 1989), pp. 240–241.
28. C. Glenn Pearce, "Learning How to Listen Empathically," *Supervisory Management*, September 1991, p. 11.
29. James G. Carr, "Dare to Share," *Pace*, June 1988, p. 22.
30. Hendric Weisinger and Norman Lobsenz, *Nobody's Perfect—How to Give Criticism and Get Results* (Los Angeles: Stratford Press, 1981), p. 39.
31. Winston Wood, "Work Week," *Wall Street Journal*, February 6, 2001, p. A1.
32. Joshua D. Macht, "How Has Technology Changed the Way You Do Your Job?," *Inc.*—[cited 23 June 2000]. Available from inc.com/inc.magazine/searchthearchives/How has technology changed the way you do your job?; INTERNET.
33. "Etiquette with Office Gadgets," *Training*, January 1999, p. 24.
34 "Etiquette with Office Gadgets," p. 24.
35. Sabrina Jones, "Employees Using E-Mail to Gossip, Kill Time or Swap Jokes Seem Blithely Unaware That They Have No Right to Privacy," *Wall Street Journal*, July 24, 1999, p. D1; Michael J. McCarthy, "Virtual Morality: A New Workplace Quandary," *Wall Street Journal*, October 21, 2000, p. B1; Michael R. McCarthy, "Your Manager's Policy on Employees' E-Mail May Have a Weak Spot," *Wall Street Journal*, April 25, 2000, p. B1; Julia Angwin, "A Plan to Track Web Use Stirs Privacy Concern," *Wall Street Journal*, May 1, 2000, p. B1; Douglas Dahlbert, "Web Surfers Beware: The Company Tech May Be a Secret Agent," *Wall Street Journal*, January 10, 2000, p. A1; Nick Wingfield, "More Companies Monitor Employees' E-Mail," *Wall Street Journal*, December 2, 1999, p. B8; David L. Wilson, "Should Bosses Be Monitoring Their Workers?" *San Jose Mercury News*, September 26, 1999, p. 1E; Stephen D. Lewis and Linda G. McGrew, "Teaching the Perils of E-Mail," *Business Education Forum*, February 2000, pp. 26–27; Michelle Conlin, "Workers, Surf at Your Own Risk," *Business Week*, June 12, 2000, p. 105; James Lardner, "Every Click You Make . . . ," *U.S. News & World Report*, November 8, 1999, p. 69; Michael Schrage, "E-Mail or E-Sting? Your Boss Knows, but He's Not Telling," *Fortune*, March 20, 2000, p. 240.
36. Kara Swisher, "Bill Gates Got an Education; So Should We," *Wall Street Journal*, June 8, 2000, p. B1.

## Chapter 3

1. Dennis M. Kalup, "Body Image, Positive or Negative, Shapes People's Lives," *The Digital Collegian*, July 10, 1997, p. 2.
2. Gene Koretz, "The Vital Role of Self-Esteem," *Business Week*, February 2, 1998; Nanci Hellmich, "Overweight Kids Thrive on Less, Not S'mores," *USA Today*, July 6, 2000, p. D1.
3. Nathaniel Branden, *The Six Pillars of Self-Esteem* (New York: Bantam, 1994), p. 7.

4. Nathaniel Branden, *Self-Esteem at Work* (San Francisco: Jossey-Bass, 1998), p. xii.
5. Kate Berry, "Starbucks Opens First Stores in Miami, Hoping to Woo Lovers of Cuban Coffee," *Wall Street Journal*, March 31, 1997, p. A9; Jennifer Reese, "Starbucks—Inside the Coffee Cult," *Fortune*, December 9, 1996, pp. 190–198.
6. David E. Shapiro, "Pumping Up Your Attitude," *Psychology Today*, May/June 1997, p. 14.
7. Richard Laliberte, "Self-Esteem Workshop," *Self*, May 1994, p. 201.
8. Branden, *The Six Pillars of Self-Esteem*, p. 39.
9. Tim Simmons and Ruth Sheehan, "Even in Earliest Years, Brain Is 'Wiring' for Life," *The News & Observer*, February 16, 1997, p. 1A.
10. Amy Bjork Harris and Thomas A. Harris, *Staying OK* (New York: Harper & Row, 1985), p. 24.
11. Margaret Henning and Ann Jardim, *The Managerial Woman* (New York: Anchor Books, 1977), pp. 106–107.
12. Ellen Graham, "Leah: Life Is All Sweetness and Insecurity," *Wall Street Journal*, February 9, 1995, p. B16.
13. Margaret S. Friedman, "Parenting for Self-Esteem"—[cited 2 July 2000]. Available from coolware.com/health/medical_reporter/parent.html. INTERNET.
14. Emmett Miller, *The Healing Power of Happiness* (Emmaus, Pa.: Rodale Press, 1989), pp. 12–13.
15. Amy Saltzman, *Downshifting* (New York: HarperCollins, 1990), pp. 15–16.
16. Miller, *The Healing Power of Happiness*, pp. 12–13.
17. Belleruth Naparstek, "About Face," *Common Boundary*, July/August 1996, p. 64.
18. Richard Ringer, David Balkin, and R. Wayne Boxx, "Matching the Feedback to the Person," *Executive Female*, November/December 1993, p. 11.
19. Arthur H. Goldsmith, Jonathan R. Veum, and William Darity, Jr., "The Impact of Psychological and Human Capital on Wages," *Economic Inquiry*, October 1997, p. 817.
20. Hyrum W. Smith, *The 10 Natural Laws of Successful Time and Life Management* (New York: Warner Books, 1994), p. 178.
21. Branden, *The Six Pillars of Self-Esteem*, p. 33.
22. Matthew McKay and Patrick Fanning, *Self-Esteem*, 2d ed. (Oakland, Calif.: New Harbinger, 1992), p. 42.
23. Ibid., pp. 18–19.
24. California State Department of Education, *Toward a State of Esteem* (Sacramento: Department of Education, January 1990), p. 19.
25. Robert J. Kriegel, with Louis Platier, *If It Ain't Broke . . . Break It!* Audiotape (Irwindale, Calif.: Barr Audio, 1992).
26. Arnold A. Lazarus and Clifford N. Lazarus, *The 60-Second Shrink* (San Luis Obispo, Calif.: Impact Publishers, 1997), p. 40.
27. Chip R. Bell, "Making Mentoring a Way of Life," *Training*, October 1996, p. 138; Lin Standke, review of *Managers as Mentors: Building Partnerships for Learning*, by Chip R. Bell, *Training*, April 1997, pp. 64–65.
28. Matt Murray, "GE Mentoring Program Turns Underlings into Teachers of the Web," *Wall Street Journal*, February 15, 2000, p. B1.
29. Hal Lancaster, "It's Harder, but You Still Can Rise Up from the Mail Room," *Wall Street Journal*, June 18, 1996, p. B1.
30. Ibid.
31. Lazarus and Lazarus, *The 60-Second Shrink*, pp. 3, 4.
32. Shakti Gawain, *Creative Visualization* (San Rafael, Calif.: Whatever Publishing, 1978), p. 14.
33. Larry King, "Quayle Had Tiger by the Tail Years Ago," *USA Today*, June 26, 2000, p. 2D.
34. Lazarus and Lazarus, *The 60-Second Shrink*, pp. 1, 2.
35. McKay and Fanning, *Self-Esteem*, pp. 33–34.
36. Herb Kindler, "Working to Change Old Habits," *Working Smart*, May 1992, p. 8.
37. Julia Flynn Siler, "The Corporate Woman: Is She Really Different?" *Business Week*, June 25, 1990, p. 14.
38. Roy J. Blitzer, Colleen Petersen, and Linda Rogers, "How to Build Self-Esteem," *Training & Development*, February 1993, pp. 58–60.
39. Rebecca Mead, "Ophelia Fights Back," *The New Yorker*, November 8, 1998, p. 19.
40. Mary Pipher, *Reviving Ophelia* (New York: Ballantine Books, 1994), p. 23.
41. David M. Garner, "The 1997 Body Image Survey," *Psychology Today*, January/February 1997, pp. 30–48; "Altering Your Image: Strategies from the Trenches," *Psychology Today*, January/February 1997, p. 80; Pipher, *Reviving Ophelia*, pp. 183–184; Rebecca Mead, "Ophelia Fights Back," p. 19; *University of California at Berkeley Wellness Letter*, May 2000, p. 1.

## Chapter 4

1. "GenXers Represent Best of American Values," from AgeVenture News Service, David Demko, ed. [cited July 1, 2000], available from www.demko.com/genx.htm.
2. Sharon Begley, "A World of Their Own," *Newsweek*, May 8, 2000, pp. 53–56.
3. Carolyn Kleiner and Mary Lord, "The Cheating Game," *U.S. News & World Report*, November 22, 1999, pp. 55–66; Chad Kaydo, "Liar, Liar," *Sales & Marketing Management*, March 1998, p. 15.
4. Michael Toms, "Investing in Character: An Interview with Sir John Templeton," *The Inner Edge*, June/July 2000, pp. 5–8.
5. David Gergen, "Candidates with Character" *U.S. News & World Report*, September 27, 1999, p. 68.
6. Patrick Smith, "You Have a Job, but How About a Life?" *Business Week*, November 16, 1998, p. 30.
7. Nathaniel Branden, *Self-Esteem at Work* (San Francisco: Jossey-Bass, 1998), p. 35.
8. Stephen R. Covey, *The 7 Habits of Highly Effective People* (New York: Simon & Schuster, 1989), p. 92.
9. Joseph Josephson and Ednah Josephson, *Character Counts Wallet Card* (Marina del Rey, Calif.: Josephson Institute of Ethics, 1994). Available from www.josephsoninstitute.com —[cited 9 July 2000]; INTERNET.
10. "Where to Learn More About Character Education," *Techniques*, May 1999, p. 29.
11. Hyrum W. Smith, *The 10 Natural Laws of Successful Time and Life Management* (New York: Warner Books, 1994), pp. 14–15.

12. J. David McCracken and Ana E. Falcon-Emmanuelli, "A Theoretical Basis for Work Values Research in Vocational Education," *Journal of Vocational and Technical Education*, April 1994, p. 4.

13. Sue Shellenbarger, "Some Top Executives Are Finding a Balance Between Job and Home," *Wall Street Journal*, April 23, 1997, p. B1.

14. Katharine Mieszkowski, "FitzGerald Family Values," *Fast Company*, April 1998, p. 194.

15. Rebecca Ganzel, "Book Reviews," *Training*, June 2000, pp. 76–77.

16. Katherine Paterson, "Family Values," *New York Times Book Review*, October 15, 1995, p. 32.

17. Toms, "Investing in Character," *The Inner Edge*, June/July 2000, pp. 5–8.

18. Chris Lee and Ron Zemke, "The Search for Spirit in the Workplace," *Training*, June 1993, p. 21.

19. Stanley M. Elam, Lowell C. Rose, and Alec M. Gallup, "The 26th Annual Phi Delta Kappa/Gallup Poll of the Public's Attitudes Toward the Public Schools," *Phi Delta Kappan*, September 1994, p. 49.

20. Sonia L. Nazario, "School Teachers Say It's Wrongheaded to Try to Teach Students What's Right," *Wall Street Journal*, April 6, 1990, p. B1.

21. Sanford N. McDonnell, "A Virtuous Agenda for Education Reform," *Wall Street Journal*, February 18, 1997, p. A22.

22. "Wellness Facts," *University of California at Berkeley Wellness Letter*, July 1998, p. 1.

23. Morris Massey, *The People Puzzle* (Reston, Va.: Reston Publishing, 1979).

24. Jeffrey L. Seglin, "Playing by the Rules," *Inc.*, November 1996, p. 39.

25. Neal Donald Walsch, *Conversations with God, Book 1 Guidebook* (Charlottesville, Va.: Hampton Roads, 1997), p. 71.

26. David Welch, "It Isn't Easy Going Green Alone," *Business Week*, May 29, 2000, p. 54.

27. Leon E. Wynter, "Business & Race," *Wall Street Journal*, June 10, 1998, p. B1.

28. "McDonnell Douglas Executive Ousted," Associated Press, *Springfield NewsLeader*, October 27, 1996, p. A1.

29. Sue Shellenbarger, "In Real Life, Hard Choices Upset Any Balancing Act," *Wall Street Journal*, April 19, 1995, p. B1.

30. Smith, *The 10 Natural Laws of Successful Time and Life Management*, pp. 68–69.

31. John Beebe, "Conscience, Integrity and Character," *The Inner Edge*, June/July 2000, pp. 9–11.

32. Vivian Arnold, B. June Schmidt, and Randall L. Wells, "Ethics Instruction in the Classrooms of Business Educators," *Delta Pi Epsilon Journal*, vol. 38, no. 4, Fall 1996, p. 185.

33. "Workers Cut Ethical Corners, Survey Finds," *Wall Street Journal*, March 10, 1995, p. A2.

34. Jennifer Reingold, "In Search of Leadership," *Business Week*, November 15, 1999, p. 176.

35. "Nearly Half of Workers Take Unethical Actions—Survey," *Des Moines Register*, April 7, 1997, p. 18B.

36. Paula Ancona, "How to Handle Unethical Situations in the Office," *San Jose Mercury News*, July 9, 1995, p. 1PC.

37. Sherwood Ross, "The Thief on the Payroll," *San Jose Mercury News*, April 14, 1996, p. 1PC. Michael J. McCarthy, "An Ex-Divinity Student Works on Searching the Corporate Soul," *Wall Street Journal*, June 18, 1999, p. B1.

38. Marian Wright Edelman, *The Measure of Our Success* (Boston: Allyn and Bacon, 1992), pp. 502–503.

39. "Long-Distance Services Target Customers' Values," *Springfield NewsLeader*, June 25, 1996, p. C1.

40. Jerry Useem, "Welcome to the New Company Town," *Fortune*, January 10, 2000, pp. 62–70.

41. Sue Shellenbarger, "Some Workers Find Bosses Don't Share Their Family Values," *Wall Street Journal*, July 12, 1995, p. B1.

42. Betsy Weisendanger, "Doing the Right Thing," *Sales & Marketing Management*, March 1991, p. 82.

43. Jerry Useem, "New Ethics . . . or No Ethics," *Fortune*, March 2000, pp. 81–86.

44. Susan Scherreik, "A Conscience Doesn't Have to Make You Poor," *Business Week*, May 1, 2000, pp. 204–206.

45. Ibid., p. 205.

46. Michael Krebs, "All the Marketing Men," *Autoweek*, February 16, 1998, p. 11.

47. "Do's and Don'ts of a Sea Cruise," *U.S. News & World Report*, August 9, 1999, p. 12.

48. Mary Ellen Egan, "Old Enough to Know Better," *Business Ethics*, January/February 1995, p. 19.

49. Bob Filipczak, "The Soul of the Hog," *Training*, February 1996, pp. 38–42.

50. Andrew Stark, "What's the Matter with Business Ethics?" *Harvard Business Review*, May/June 1993, p. 38.

51. "Tom Chappell—Minister of Commerce," *Business Ethics*, January/February 1994, p. 17.

52. "Ethical Programs and Personal Values Are Still Not Enough," *Business Ethics*, May/June 1996, p. 12.

53. Joshua Hyatt, "How to Hire Employees," *Inc.*, March 1990, p. 2.

54. Phillip Barnhart, "The Ethics Game," *Training*, June 1993, pp. 65, 66.

55. Ellen Neuborne, "Whistle-Blowers Pipe Up More Frequently," *USA Today*, July 22, 1996, p. 2B; Edward T. Pound, "Nurse's Clues Shut Down Research," *USA Today*, July 13, 2000, p. 3A; Lee Gomes, "A Whistle-Blower Finds Jackpot at the End of His Quest," *Wall Street Journal*, April 27, 1998, p. B1.

56. Jan Yager, *Business Protocol—How to Survive and Succeed in Business*, 2d ed. (Stanford, Conn.: Hannacroix Creek Books, 2001), pp. 109–119.

57. Chris Hill and Toby Hanlon, "26 Simple Ways to Change How You Feel," *Prevention*, August 1993, p. 126.

58. Jennifer J. Laabs, "Beef About Employee Benefits Causes Religious Group to Boycott Disney," *Personnel Journal*, August 1996, p. 11; "Southern Baptists Take on Disney," *U.S. News & World Report*, June 24, 1996, p. 18; Kate Clinton, "The Lull Before the Lull," *Progressive*, August 1996, p. 46.

## Chapter 5

1. Peter Carbonara, "Hire for Attitude, Train for Skill," *Fast Company*, August 1996, pp. 73–75; Eileen P. Gunn, "How Mirage Resorts Sifted 75,000 Applicants to Hire 9,600 in

24 weeks," *Fortune*, October 12, 1998, p. 195; Timothy Aeppel, "Toyota Plant Roils the Hiring Hierarchy of an Indiana Town," *Wall Street Journal*, April 6, 1999, p. A1.

2. Carbonara, "Hire for Attitude, Train for Skill," p. 74.
3. "A Matter of Attitude," *Royal Bank Letter,* May/June 1994, p. 2.
4. Tom Lopp, "Attitude Makes a Difference," *Vocational Education Journal*, January 1996, p. 8.
5. Price Pritchett, *Teamwork—The Team Member Handbook* (Dallas, Tex.; Pritchett & Associates, Inc., 1992), p. 26.
6. Carol Kleiman, "Workers Who Quit Aren't Traitors; They're Targets for Re-Recruitment," *San Jose Mercury News*, May 14, 2000, p. PC1.
7. Jerome Kagan, *Psychology: An Introduction* (New York: Harcourt Brace Jovanovich, 1984), p. 548.
8. William F. Schoell and Joseph P. Guiltinan, *Marketing*, 5th ed. (Boston: Allyn and Bacon, 1992), pp. 166–167; William M. Pride and O. C. Ferrell, *Marketing* (Boston: Houghton Mifflin, 2000), p. 211.
9. Joan Hamilton, "Net Work: At Icarian, It's All Work and Some Play," *Business Week E.BIZ*, April 3, 2000, p. EB116.
10. John Case, "Corporate Culture," *Inc.*, November 1996, pp. 42–53.
11. Thomas E. Ricks, "New Marines Illustrate Growing Gap Between Military and Society," *Wall Street Journal*, July 27, 1995, p. A1.
12. Shawn Cavence, "Spiritual Doctor Sets Up Shop," *Collegiate Times*, February 20, 1990, p. A6.
13. Nathaniel Branden, *Self-Esteem at Work* (San Francisco: Jossey-Bass, 1998), pp. 94–97; "Adjusting an Attitude," *San Jose Mercury News*, August 20, 1997, p. G6.
14. Nancy L. Mueller, "Wisconsin Power and Light's Model Diversity Program," *Training & Development*, March 1996, p. 57.
15. His Holiness the Dalai Lama and Howard C. Cutler, *The Art of Happiness* (New York: Riverhead Books, 1998), pp. 16–17.
16. Michael Crom, "Live Enthusiastically and You'll Live Successfully," *Training*, April 1999, p. 6.
17. His Holiness the Dalai Lama and Howard C. Cutler, *The Art of Happiness*, p. 22.
18. Ibid., p. 23.
19. Patricia Sellers, "Now Bounce Back!" *Fortune*, May 1, 1995, p. 57.
20. Martin Seligman, *Learned Optimism* (New York: Knopf, 2001), p. 4.
21. Redford Williams and Virginia Williams, *Anger Kills* (New York: Harper Perennial, 1993), p. 12.
22. Bob Wall, *Working Relationships* (Palo Alto, Calif.: Davies-Black, 1999), pp. 11–12.
23. Ibid., p. 17.
24. Harry E. Chambers, *The Bad Attitude Survival Guide* (Reading, Mass.: Addison-Wesley, 1998), pp. 6–7.
25. Nathaniel Branden, *Self-Esteem at Work* (San Francisco, Calif.: Jossey-Bass, 1998), pp. 111–112.
26. Hamilton, "Net Work," p. EB117.
27. Quoted in Nancy W. Collins, Susan K. Gilbert, and Susan Nycum, *Women Leading: Making Tough Choices on the Fast Track* (Lexington, Mass.: Stephen Greene Press, 1988), p. 1.

28. Candace Goforth, "Why J. M. Smucker Is Such a Sweet Place to Work," *San Jose Mercury News*, May 9, 2000, p. 3F.
29. Shelly Branch, "The 100 Best Companies to Work For in America," *Fortune*, January 11, 1999, p. 121.
30. Ibid.
31. Timothy Aeppel, "Not All Workers Find Idea of Empowerment as Neat as It Sounds," *Wall Street Journal*, September 8, 1997, p. A1; Barbara Moses, *Career Intelligence* (San Francisco: Berrett-Koehler, 1998). Available from www.go.com/workingwounded/SoLongStability—[cited 14 July 2000]; INTERNET.

## Chapter 6

1. John Hechinger, "Quick-Change Artists: In the Casual Office, Keep a Suit on Hand," *Wall Street Journal*, August 2, 2000, p. A1.
2. Ibid.
3. Ibid., p. A10.
4. Stephen R. Covey, *The 7 Habits of Highly Effective People* (New York: Simon & Schuster, 1989), pp. 22, 34.
5. Susan Bixler, *Professional Presence* (New York: G. P. Putnam's Sons, 1991), p. 16.
6. "Author: Success Pivots on First Impressions," *San Jose Mercury News*, November 8, 1992, p. 2PC.
7. Douglas A. Bernstein, Alison Clarke-Stewart, Louis A. Pence, Edward J. Roy, and Christopher D. Wickens, *Psychology*, 5th ed. (Boston: Houghton Mifflin, 2000), pp. 226–227.
8. "Dress Codes for Presidential Candidates," *Parade Magazine*, November 5, 1995, p. 17.
9. Malcolm Fleschner, with Gerhard Gschwandtner, "Power Talk," *Personal Selling Power*, July/August 1995, p. 14.
10. Leonard Zunin and Natalie Zunin, *Contact—The First Four Minutes* (New York: Ballantine Books, 1972), p. 17.
11. Clyde Haberman, "No Offense," *New York Times Book Review*, February 18, 1996, p. 11.
12. Diane E. Lewis, "Some Firms in a Twist over Braids," *San Jose Mercury News*, May 25, 1997, p. 1PC. For an update on this hairstyle issue see Ray A. Smith, "Cornrows for Men Built Momentum, Exploded into Mainstream This Year," *Wall Street Journal*, July 31, 2000, p. B11.
13. Haberman, "No Offense," p. 11.
14. Bixler, *Professional Presence*, p. 141.
15. Haidee E. Allerton, "Dress Code Backlash," *Training & Development*, August 1997, p. 8.
16. Dave Knesel, "Image Consulting—A Well-Dressed Step Up the Corporate Ladder," *Pace*, July/August 1981, p. 74.
17. Cora Daniels, "The Man in the Tan Khaki Pants," *Fortune*, May 1, 2000, p. 338.
18. Megan Schnabel and Amy Kane, "Toss the Tie, Lose the Suit—The Casual Look Is In," *The Roanoke Times*, September 5, 1999, pp. B1, B2.
19. Wendy Bounds, Rebecca Quick, and Emily Nelson, "In the Office, It's Anything Goes," *Wall Street Journal*, August 26, 1999, pp. B1, B4.
20. Anne Fisher, "Ask Annie," *Fortune*, May 15, 2000, p. 504; Frederic M. Biddle, "Work Week," *Wall Street Journal*, February 15, 2000.

21. "HR Sows Its Fall Collection," *Training*, August 1996, p. 14; Bounds, Quick, and Nelson, "In the Office, It's Anything Goes."

22. Deborah Blum, "Face It!" *Psychology Today*, September/October 1998, pp. 34 and 69.

23. Susan Bixler, *The Professional Image* (New York: Perigee Books, 1984), p. 217.

24. Ibid., p. 219.

25. Marc Hequet, "Giving Good Feedback," *Training*, September 1994, p. 74.

26. Adapted from Zunin and Zunin, *Contact*, pp. 102–108; "Handshake 101," *Training & Development*, November 1995, p. 71.

27. Amy Gamerman, "Lunch with Letitia: Our Reporter Minds Her Manners," *Wall Street Journal*, March 3, 1994, p. A14.

28. Barbara Pachter and Mary Brody, *Complete Business Etiquette Handbook* (Englewood Cliffs, N.J.: Prentice-Hall, 1995), p. 3.

29. Kevin Dobbs, "Mind Your Manners—It's Big Business," *Training*, May 2000, pp. 48–52.

30. Jacqueline Thompson, *Image Impact* (New York: Ace Books, 1981), p. 8.

31. Bob Greene, "Why Must We Say Things Like . . . and . . . ?" *Roanoke Times & World-News*, April 27, 1980, p. 7.

32. Ann Marie Sabath, "Meeting Etiquette: Agendas and More," *DECA Dimensions*, January/February 1994, p. 8.

33. Susan Bixler, "Your Professional Presence," *Training Dimensions*, vol. 9, no. 1, 1994, p. 1.

34. Letitia Baldrige, *Letitia Baldrige's Complete Guide to Executive Manners* (New York: Rawson Associates, 1985), p. 13.

35. Nancy K. Austin, "What Do America Online and Dennis Rodman Have in Common?" *Inc.*, July 1997, p. 54.

36. Stephanie G. Sherman, *Make Yourself Memorable* (New York: American Management Association, 1996), pp. 3–4; Michael J. McCarthy, "America Saw Itself in DiMaggio, and It Liked What It Saw," *Wall Street Journal*, March 9, 1999, pp. A1 and A8; "People in the News," *U.S. News & World Report*, November 8, 1999, p. 12; Ann Landers, "If You've Got Class, Nothing Else Matters," *The News & Observer*, July 11, 1998, p. 2E.

**Chapter 7**

1. Kenneth Labich, "No More Crude at Texaco," *Fortune*, September 6, 1999, pp. 205–212; "Rooting Out Racism," *Business Week*, January 10, 2000, p. 86; Carol Memmott, "Author Offers Ugly Account of Texaco Lawsuit," *USA Today*, April 13, 1998, p. 6B.

2. Wendy Zellner, Michael Arndt, and Amy Borrus, "Keeping the Hive Humming," *Business Week*, April 24, 2000, pp. 50–52.

3. Marilyn Loden and Judy B. Rosener, *Workforce America!* (Homewood, Ill.: Business One Irwin, 1991), p. 18.

4. Ibid., p. 21.

5. Dudley Weeks, *The Eight Essential Steps to Conflict Resolution* (New York: G. P. Putnam's Sons, 1992), pp. 114–115.

6. Marcus Wynne, "From the '70s to the '90s," *Psychology Today*, November/December 1998, p. 8.

7. Michael Hughes and Tonnisha Bell, "The Stereotype and the Reality: Substance Problems and African Americans," *Spectrum*, March 31, 2000, p. 4.

8. Daniel Goleman, *Emotional Intelligence* (New York: Bantam Books, 1995), pp. 156–157.

9. Lewis Brown Griggs and Lente-Louise Louw, *Valuing Diversity* (New York: McGraw-Hill, 1995), pp. 3–4, 150–151.

10. Deborah Kong, "Hispanics Facing Backlash After Demographics Leap," *News-Leader*, August 4, 2001, p. 3A.

11. Griggs and Louw, *Valuing Diversity*, p. 151.

12. Yochi J. Dreazen, "U.S. Racial Wealth Gap Remains Huge," *Wall Street Journal*, March 14, 2000, p. A2.

13. Horace B. Deets, "Age Discrimination Still on the Rise," *Modern Maturity*, May/June 1999, p. 80.

14. Larry Anderson, "A Workplace in Transition," *Inside ACTE*, February 1999, p. 57; "Fifty-Something," *Training & Development*, May 1994, p. 143.

15. James Q. Wilson, "A Long Way from the Back of the Bus," *New York Times Book Review*, November 16, 1997, p. 10; Orlando Patterson, "Why Conduct a Racial Census?" *The News & Observer*, July 13, 1997, p. 29A.

16. Robert S. Boynton, "Color Us Invisible," *New York Times Book Review*, August 17, 1997, p. 13.

17. Stephen Magagini, "A Race Free Consciousness," *The News & Observer*, November 23, 1997, pp. 25a–26a.

18. Wilson, "A Long Way from the Back of the Bus," p. 10.

19. G. Pascal Zachary, "A Mixed Future," *Wall Street Journal*, January 1, 2000, p. R43. A recent book entitled *One Drop of Blood—The American Misadventure of Race* by Scott L. Malcomson provides an excellent review of America's separatist history.

20. Lynette Clemetson, "Color My World," *Newsweek*, May 8, 2000, p. 70.

21. Lawrence Lindsey, "This Is a Political Matter," *Wall Street Journal*, December 26, 1996, p. 16A.

22. John Williams, "The New Workforce," *Business Week*, March 20, 2000, p. 65.

23. Thomas Petzinger, Jr., "AT&T Class Teaches an Open Workplace Is Profitably Correct," *Wall Street Journal*, November 10, 1995, p. B1.

24. Rachel Emma Silverman, "Wall Street, a New Push to Recruit Gay Students," *Wall Street Journal*, February 9, 2000, p. B1.

25. U.S. Commission on Civil Rights, *Promise and Perceptions: Federal Efforts to Eliminate Employment Discrimination Through Affirmative Action* (Washington, D.C.: U.S. Government Printing Office, October 1981), p. 17.

26. Loden and Rosener, *Workforce America!* p. 12.

27. *101 Tools for Tolerance* (Montgomery, Ala.: Southern Poverty Law Center), pp. 4–7.

28. Alex Markels, "A Diversity Program Can Prove Divisive," *Wall Street Journal*, December 4, 1996, p. B1.

29. Adapted from Leone E. Wynter, "Do Diversity Programs Make a Difference?" *Wall Street Journal*, December 4, 1996, p. B1.

30. Nicole Harris, "A New Denny's—Diner by Diner," *Business Week*, March 25, 1996, pp. 166–168.

31. "From a Diversity Whoops! To a Diversity Model: The Denny's Story," *The Inner Edge*, April/May 2000, p. 22.

32. Dean Foust, "Coke: Say Good-Bye to the Good Ol' Boy Culture," *Business Week*, May 29, 2000, p. 58.

33. Faye Rice, "How to Make Diversity Pay," *Fortune*, August 8, 1994, p. 82.

34. Stan Crock and Michele Galen, "A Thunderous Impact on Equal Opportunity," *Business Week*, June 26, 1995, p. 37.

35. Stephen M. Paskoff, "Ending the Workplace Diversity Wars," *Training*, August 1996, p. 44.

36. Paskoff, "Ending the Workplace Diversity Wars," pp. 46–47.

37. Joanne L. Symons, "Is Affirmative Action in America's Interest?" *Executive Female*, May/June 1995, p. 52.

38. Robert Kreitner, *Management*, 8th ed. (Boston: Houghton Mifflin, 2001), pp. 334–335.

39. Symons, "Is Affirmative Action in America's Interest?" p. 52.

40. Terry Eastland, "Endgame for Affirmative Action," *Wall Street Journal*, March 28, 1996, p. A15.

41. Michael K. Frisby, "Powell Reshapes Debate on Affirmative Action, Deepening Divisions Among Black Republicans," *Wall Street Journal*, August 13, 1996, p. A14.

42. Paul Berman, "Redefining Fairness," *New York Times Book Review*, April 14, 1996, p. A14.

43. Arthur A. Fletcher, "Business and Race: Only Halfway There," *Fortune*, March 6, 2000, pp. F75–F78; Gene Koretz, "Does Hiring Minorities Hurt?" *Business Week*, September 14, 1998, p. 26.

44. Geoffrey Brewer, "Why We Can't All Get Along," *Sales & Marketing Management*, December 1995, p. 32.

45. Katherine Roth, "God on the Job," *Working Woman*, February 1998, pp. 65–66.

46. Benjamin A. Holden, "Denny's Chain Settles Suits by Minorities," *Wall Street Journal*, May 24, 1994, p. A3; Stephen Labaton, "Civil Rights Milestone," *Denver Post*, May 25, 1994, p. 2A; Nicole Harris, "A New Denny's—Diner by Diner," *Business Week*, March 25, 1996, pp. 166–168; Jim Adamson, "The Denny's Story," book review, *Training*, August 2000, pp. 74–76; "From a Diversity Whoops! To a Diversity Model: The Denny's Story," *The Inner Edge*, April/May 2000, p. 22.

**Chapter 8**

1. Carol Hymowitz, "Damark's Unique Post: A Manager Who Helps Work on Relationships," *Wall Street Journal*, September 12, 1999, p. B1; "Mark Johansson, Relationship Manager," *Training*, December 1999, p. 20.

2. Dudley Weeks, *The Eight Essential Steps to Conflict Resolution* (New York: G. P. Putnam's Sons, 1992), p. 7.

3. Ibid., pp. 7–8.

4. Anne Fisher, "Which One Should I Fire? . . . Is My Voice Mail Monitored? . . . and Other Queries," *Fortune*, November 25, 1996, p. 173.

5. Rebecca Blumenstein and Gregory L. White, "The $2 Billion Tag May Seem a Rather High Price for Some Labor Peace," *Wall Street Journal*, July 30, 1998, p. 31.

6. David Leonhardt and Aaron Bernstein with Wendy Zellner, "UAL: Labor Is My Co-Pilot," *Business Week*, March 1, 1999.

7. David Stiebel, "The Myth of Hidden Harmony," *Training*, March 1997, p. 114.

8. Yochi J. Dreazen and Deborah Soloman, "Forced Overtime Is Sticking Point in Verizon Talks," *Wall Street Journal*, August 8, 2000, p. B1; David Field, "Boeing, Union Angle for Contract," *USA Today*, August 26, 1999, p. B3; Tara Parker-Pope and Kyle Pope, "Family-Friendly, Singles-Unfriendly," *Wall Street Journal*, October 31, 1999.

9. Carol Kleiman, "How to Deal with a Co-worker Who's Getting on Your Nerves," *San Jose Mercury News*, October 3, 1999, p. PC1.

10. "Assertiveness: More Than a Forceful Attitude," *Supervisory Management*, February 1994, p. 3.

11. Stephen Ash, "How to Make Assertiveness Work for You," *Supervisory Management*, p. 8.

12. Albert Ellis, *Effective Self-Assertion*, Psychology Today audiotape, 1985.

13. Cheryl Shavers, "Strategy, Not Tactics, Is the Better Approach for a Winning Negotiator," *San Jose Mercury News*, January 24, 1999, p. 5E.

14. Weeks, *The Eight Essential Steps to Conflict Resolution*, pp. 127–129.

15. David Stiebel, *When Talking Makes Things Worse!* (Dallas: Whitehall & Nolton, 1997), p. 17.

16. Roger Fisher and Alan Sharp, *Getting It Done* (New York: Harper Business, 1998), pp. 81–83.

17. Roger Fisher and William Ury, *Getting to Yes* (New York: Penguin Books, 1981), p. 59.

18. Weeks, *The Eight Essential Steps to Conflict Resolution*, p. 228.

19. Ibid., p. 223.

20. Carol S. Pearson, "The Emotional Side of Workplace Success," *The Inner Edge*, December 1998/January 1999, p. 3.

21. Daniel Goleman, *Emotional Intelligence* (New York: Bantam Books, 1995), p. 34.

22. Daniel Goleman, *Working with Emotional Intelligence* (New York: Bantam Books, 1998), pp. 24–28.

23. John Selby, *Conscious Healing* (New York: Bantam Books, 1989), p. 32.

24. Ibid.

25. James Georges, "The Not-So-Stupid Americans," *Training*, July 1994, p. 90.

26. Margaret A. Jacobs, "Brutal Firings Can Backfire, Ending in Court," *Wall Street Journal*, October 24, 1994, p. B1.

27. Gerald L. Manning and Barry L. Reece, *Selling Today— Building Quality Partnerships*, 8th ed. (Englewood Cliffs, N.J.: Prentice-Hall Business Publishing, 2001), p. 15.

28. Ron Zemke, "Contact! Training Employees to Meet the Public," *Service Solutions* (Minneapolis: Lakewood Books, 1990), pp. 20–23.

29. Georges, "The Not-So-Stupid Americans," p. 90.

30. Douglas A. Bernstein, Edward J. Roy, Louis A. Penner, Alison Clark-Stewart, and Christopher D. Wickens, *Psychology*, 5th ed. (Boston: Houghton Mifflin, 2000), p. 424.

31. Ibid.

32. William C. Menninger and Harry Levinson, *Human Understanding in Industry* (Chicago: Science Research Associates, 1956), p. 29.

33. Joan Borysenko, *Guilt Is the Teacher, Love Is the Lesson* (New York: Warner Books, 1990), p. 70.

34. Donella H. Meadows, "We Are, to Our Harm, What We Watch," *Roanoke Times & World-News*, October 16, 1994, p. G3.

35. Bernstein *et al.*, *Psychology*, p. 23.

36. Tori DeAngelis, "Women's Safety Illusory When Males Turn Violent," *APA Monitor*, September 1994, p. 1.

37. Jan E. Stets and Debra A. Henderson, "Contextual Factors Surrounding Conflict Resolution While Dating: Results from a National Study," *Family Relations*, January 1991, pp. 29–36.

38. Harold H. Bloomfield and Robert K. Cooper, *The Power of 5* (Emmaus, Pa.: Rodale Press, 1995), p. 334.

39. Redford Williams and Virginia Williams, *Anger Kills* (New York: HarperCollins, 1993), p. 3.

40. Kimes Gustin, *Anger, Rage, and Resentment* (West Caldwell, N.J.: St. Ives' Press, 1994), p. 1.

41. Art Ulene, *Really Fit Really Fast* (Encino, Calif.: HealthPoints, 1996), pp. 170–174.

42. Chip Alexander, "Punch Shot Undoes Olazabal," *The News & Observer*, June 19, 1999, p. C3.

43. Susan Bixler, *Professional Presence* (New York: G. P. Putnam's Sons, 1991), pp. 190–191.

44. Rolland S. Parker, *Emotional Common Sense* (New York: Barnes & Noble Books, 1973), pp. 80–81.

45. Pamela Kruger, "Betrayed by Work," *Fast Company*, November 1999, p. 186.

46. Gustin, *Anger, Rage, and Resentment*, p. 37.

47. Les Giblin, *How to Have Confidence and Power in Dealing with People* (Englewood Cliffs, N.J.: Prentice-Hall 1956), p. 37.

48. William J. Crockett, "Our Two Worlds," *Training & Development*, May 1982, p. 60.

49. Sam Keen, *Fire in the Belly—On Being a Man* (New York: Bantam Books, 1991), p. 242.

50. Lazarus and Lazarus, *The 60-Second Shrink*, pp. 10–11.

51. Borysenko, *Minding the Body, Mending the Mind*, p. 169.

52. Ellen Safier, "Our Experts Answer Your Questions," *Menninger Letter*, May 1993, p. 8.

53. Leo F. Buscaglia, *Loving Each Other* (Thorofare, N.J.: Slack, 1984), p. 160.

54. Keen, *Fire in the Belly*, p. 242.

55. Perri Capell, "Salvaging the Careers of Talented Managers Who Behave Badly," *Wall Street Journal*, December 24, 1996, p. B1; Thomas A. Stewart, "Looking Out for Number 1," *Fortune*, January 15, 1996, p. 36; Edward Felsenthal, "Potentially Violent Employees Present Bosses with a Catch-22," *Wall Street Journal*, April 5, 1995, p. B1.

## Chapter 9

1. Timothy Aeppel, "Living Overtime: A Factory Workaholic," *Wall Street Journal*, October 13, 1998, p. B1.

2. Nancy Ann Jeffrey, "The New-Economy Family," *Wall Street Journal*, September 8, 2000, p. W1.

3. Robert M. Strozier, "The Job of Your Dreams," *New Choices*, April 1998, p. 25.

4. Richard Simon, "From the Editor," *Network*, January/February 1998, p. 2.

5. Amy Saltzman, *Downshifting* (New York: HarperCollins, 1991), p. 16.

6. Marc Heguet, "Flat and Happy?" *Training*, April 1995, pp. 29–34.

7. Lynn Lannon, "Giving Back: The Secret of Creating Success," *Training & Development*, April 1990, p. 58.

8. Robert McGarvey, "Softening the Blow," *U.S. Air*, September 1991, p. 18.

9. Sue Shellenbarger, "Keeping Your Career a Manageable Part of Your Life," *Wall Street Journal*, April 12, 1995, p. B1; "Career vs. Family: Companies Respond," *Fortune*, April 28, 1997, p. 22.

10. "When Success Fails to Make You Happy," *Working Smart*, September 1991, p. 1.

11. Albert R. Karr, "Boot Camp for Job Hoppers," *Wall Street Journal*, July 11, 2000, p. B1; Ann Claycombe, "Spa for Doggies Features Play Groups and NPR," *The Chapel Hill News*, August 25, 2000, p. A6; Robert M. Strozier, "Get Ready for the Job of Your Dreams," *New Choices*, April 1998, p. 28.

12. Yvonne V. Chabrier, "Focus on Work," *New Age*, 1998, p. 95.

13. Ronald Henkoff, "So You Want to Change Your Job," *Fortune*, January 15, 1996, p. 52.

14. Marsha Sinetar, *Do What You Love . . . The Money Will Follow* (New York: Dell, 1987), p. 11.

15. Ibid., pp. 11–12.

16. Anne Fisher, "Six Ways to Supercharge Your Career," *Fortune*, January 13, 1997, pp. 46–48; John Epperheimer, "If It Feels Good, Do It and Change Your Career," *San Jose Mercury News*, July 17, 1996, p. 7G.

17. Michael Phillips, *The Seven Laws of Money* (Menlo Park, Calif.: Word Wheel and Random House, 1997), p. 9.

18. Sinetar, *Do What You Love*, pp. 14–15.

19. Sue Shellenbarger, "New Job Hunters Ask Recruiters, Is There a Life After Work?" *Wall Street Journal*, January 29, 1997, p. B1.

20. Carole Kanchier, "Dare to Change Your Job and Your Life in 7 Steps" *Psychology Today*, March/April 2000, pp. 64–67.

21. Aeppel, "Living Overtime: A Factory Workaholic," p. B1.

22. Peter T. Kilborn, "Splurge," *New York Times Book Review*, June 21, 1998, p. 34.

23. Michael Toms, "The Soul of Money—A Conversation with Lynne Twist," *New Dimensions*, January/February 1997, pp. 7–8; Carol S. Pearson, "Money Is Power," *The Inner Edge*, June/July 1999, pp. 3–4.

24. Ibid., p. 8.

25. Carol Frey, "Some Two-Income Couples Wonder Whether One Will Do," *The News & Observer*, May 24, 1998, p. E1; Jaine Carter and James D. Carter, "Book Helps Couples End Money War," *The News & Observer*, May 5, 2000, p. 3E.

26. Teri Lammers Prior, "If I Were President . . . ," *Inc.*, April 1995, pp. 56–60.

27. Michael Toms, "Money: The Third Side of the Coin" (interview with Joe Dominguez and Vicki Robin), *New Dimensions*, May/June 1991, p. 7.

28. Susan Smith Jones, "Choose to Be Healthy and Celebrate Life," *New Realities*, September/October 1988, pp. 17–19.

29. Ibid., p. 18.

30. Don Jacobson, "Nonstop Learning, Dead-End Jobs," *Training*, September 1998, p. 16.

31. Hal Lancaster, "Re-Engineering Authors Reconsider Re-Engineering," *Wall Street Journal*, January 17, 1995, p. B1.

32. Derwin Fox, "Career Insurance for Today's World," *Training & Development*, March 1996, pp. 63–64.

33. Ibid., p. 63.

34. Ron Zemke, "Why Organizations Still Aren't Learning," *Training*, September 1999, p. 43.

35. His Holiness the Dalai Lama and Howard C. Cutler, *The Art of Happiness* (New York: Riverhead Books, 1998), pp. 227–228.

36. Saltzman, *Downshifting*, p. 23.

37. Jay T. Knippen, Thad B. Green, and Kurt Sutton, "Asking Not to Be Overworked," *Supervisory Management*, February 1992, p. 6.

38. Art Ulene, *Really Fit Really Fast* (Encino, Calif.: Health-Points, 1996), pp. 198–199.

39. Ulene, *Really Fit Really Fast*, p. 199.

40. Marilyn Chase, "Weighing the Benefits of Mental-Health Days Against Guilt Feelings," *Wall Street Journal*, September 9, 1996, B1.

41. Leo Booth, "When God Becomes a Drug," *Common Boundary*, September/October 1991, p. 30; David N. Elkins, "Spirituality," *Psychology Today*, September/October, 1999, pp. 45–48.

42. Harold H. Bloomfield and Robert K. Cooper, *The Power of 5* (Emmaus, Pa.: Rodale Press, 1995), p. 484.

43. "Making the Spiritual Connection," *Lears*, December 1989, p. 72.

44. Robert Bolton and Dorothy Grover Bolton, *People Styles at Work* (New York: AMACOM, 1996), pp. 110–111.

45. Barnaby J. Feder, "Clergymen on the Job to Help Workers Deal with Problems," *Roanoke Times*, October 13, 1996. p. A6.

46. G. Paul Zachary, "The New Search for Meaning in Meaningless Work," *Wall Street Journal*, January 9, 1997, p. B1.

47. Judith Valente, "Some Employ Faith to Get the Job Done," *USA Today*, June 16, 1995, p. B1.

48. Ibid., p. B2.

49. Redford Williams and Virginia Williams, *Anger Kills* (New York: HarperCollins, 1993), pp. 181–182.

50. Chris Lee and Ron Zemke, "The Search for Spirit in the Workplace," *Training*, June 1993, p. 25.

51. *Dietary Guidelines for Americans* (Washington, D.C.: U.S. Department of Health and Human Services, December 1995), pp. 3–21.

52. "What Makes a Diet 'Varied'?" *University of California at Berkeley Wellness Letter*, December 1998, p. 6.

53. *Dietary Guidelines for Americans,* p. 36.

54. Ibid., pp. 40–41.

55. Ulene, *Really Fit Really Fast*, pp. 20–21; Robert Langreth, "Every Little Bit Helps," *Wall Street Journal*, May 1, 2000, p. R5.

56. "One Small Step . . . ," *University of California at Berkeley Wellness Letter*, January 1991, p. 1.

57. Robert A. Gleser, *The Healthmark Program for Life* (New York: McGraw-Hill, 1988), p. 147.

58. *Fitness Fundamentals* (Washington, D.C.: Department of Health and Human Services, 1988), p. 2.

59. Stephen R. Covey, *The Seven Habits of Highly Effective People* (New York: Simon & Schuster, 1989), p. 46.

60. James Fadiman, *Be All That You Are* (Seattle: Westlake Press, 1986), p. 25.

61. Robert McGarvey, "Getting Your Goals," *U.S. Air*, July 1989, p. 28.

62. Fadiman, *Be All That You Are*, p. 45.

63. Mike Hernacki, *The Ultimate Secret of Getting Absolutely Everything You Want* (New York: Berkley Books, 1988), p. 35.

64. Adapted from Bloomfield and Cooper, *The Power of 5*, pp. 492–493.

65. Sue Shellenbarger, "Work & Family," *Wall Street Journal*, January 12, 2000, p. B1; Edward M. Hallowell, *Connect* (New York: Pantheon Books, 1999), p. 3; His Holiness the Dalai Lama and Howard C. Cutler, *The Art of Happiness*, pp. 126–127.

# CREDITS

## Career Corner Credits

**Chapter 1:** Louis S. Richman, "How to Get Ahead in America," *Fortune,* May 16, 1994, pp. 46–54; Ronald Henkoff, "Winning the New Career Game," *Fortune,* July 12, 1993, pp. 46–49.

**Chapter 2:** Barry L. Reece and Gerald L. Manning, *Supervision and Leadership in Action* (New York: Glencoe, 1990); Camille Wright Miller, "Working It Out," *Roanoke Times & World-News,* July 17, 1994, p. F-3.

**Chapter 3:** Maxwell Maltz, *Psycho-Cybernetics* (New York: Pocket Books, 1972), pp. 6–7.

**Chapter 4:** Hal Lancaster, "You Have Your Values; How Do You Identify Your Employer's?" *Wall Street Journal,* April 8, 1997, p. B1.

**Chapter 6:** "How Much Can Employer Dictate Your Lifestyle?" *San Jose Mercury News,* May 2, 1993, pp. 1 PC and 2 PC; Susan Barciela, "Looks and Dress Still Count, Though the Lawyers Might Argue," *Roanoke Times & World-News,* June 19, 1993, p. D2; Susan Bixler, "Your Professional Presence," *Training Dimensions,* Vol. 9, No. 1, 1994, p. 1.

**Chapter 7:** "Good Customer Phone Form," *Training & Development,* December 1992, p. 9.

**Chapter 8:** Sue Shellenbarger and Carol Hymowitz, "As Population Ages, Older Workers Clash with Younger Bosses," *Wall Street Journal,* June 3, 1994, pp. A1 and A5.

**Chapter 9:** Carol Kleiman, "It's Never Too Late to Get 'Unstuck' from a Career," *San Jose Mercury News,* January 28, 2001, p. 2PC; Cheryl Shavers, "How to Decide When It Is Time to Move On," *San Jose Mercury News,* January 10, 1999, p. 3E.

## Total Person Insight Credits

### Chapter 1

**p. 5:** Harry E. Chambers, *The Bad Attitude Survival Guide* (Reading, Mass.: Addison-Wesley, 1998), p. 1; **p. 9:** Anne Fisher, "Success Secret: A High Emotional IQ," *Fortune,* October 26, 1998, p. 293; **p. 12:** William Raspberry, "Topmost Priority: Jobs," *Washington Post,* (n.d.), 1977; **p. 15:** James Baughman quote from Frank Rose, "A New Age for Business?" *Fortune,* October 8, 1990, p. 162.

### Chapter 2

**p. 29:** Paul R. Timm, "The Way We Word," in *Effective Communication on the Job,* ed. William K. Fallon (New York: AMACOM, 1981), p. 74; **p. 40:** Gerry Mitchell quote from "Listen, Listen, Listen," *Business Week,* September 14, 1987, p. 108; **p. 43:** Aaron Lazare, "Go Ahead—Say You're Sorry," *Psychology Today,* January/February 1995, p. 40.

### Chapter 3

**p. 60:** Oprah Winfrey, "You Are the Dream," *O, The Oprah Magazine,* March 2001, p. 39; **p. 62:** Belleruth Naparstek, "About Face," *Common Boundary,* July/August 1996, p.64; **p. 66:** Fran Cox and Louis Cox, *A Conscious Life* (Berkeley, Calif.: Conari Press, 1996), p. 12.

### Chapter 4

**p. 83:** Peter Senge quote from Brian Dumaine, "Mr. Learning Organization," *Fortune,* October 17, 1994, p. 147; **p. 90:** www.josephsoninstitute.org, 7/1/00; **p. 94:** Dan Rice and Craig Dreilinger, "Rights and Wrongs of Ethics Training," *Training & Development,* May 1990, p. 105; **p. 100:** www.josephsoninstitute.org, 7/12/01.

### Chapter 5

**p. 109:** Price Pritchett, *New Work Habits for the Next Millennium* (Dallas, Tex.: EPS Solutions, 1999), p. 2; **p. 120:** His Holiness the Dalai Lama and Howard C. Cutler, *The Art of Happiness* (New York: Riverhead Books, 1998), p. 37.

### Chapter 6

**p. 135:** Susan Bixler and Nancy Nix-Rice, *The New Professional Image* (Holbrook, Mass.: Adams Media Corporation, 1997), p. 3; **p. 145:** Judith Martin, "Low Income Is Not Low-Class," *Roanoke Times & World-News,* March 13, 1988, p. E 10.

### Chapter 7

**p. 155:** Keith H. Hammonds, "Difference Is Power," *Fast Company,* July 2000, p. 260; **p. 157:** Vernon E. Jordan, Jr., "Look Outward, Black America," *Wall Street Journal,* October 27, 1995, p. A14.

### Chapter 8

**p. 184:** Cheryl Shavers, "Some Positive Steps That You Can Take to Resolve Conflicts," *San Jose Mercury News,* March 21, 1999, p. 3E; **p. 194:** Roger Fisher and William Ury, *Getting to Yes* (New York: Penguin Books, 1981), p. 4; **p. 203:** James Georges, "The Not-So-Stupid Americans," *Training,* July 1994, p. 90; **p. 208:** Kimes Gustin, *Anger, Rage, and Resentment* (West Caldwell, N.J.: St. Ives' Press, 1994), p. 13; **p. 212:** Gerard Egan, *You and Me* (Monterey, Calif.: Brooks/Cole, 1977), p. 73.

### Chapter 9

**p. 220:** Amy Saltzman, *Downshifting: Reinventing Success on a Slower Track* (New York: HarperCollins Publishers, 1990), p. 15; **p. 222:** Cheryl Shavers, "Set a Pace That Lets You Enjoy the Fruits of Your Labor," *San Jose Mercury News,* October 19, 1997, p. 30; **p. 229:** Julie Connelly, "How to Choose Your

Next Career," *Fortune,* February 6, 1995, p. 45; **p. 234:** Robert Wuthnow, "Roots & Wings," *Common Boundary,* January/February 1999, pp. 24–31; **p. 235:** Patricia Sellers, "Don't Call Me Slacker!" *Fortune,* December 12, 1994, p. 196.

## Human Relations in Action Credits

### Chapter 1

**p. 7:** Chris Lee, "The Death of Civility," *Training,* July 1999, p. 25; **p. 12:** George Gendron, "That Magic Moment," *Inc,* June 2000, p. 11; Shelly Branch, "The 100 Best Companies to Work For in America," *Fortune,* January 11, 1999, p. 123; **p. 19:** "Business Bulletin," *Wall Street Journal,* September 30, 1999; "Job-Turnover Tab," *Business Week,* April 20, 1998.

### Chapter 2

**p. 31:** "The Born-Again Techies Are Percussing Again," *Training,* March 2000, p. 24; "Jargonese," *Training and Development,* July 1998, p. 21; "Do You Speak Business?" *Business Week,* November 16, 1998, p. 6; **p. 39:** Excerpt adapted from "Ask Annie," *Fortune,* July 19, 1999. Copyright © 1999 Time Inc. All rights reserved; **p. 47:** Adapted from "The 10 Commandments of E-MAIL," *Harvard Communications Update,* Vol. 2, No. 3, March 1999, pp. 7–8; Carolyn Kleiner, "Online Buffs Hit and Miss on Manners," *U.S. News and World Report,* March 22, 1999, p. 60; "Etiquette with Office Gadgets," *Training,* January 1999, p. 24; **p. 49:** "Telephone Tips," *The Office Professional,* see www.hardatwork.com; INTERNET.

### Chapter 3

**p. 57:** *www.es.emory.edu/mfp/efficacynotgiveup.html.* Accessed November 17, 2000; **p. 67:** Anne Fisher, "Ask Annie," *Fortune,* October 12, 1998, p. 208.

### Chapter 4

**p. 82:** James P. Miller, "Work Week," *Wall Street Journal,* February 1, 2000, p. A1; **p. 87:** Sue Shellenbarger, "In Cataclysmic Times, Workers Need Room to Rethink Priorities," *Wall Street Journal,* September 19, 2001, p. B1. **p. 91:** Dennis T. Jaffe and Cynthia P. Scott, "How to Link Personal Values with Team Values," *Training & Development,* March 1998, pp. 24–26; **p. 101:** Burton L. Visotzky, "Bible in the Boardroom?" *Inc.,* July 1998, pp. 29–30; Corine McLaughlin, "Workplace Spirituality Transforming Organizations from the Inside Out," *The Inner Edge,* August/September 1998, pp. 25–27.

### Chapter 5

**p. 111:** Ellen Joan Pollack, "The Selling of a Golden Speech," *Wall Street Journal,* March 31, 1999, p. B1; **p. 114:** Phaedra Hise, "Avoid the Stuff That Sucks," *Inc. 500,* 1999, pp. 195–196; **p. 118:** "The Flip Side of Disaster," *Psychology Today,* March/April 1998, p. 18.

### Chapter 6

**p. 133:** "Job Titles of the Future," *Fast Company,* June 1999, p. 82; **p. 144:** Jean Nash Johnson, "Etiquette Book Tackles Code of Manners for Blacks," *The News & Observer,* April 25, 1999, p. 80.

### Chapter 7

**p. 159:** "Tools for Tolerance: Personal," excerpted, with permission, from *Teaching Tolerance.* Copyright © 2000, Southern Poverty Law Center, Montgomery, AL. *101 Tools for Tolerance* is available free from the SPLC. For more information, visit www.splcenter.org or send a fax to (334) 264-7310; **p. 165:** "When Meeting Someone With a Disability", adapted from "Communication Solutions." Reprinted by permission of Progressive Business Publications; **p. 176:** "Tools for Tolerance: Community," excerpted, with permission, from *Teaching Tolerance.* Copyright © 2000, Southern Poverty Law Center, Montgomery, Al. *101 Tools for Tolerance* is available free from the SPLC. For more information, visit www.splcenter.org or send a fax to (334) 264-7310.

### Chapter 8

**p. 185:** Excerpt adapted from "In the Lead: How to Avoid Hiring the Prima Donnas Who Hate Teamwork" by Carol Hymowitz, from the *Wall Street Journal,* February 15, 2000. Copyright © 2000 by Dow Jones & Co. Inc. Reproduced with permission of Dow Jones & Co. Inc. via Copyright Clearance Center, p. C19; **p. 188:** Excerpt adapted from "More Firms, Siding With Employees, Bid Bad Clients Farewell" by Sue Shellenbarger, from the *Wall Street Journal,* February 26, 2000. Copyright © 2000 by Dow Jones & Co. Inc. Reproduced via Copyright Clearance Center, p. B1; **p. 202:** Daniel Goleman, *Working with Emotional Intelligence* (New York: Bantam Books, 1998), p. 23; **p. 207:** Ira Podell, "Caught in the Act," *The Herald Sun,* February 23, 2000, p. D-1; "Detail of Sprewell Hearing Revealed," *The News & Observer,* March 7, 1998, p. 9-C; Jason Silverman, "The Art of Trash Talk," *Psychology Today,* September/October 1999, p. 10.

### Chapter 9

**p. 224:** Almar Latour, "Detroit Meets a 'Worker Paradise,'" the *Wall Street Journal,* March 3, 1999, p. B1; **p. 228:** "Who Wants to Be a Millionaire?" *San Jose Mercury News,* Weekly Tip. **p. 239:** Carole Kanchier, "Dare to Change Your Job and Your Life in 7 Steps," *Psychology Today,* March/April 2000, pp. 64–67.

## Photo and Cartoon Credits

### Chapter 1

**p. 2:** © Brian Coats. All Rights Reserved; **p. 4:** © 1999 Ted Rall. All Rights Reserved; **p. 6:** © David Zadig; **p. 13:** Jeff Greenberg/Index Stock; **p. 20:** © The St. Paul.

### Chapter 2

**p. 28:** Cartoon by Dave Carpenter; **p. 32:** AP/Wide World; **p. 36:** Courtesy Benton Foundation; **p. 41:** KRT photo by Kent Phillips; **p. 45:** © Will McIntyre.

### Chapter 3

**p. 59:** Courtesy Stuttering Foundation of America; **p. 61:** © Lynn Johnston Productions, Inc./Distributed by United Feature Syndicate, Inc.; **p. 69:** © Gail Albert Halaban/SABA.

**Chapter 4**

**p. 81:** Ron McQueeney Photography; **p. 85:** Bob Daemmrich/ Stock Boston; **p. 87:** © Stan Honda/AFP; **p. 90:** AP/Wide World; **p. 96:** from the *Wall Street Journal/* Permission, Cartoon Features Syndicate; **p. 98:** Courtesy Sears, Roebuck and Co.

**Chapter 5**

**p. 108:** Spencer Grant/Stock Boston; **p. 113:** © Danny Turner; **p. 115:** Courtesy Harrell Performance Systems; **p. 119:** from the *Wall Street Journal/*Permission, Cartoon Features Syndicate Inc.; **p. 124:** David Woo Photo.

**Chapter 6**

**p. 133:** © Francisco Rangel; **p. 138:** Dana White/PhotoEdit; **p. 141:** Chernus/FPG; **p. 143:** *Dilbert* reprinted by permission of United Features Syndicate, Inc.

**Chapter 7**

**p. 157:** Reprinted with permission of General Motors; **p. 160:** ACLU/DeVito Verdi; **p. 166 (top):** Lynn Johnston Produc-

tions, Inc./Distributed by United Features Syndicate, Inc.; **p. 166:** AP/Wide World; **p. 173:** © Robert Wright; **p. 175:** from the *Wall Street Journal/*Permission, Cartoon Features Syndicate.

**Chapter 8**

**p. 187:** Andy Freeburg; **p. 193:** Anna Curtis; **p. 195:** Reprinted with permission from *Modern Maturity.* American Association of Retired Persons; **p. 198:** Courtesy American Arbitration Association; **p. 201:** Damian Strohmeyer/*Sports Illustrated;* **p. 206:** Courtesy Skyrage Foundation; **p. 209:** AP/Wide World.

**Chapter 9**

**p. 221:** © Cheryl Himmelstein Photography; **p. 222:** © Joe A. Sumrall, author of *Lighten-Up, A Book of Enlightened Humor* (Bear & Co. Santa Fe, NM); **p. 225:** © Michael Schwarz; **p. 233:** © Michael Lewis; **p. 236:** Jon Riley/Tony Stone Images.